Human Resources and the Adjustment Process

Ricardo Paredes
Luis A. Riveros
Editors

Published by the Inter-American Development Bank
Distributed by The Johns Hopkins University Press

Washington, D.C.
1994

Human Resources and the Adjustment Process

© Copyright 1994 by the Inter-American Development Bank

1300 New York Avenue, N.W.
Washington, D.C. 20577

Distributed by
The Johns Hopkins University Press
2715 North Charles Street
Baltimore, MD 21218-4319

Library of Congress Catalog Card Number: 94-72902
ISBN: 0-940602-90-3

AUTHORS

Amadeo, Edward
Professor, Pontificia Universidad Católica, Rio de Janeiro, Brazil.

Bucheli, Marisa
Professor, Economics Department, School of Social Sciences, Universidad de la República, Uruguay.

Camargo, José Márcio
Professor, Economics Department, Pontificia Universidad Católica, Rio de Janeiro, Brazil.

Cassoni, Adriana
Professor, Economics Department, School of Social Sciences, Universidad de la República, Uruguay.

Diez de Medina, Rafael
Economist, Professor, Economics Department of the School of Social Sciences, Universidad de la República, Uruguay. Technical Coordinator at ECLAC, Montevideo, Uruguay.

Paes de Barros, Ricardo
Researcher, Instituto de Pesquisa Econômica Aplicada, Rio de Janeiro, Instituto de Economia Industrial/Universidade Federal do Rio de Janeiro (IEI/UFRJ), Instituto Universitario de Pesquisas do Rio de Janeiro (IUPERJ), Brazil, and at Yale University.

Paredes, Ricardo
Associate Professor, Economics Department, University of Chile.

Pero, Valéria
Research Assistant, Instituto de Pesquisa Econômica Aplicada, Rio de Janeiro, Brazil.

Pinto de Mendonça, Rosane
Research Assistant, Instituto de Pesquisa Econômica Aplicada, Rio de Janeiro, Brazil.

Riveros, Luis A.

Principal Professor, Economics Department, University of Chile.

Rossi, Máximo

Economist. Professor, Economics Department of the School of Social Sciences, Universidad de la República, Uruguay. Consultant at ECLAC, Montevideo, Uruguay.

Urani, André

Professor, School of Business and Economics, UFRJ and Consultant at IUPERJ, Brazil.

Zerda, Alvaro

Professor, Universidad Nacional de Colombia and Principal Researcher at the Centro de Investigaciones para el Desarrollo, Colombia.

FOREWORD

Human Resources and the Adjustment Process is the tenth book of a series published under the Centers for Research in Applied Economics Project sponsored by the Inter-American Development Bank. In keeping with the centers' objective of addressing the major economic and social problems affecting Latin America and the Caribbean, this volume examines the effects of the adjustment process on human resources and the ability of workers to adapt (or fail to adapt) to the requirements imposed by structural change.

The overall study is divided into three parts. First, the authors examined the processes of adjustment and crisis to determine whether drops in output could be associated with structural adjustment, macroeconomic crisis, or a combination of the two. Second, they identified the labor categories hardest hit in terms of intrasector mobility, wages, and employment. Finally, they analyzed the efforts of national institutions to retrain the work force and to cushion the impact of adjustment.

This book analyzes the situations in Brazil, Chile, Colombia, and Uruguay, countries whose experiences are particularly illustrative of the nature of structural adjustments in Latin America. Because adjustment has affected countries differently, each case study carries with it specific policy lessons for the future design and evaluation of training programs and institutions. Evident from all four studies is the need to adopt flexible training programs that are driven by and adapt to private sector needs. Also recommended is a shift away from the procyclical nature of funding for training programs, whereby human resource development surges during boom periods but is left to wither during recessionary cycles. The idea is to create an institutional mechanism to track demand for different types of labor and to ensure that the national training program is a dynamic one that not only meets the current demand but anticipates labor needs in the near term.

In this book, structural adjustment is understood as a process in which shrinking industrial sectors coexist with expanding ones in a way which spurs economic activity and employment. Macroeconomic crisis, on the other hand, is understood as a situation in which the economy as a whole is contracting. Structural adjustments and macroeconomic crises result in production declines. However, the studies clearly show that structural adjustments require greater flexibility and mobility of production factors than do macroeconomic crises. Also, it was found that the deeper the structural changes, the greater the requirements for adaptation of human resources.

According to the research, the situation in each country has called for substantially different adaptations. Unfortunately, no country has yet designed a structure for retraining workers that deals adequately with all the effects of adjustment.

The results of the studies suggest that it is necessary to improve communication and coordination between restructured firms and the educational system. Also, the studies show that countries attempting to weather the storms of adjustment with rudimentary or nonexistent institutional training schemes do not really adjust. Thorough economic adjustments require adaptable retraining plans characterized by dependable financing curricula that are responsive to private sector requirements, as well as worker assistance during the adjustment period.

Nohra Rey de Marulanda, Manager
Integration and Regional Programs Department

CONTENTS

Chapter One
Human Resources and the Adjustment Process: An Overview 1
Ricardo Paredes
Luis A. Riveros

Chapter Two
Brazil 13
Edward Amadeo
Ricardo Paes de Barros
José Márcio Camargo
Rosane Pinto de Mendonça
Valéria Pero
André Urani

Chapter Three
Chile 63
Ricardo Paredes
Luis A. Riveros

Chapter Four
Colombia 109
Alvaro Zerda

Chapter Five
Uruguay 147
Marisa Bucheli
Adriana Cassoni
Rafael Diez de Medina
Máximo Rossi

Index 197

CHAPTER ONE

HUMAN RESOURCES AND
THE ADJUSTMENT PROCESS: AN OVERVIEW

Ricardo Paredes[1]
Luis A. Riveros

A key factor for success in structural adjustment programs is human resource mobility and adaptability. Mobility of productive factors is an imperative, particularly when adjustments are linked to increasing economic transparency and promoting the tradable goods sectors. Furthermore, the ability of human resources to adapt to changing economic conditions has a critical bearing on the costs incurred. These costs can translate into sectoral unemployment, reductions in real salaries, and underemployment.

A critical factor for determining the level of intersectoral and interindustrial mobility of production elements—especially human resources—relates to education and training. These elements determine the human capital embodied in each individual. The pool of human capital created is therefore strictly dependent on the performance of the training institutions which ultimately convert and rebuild abilities, know-how, and skills rendered obsolete by structural adjustment processes. The main objective of the studies in this volume is to understand how human resources have adapted (or failed to adapt) to structural changes in the economies of Brazil, Colombia, Chile, and Uruguay. Each country study is divided into three sections: 1) analysis of adjustment processes or macroeconomic crises; 2) assessments of human resources most severely affected by adjustment processes or by macroeconomic crises as these relate to interindustrial mobility, real salaries, and levels of employment; and 3) analysis of the role played by training institutions in adapting human resources to production needs that arise during an adjustment process, as well as policies aimed at alleviating related impacts on specific groups.

[1] The authors wish to thank Fred Jaspersen, Robert Kestell, and Juan Gabito for their comments and suggestions. They are also grateful to the participants at the seminar held in Montevideo in March, 1993.

This chapter summarizes the key characteristics of each case study and presents several general recommendations. While it is clear that the conclusions derived from the country studies relate to specific situations and must not be generalized, the findings of the analyses can yield multiple policy lessons. These lessons can provide important guidelines for future design and evaluation of training programs and institutions.

Structural Adjustments and Macroeconomic Crises

The analysis of the Brazilian, Colombian, Chilean, and Uruguayan experiences is particularly interesting for understanding the nature of structural adjustments in Latin America, their problems, and the policies enacted to improve the performance of training institutions. This analysis clearly shows that both structural adjustment processes and macroeconomic crises result in production declines. However, structural adjustments require greater flexibility and mobility of production factors than do macroeconomic crises. Also, the cause of the crises—external shocks or problems in balance of payments—determines the reaction of the labor market. In turn, as Jaspersen (1981) has shown, the optimum economic policy response is determined by the nature of the shocks, thus implying that human resources need to adapt in different ways. The extent to which human resources can actually be molded also depends on the flexibility of institutional training programs.

In the following country studies, structural adjustment processes are defined as situations in which contracting industrial sectors coexist with expanding sectors that spur economic activity and employment. However, sectoral growth depends on the availability and mobility of production factors. This implies adaptability on the part of human resources. A macroeconomic crisis, on the other hand, is defined as a situation in which the economy as a whole is contracting. Therefore, flexibility requirements for moving production factors among different activities and adapting them to different conditions are less important for macroeconomic crises than for structural adjustments. This study does not deal with optimum economic policy options.[2] Rather it focuses on the impacts that different adjustment strategies have had on human resources.

The fact that the structural adjustment experiences described in the country studies differ considerably represents a limitation. Indeed, it could be argued that few conclusions can be drawn from such a comparison. However, a contrast of the different experiences can yield useful lessons in policy analysis.

---

[2] A good treatment of this subject can be found in Jaspersen and Shariff (1990).

The Brazilian study shows that the country never adopted a true adjustment program. Although Brazil underwent four major economic shocks between 1970 and 1990, the crises were mainly caused by balance of payment problems. Policies introduced in response to the external shocks were, in fact, quickly revoked. Furthermore, despite the generation of foreign trade surpluses in reaction to the crises, it appears that Brazil's industrial sectors did not undergo significant changes. This suggests that domestically marketed goods did not require improvements in quality in order to be exported. Therefore, the Brazilian experience may not apply to other Latin American countries where production methods needed to be greatly improved in order to expand nontraditional exports. However, Brazil's economic liberalization process has slowed down in the last 20 years because of increased government intervention in the market. This has diminished the country's efficiency and ability to implement future structural changes that could avoid onerous demands on human resource mobility.

Colombia as well did not introduce a true structural adjustment program. In contrast to Brazil, however, Colombia had no pressing need to do so. Indeed, during the past 20 years Colombia underwent three periods characterized by successive economic booms and recessions. These periods were mainly induced by temporary external events (for example, a severe frost in Brazil that temporarily raised coffee prices). Consequently, both the booms and the crises were short-lived and the country's industrial structure and production sectors were only slightly affected by the economic fluctuations. Lack of dynamism evidently did not affect the industrial structure of production. Nevertheless, the country faced increasing levels of poverty. Since 1990, Colombia has shown a clear determination to start a structural adjustment process, which raises interesting questions about the future impact of the process on human resources.

Uruguay's relative success in dealing with its crisis and in converting its human resources over the 20-year period analyzed in the study is mainly due to a gradually implemented adaptation process and a highly educated population, which reduced the need for flexibility and mobility. However, the gradual nature of the changes in Uruguay's productive structure caused greater pressure on interindustrial labor mobility and human resource conversion than in Brazil and Colombia. Among the major changes that took place were greater financial liberalization, a decline in organized labor pressures, and a significant reduction in tariffs. These changes are insignificant, however, when compared with those that Uruguay will face in its future accession to the Southern Cone Common Market (MERCOSUR).

Finally, and in sharp contrast with the Brazilian and Colombian experiences, Chile introduced the most radical and consistent structural adjustment changes. The range and depth of these mid-1970 changes have made Chile's experience the most important among the case studies. The changes brought about an important restructuring in production, which exerted significant pressures on production factors, particularly on skill requirements and interindustrial mobility of human resources. Chile's 1982-85 economic crisis had a distinctly different impact on human resource requirements than previous crises. This contrast makes the Chilean experience particularly interesting, being in turn explained by the institutional framework and the economic policies adopted during the 1970s, which were in tune with long-term economic objectives related to market priorities. These priorities pertain to resource allocation and to the private sector's role as the leading agent for economic development.

Effects on Human Resources

When structuring job conversion and training programs, facilitating the mobility of human resources, and paring incurred and social costs of structural adjustments, it is helpful to identify the population groups most affected by the adjustment process in terms of frequency and duration of unemployment and losses in real salaries. Moreover, focusing on the needs of individual groups allows for the recommendation of short-term assistance measures that could supplement human resource training programs. Thus, differentiating among human resources make it possible to adopt policies that enhance the efficiency and fairness of the adjustment process.

Not surprisingly, a general conclusion of all the case studies is that the unskilled, the young, and the least educated exhibit the highest levels of unemployment. Nonetheless, it is not the purpose of this study to analyze the long-term status of human resources, though this may be an interesting issue. This volume's main objective is to analyze the impact of the adjustment process (or macroeconomic crisis) on levels and duration of unemployment, real salaries, and the status of human resources in general.

The country studies confirm the hypothesis that macroeconomic crises and adjustment processes do not necessarily affect the same groups. This is a consequence of two factors: the severity of the crises and their effect on output levels; and the private sector's response to changes in aggregate demand which are seen as transitory in the case of macroeconomic crises, and permanent in the case of structural adjustments. Therefore, policies aimed at alleviating the effects of the economic adjustment program on human resources and accelerating the transition process will differ according to the nature of the economic crisis. Consequently, countries tend to rely on different labor conversion and mobility schemes according to the type and severity of the crises they face.

This notion has underpinned the analysis of the country studies. It supports the thesis that different types of economic changes call for different responses. While our comparative analysis supports the hypothesis that both macroeconomic crises and structural adjustment processes reduce real salaries and employment, it also shows that structural adjustment changes are relatively more apt to impair skills which had previously been in high demand. Rather than simply waiting out the crisis, the situation requires implementation of special assistance policies.

The Brazilian case shows that the crises of the last 20 years, particularly those in the 1980s, mainly affected job quality as opposed to quantity. Despite a practically stagnant economy, a significant number of jobs were created in the 1980s. Brazilian policies, however, resulted in a decline in employment in the tradable goods sector, as opposed to the nontradable goods sector, despite subperiods in which the promotion of exports was key to economic policy. This suggests, therefore, that despite changes in output and variations in the severity of economic cycles, the economy did not undergo an adjustment process that would have required a significant restructuring of employment.

Colombia's failure to adopt a structural adjustment policy also affected its labor market. Employment and salary trends closely paralleled those of output. However, the country's highly regulated labor market (only recently deregulated) resulted in increasing labor shifts from the formal to the informal sector. This phenomenon would explain both the seemingly minor impact that changes in the level of economic activity have had on the employment rate and the significant salary deterioration in unregulated economic sectors. The Colombian case shows the eventual consequences of labor regulations which, while enacted for the purpose of protecting workers, actually have the effect of constraining employment, salaries, and economic development. For example, Colombia experienced growth in temporary employment, with worker turnovers occurring every 14 months on the average. The high turnover rate implies that companies are systematically dismissing older workers and replacing them with younger ones. This allows companies to avoid severance payments that increase with every year of employee service. Obviously, this practice impairs workers' productivity since it limits work-related experience, a major source of increased productivity.

In Uruguay the crises have mostly affected groups endowed with less human capital—young people, seniors, and women (the latter because they have less continuous job experience). This situation suggests that Uruguay underwent a structural adjustment process rather than a macroeconomic crisis. If this is true, it is possible that the gradual nature of the changes resulted in relatively smaller losses in salaries and employment for the more skilled workers. The notably small impact of lower output on average employment and wages can be attributed to Uruguay's highly educated labor force, which was better equipped to adapt to changes in work conditions.

Finally, Chile's structural adjustment had a major impact on employment and salaries in the 1970s. This had long-term consequences, as evidenced by the fact that the recovery in output of the late 1980s did not alleviate deteriorated employment and salary conditions. This situation is in marked contrast not only to the experiences of the other countries under study, but also to Chile's own situation during the 1980s crisis. In this second crisis, employment responded remarkably well to output recovery, especially when the response is compared to the historically low elasticities in output-related employment which have doubled since the 1980s.

The direct impact that macroeconomic crises have on specific population groups supports, to a large extent, the hypothesis that the crises mainly affect unskilled workers. In the Colombian case, for example, the crisis clearly had a more severe impact on women in the work force.[3] Workers with fewer than four years of education in metropolitan Brazil were similarly singled out as the group most affected by the cyclical crises.[4]

Chile's structural adjustment process of the 1970s mostly affected workers with relatively high specific skills, that is, middle-aged men. This can be explained by a deterioration in skills predating the adjustment period. In contrast, this adjustment process had a milder impact on employment and salary levels of workers with low specific skills, such as women and young people. This situation completely reversed itself during the 1980s crisis. As previously mentioned, the latter crisis exhibited characteristics that were different from those of the 1970s structural adjustment. While unemployment in Chile during the 1980s crisis reached record levels, the crisis mostly affected young people, women, and uneducated workers.

In summary, the crises in Colombia and Brazil mainly affected those groups endowed with the least human capital. This, however, was not the case in Chile during the 1970s, when declines in output were linked to structural changes in the economy.

It is worthwhile noting here some structural characteristics that help explain the lack of mobility and resource adaptation. This shortcoming, in turn, requires the implementation of tailored policy initiatives. In Brazil, for example, a generally low education level constitutes an actual barrier to the mobility and adaptability of human resources, since individuals with low levels of education are more difficult to train.[5] Moreover, a country's labor laws determine, in part, the ability of its economy to adapt human resources to structural changes. In Brazil and Colombia, the use of hiring and firing clauses in work contracts (contrary to protection provisions in the law) seems to explain the high employment turnover which, in turn, prevents the development of human capital within corporate struc-

---

[3] Seniors particularly were impacted. More than a human capital trait, the phenomenon is due to the fact that early retirement helps companies avoid paying increasing retirement benefits.

[4] Unemployment, however, did not affect any of the country's poorest groups, a fact that seems to be related to the decline in job quality.

[5] Brazil's most important training institution, the National Service for Industrial Training (Serviço Nacional de Aprendizagem Industrial—SENAI), requires that its program enrollees have more than four years of education, a level which is higher than the national educational average.

tures. Chile and Uruguay are different, however, since modifications in the labor laws of both countries have practically eliminated restrictions on mobility. Finally, the analysis finds that the growing informality of the Brazilian and Colombian labor markets is a phenomenon deserving attention and decisive policy actions. These countries did not actually implement a structural adjustment policy. Despite the fact that their labor markets were not directly impacted by the adjustment processes, these markets showed signs of gradual deterioration. This can be attributed to lack of structural adjustment in the presence of declining productivity. In conclusion, a structural adjustment process implies potential adverse impacts on certain segments of the labor force. These impacts could be alleviated through the implementation of appropriate policies. Arguments to the effect that labor interests can best be served by avoiding economic adjustment are, therefore, invalid.

Institutional Framework for Structural Adjustment

An interesting issue discussed in the case studies, and one from which valuable lessons can be drawn, relates to the way countries have faced the need to organize a national training system. The Brazilian and Colombian training systems, which rely on public infrastructures, were created in a framework of stable economic growth rather than in one requiring labor conversion as part of structural adjustment programs. In fact, these systems organize programs and courses, structure formal training, and finance their operations mostly with a focus on training employees of large companies. The studies for both countries show that program coverage for these institutions is small when compared to their objectives and resources. For example, in Colombia only slightly more than 10 percent of training program enrollees receive apprentice training. Moreover, thanks to the substantial resources that are raised through taxes levied on the wage bill of formal firms, these training institutions have been refocusing their attention on other areas such as aid to small businesses, reducing the size of the informal sector, farmer assistance, and financing of unrelated central government operations.

Regarding assistance provided to human resources affected by the adjustment process, it is interesting to note that in Brazil, the National Confederation of Industries and the National Federation of Industries are the entities responsible for managing SENAI. This is clearly an advantage and illustrates the training and coordination role that the training entity (in this case the state) should play vis-à-vis the private sector. It must be recognized, however, that such a system is ill-suited to structural adjustments since an adjustment program should focus mainly on retraining and providing assistance to the unemployed. Furthermore, an analysis of the Brazilian and Colombian systems shows that their national training institutions are highly inflexible. New companies and small but growing ones are not in a position to influence decisions affecting training activities, and excessive state intervention and bureaucratized training services prevail. The Chilean and the Uruguayan systems are plagued with similar problems. The Chilean system, though more flexible because of its strong ties to the private sector, does not focus on the unemployed or on general training which theoretically is the purpose of state-sponsored training.

In summary, Brazil and Colombia are typical examples of training systems that are inefficient because of excessive state intervention. The traditional development strategy followed by these countries involved state planning, focusing training on expanding economic sectors where uncertainty or risks are limited and, therefore, little flexibility is required. Furthermore, these systems are geared to the needs of established rather than new companies. They do not address unemployment resulting from adjustment processes or the problems of young people entering the work force. The Colombian study also shows that the National Training Service (Servicio Nacional de Aprendizaje—SENA), despite its large budgetary allocations, has major weaknesses because of its obsolete techniques and technologies. SENA's extremely rigid administrative structures also prevent institutions from undertaking appropriate initiatives and program modifications.

Uruguayan state institutions have not played a clear role in training and labor reconversion. These institutions, and the private ones that have since emerged, have not completely focused on training or rebuilding the skills of workers displaced during the adjustment period. This is evidenced by the fact that 80 percent of the courses are financed through tuition fees. It must be noted, however, that Uruguay's state-run Vocational Training Center (Centro de Capacitación Profesional—COCAP) is partly funded by the private sector. The center was created in 1978 mainly to provide accelerated training to workers in the export sector in response to expectations that the sector would grow.

Also noteworthy are two types of training courses provided by Uruguay's COCAP. In-house courses (23 percent) are primarily provided by companies as career-oriented training. While this type of training may yield high social returns, it is not particularly useful from the point of view of structural adjustment. Public enrollment courses (77 percent), whose basic curriculum is general education, apply to a wide range of employment skills. Part of the latter training is financed by voluntary contributions, an approach which training policies of this type should obviously pursue.

While the Uruguayan case illustrates an interesting private sector response to a shortfall in public sector programs, it should be pointed out that surveys conducted among private companies view the training as inadequate.

The Chilean training system is highly decentralized and flexible. The almost total elimination of onerous state structures has effectively debureaucratized the system. This was achieved by privatizing the state and relieving it of virtually all nonessential activities. While this system is highly responsive to the actual needs of the private sector, its training program is company-specific. Companies that receive subsidies are free to decide which training courses to provide. Thus, it can be concluded that the Chilean subsidy mechanism was not specifically meant to foster mobility during the adjustment process. This observation is based on two facts. First, the training system's subsidies are for the most part channeled directly to companies (not to the trainees), thus favoring specific rather than general training. Second, the nature of the tax breaks provided to the companies, unlike state subsidies with broader coverage, is highly procyclical.

In summary, while the countries under study have chosen different approaches to training, all of the systems adopted appear to be ill-suited to structural adjustment. Thus, one conclusion is that despite different situations, institutional structures, degrees of private sector participation, and financing approaches, none of the countries has adopted a labor conversion or reconversion system suited to an ongoing or potential structural adjustment process.

Policy Recommendations

The policy recommendations made in the four country studies apply mainly to general issues. Although some can only be implemented in the long term, they are still important. The implementation of other policy proposals appears more straightforward and feasible in the short term. The long-term, and by far the most important recommendation, relates to the strong connection that must be encouraged between general education and training. Countries that have highly educated populations find it easier to retrain their work forces, making the process of skill-conversions associated with a structural adjustment program less costly. Thus, the advantage inherent in a better educated population should be evaluated in the context of the eventual need to adapt human resources to new economic conditions. This makes the country's level of general education a highly valuable asset. Likewise, in countries where the general level of education is low or uneven and where a high percentage of the work force is uneducated, education systems must be structured to include training or skill-conversion programs targeted to the uneducated.

The above recommendation suggests the creation of training programs aimed primarily at high priority segments of the population. Underlying this recommendation is the observation that the training systems described in the studies do not benefit those most severely affected by structural adjustment (the unemployed) or macroeconomic crises (those endowed with lesser human capital). Therefore, it is recommended that the coverage of subsidized training programs be extended to include the unemployed by subsidizing training directly to the beneficiary. To prevent subsidies from benefitting individuals outside the targeted groups or from resulting in training that does not correspond to private sector needs, this policy should require that course work be supplemented by a guaranteed practice stint within the company that provides the training.

Another key element concerns the financing of training and labor reconversion. It is important to recognize that, during a structural adjustment process, the highest training requirements coincide with the lowest levels of economic activity. Reliance on voluntary financial contributions (as in Uruguay) or recourse to budget-allocated subsidies (as in Uruguay and Chile) make these financing approaches clearly procyclical.

A further recommendation is to urgently address the discrepancy between existing skill training programs and those needed in the marketplace. Therefore, it is not sufficient to create programs, such as in Chile, where most of the training is carried out by companies receiving direct subsidies. Although such programs guarantee training in areas of growth and in areas in which companies have a vested interest, they only focus on topics that are germane to the companies' specialized operations. This is not the type of subsidized training the state should support, since it diminishes rather than promotes flexibility and mobility. Furthermore, the Chilean subsidies, whose disbursements are tied to corporate decisions, often translate into nonmonetary benefits for company executives. This would explain why a significant percentage of training courses in Chile are being attended by high company executives and high-income employees. At the same time, the experiences in Brazil and Colombia suggest that their institutional approaches—which are better suited to the economic environment that prevailed in Latin America in the early 1930s than to the current one—should be replaced by more flexible approaches. This may be achieved by a better understanding of the production needs of the private sector.

In a certain way, the Brazilian approach, which bestows on company consortia greater decision-making power, has an advantage over less flexible schemes such as those in Colombia because it eliminates problems associated with general training. Indeed, from a sectoral perspective, the investment loss companies face when employees they have trained quit disappears. Transfers of skilled workers from companies that trained them to others that do not provide such training may represent losses for the former, but this is clearly not true for the industrial sector as a whole. Instead of a totally centralized system that eventually generates costs that are as large or greater than those of a totally decentralized system, it is therefore reasonable to give consideration to the advantages of a mixed scheme.

The most critical aspect in tax-subsidized institutional programs that allow the company leadership to determine curricula and training activities is that the beneficiaries of the training can exert the greatest pressure on the training entity. This creates a bias benefitting the largest companies which, because they receive net subsidies, usually encourage the permanence of such training structures. The clearest policy recommendation in this regard would, therefore, aim at an equilibrium between the decentralization of training decisions and training requirements in general. Mixed mechanisms, such as those which are currently carried out in Chile under the Youth Training Program (Programa de Capacitación de Jóvenes) financed by the Inter-American Development Bank, seem to be a logical approach.

Also recommended is close coordination between training and social assistance systems. These systems are crucial for alleviating the impact of net declines in labor demand which are inevitable by-products of structural adjustment. Such coordination should help reduce administrative costs and would take advantage of the close complementarity of the two systems. The experiences analyzed in the country studies demonstrate that assistance programs, usually enacted on an emergency basis, waste significant resources and fail to directly benefit their targeted beneficiaries. For example, in Chile a category of unemployment subsidies went to individuals who did not even belong to the labor force. Such wasteful practices could be substantially reduced if subsidy deliveries were conditioned on attendance in labor training courses.

Finally, the research in this volume implies that countries such as Uruguay can successfully endure an adjustment process with little or no emphasis on institutional training programs. Nevertheless, it is suggested that such success is mainly due to the lack of an effective structural adjustment as well as to the population's generally high educational level. As these circumstances may not be duplicated, at least in the short term, it is imperative that flexible programs be adopted in most countries where adjustment processes may eventually occur. These programs should avoid procyclical fund allocations, ensure that training curricula conform strictly to private sector requirements, and closely coordinate and integrate the different labor reconversion and assistance programs designed to reduce the social burden of groups affected by the adjustment.

Bibliography

Jaspersen, F. Z. 1981. *Adjustment Experience and Growth Prospects of the Semi-Industrial Economics.* Staff Working Paper No. 477. World Bank, Washington, D.C.

Jaspersen, F. Z., and K. Shariff. 1990. *The Macroeconomic Underpinnings of Adjustment Lending.* Policy, Research, and External Affairs Working Papers. World Bank, Washington, D.C.

CHAPTER TWO

BRAZIL

Edward Amadeo
Ricardo Paes de Barros
José Márcio Camargo
Rosane Pinto de Mendonça
Valéria Pero
André Urani

By the end of the 1980s, Brazil faced a major challenge: how to carry out structural reforms to control the fiscal deficit and increase international competitiveness. Since 1990, the country has adopted a series of economic policies to meet this challenge. It is hoped that these policies will improve economic productivity in Brazil and enhance the performance of its labor market.

Structural reforms can bring about significant adjustment costs that are unevenly distributed and impact selectively on labor. These costs result from structural changes that eliminate and create jobs at the same time and require considerable labor mobility. The size of the costs and their impact is inversely proportional to a labor market's flexibility. In other words, labor market flexibility depends on: (a) the skill level of the labor force and the availability and cost of retraining programs; (b) institutional constraints resulting from labor contracts and laws; and (c) structural characteristics of the labor market such as its level of regional integration and informality.

The first two sections of this chapter identify the needs and range of structural changes in relation to those which occurred in the 1980s. The third section assesses the extent and impact of the adjustment costs caused by economic fluctuations in the 1980s. The fourth section discusses the skill level of Brazil's work force and the country's education system, with emphasis on technical and professional training. The fifth section examines several policies that could affect labor market performance and identifies those policies that could reduce adjustment costs by increasing labor market flexibility. The final section presents a summary of the conclusions reached.

Brazil's Structural Adjustment Process

In the last 20 years, Brazil's economy experienced four external shocks and several significant political changes. The external shocks were the oil crises of the mid-1970s and the late 1970s, the increase in international interest rates during the late 1970s and early 1980s, and the interruption of foreign capital inflows. The country also experienced a gradual process of democratization during the 1980s, which was accompanied by heightened concern over issues of social inequality and poverty and by stronger business and labor influences.

In response to these changes, a significant number of economic policies were implemented. While these policies greatly influenced Brazil's macroeconomic and labor conditions, their results were, at best, mixed. On the one hand, the policies were successful in eliminating most external imbalances; on the other, they created some domestic imbalances and were unable to do away with others.

The early 1970s represented a period of rapid economic growth for Brazil. GDP grew at an annual rate of 10 to 12 percent, while inflation (15 to 20 percent annually)[1] and the trade deficit (never above 2 percent of GDP) were moderate (Tables 2.1 and 2.2).

The First Oil Crisis: 1973-78

The first oil crisis caused an enormous trade deficit in 1974 (5.6 percent of GDP), raising import levels from 9 percent of GDP in 1973 to 13.3 percent in 1974, while export levels remained steady at approximately 8 percent of GDP. As a result, the net external debt rose from 4 percent of GDP in 1973 to 7 percent in 1974.

Two types of economic policy measures were implemented. First, because of easy access to low interest credit in the international marketplace, the trade account was adjusted without carrying out a devaluation in the real exchange rate of the cruzeiro. Thus the country adopted a growth strategy based on foreign borrowing. Also adopted was a structural adjustment program that consisted of a daring investment plan aimed at reducing the country's dependence on imported capital and intermediary goods, and at promoting the export of manufactured goods. The result was a gradual reduction of Brazil's trade deficit, from 5.6 percent of GDP in 1974 to 1.2 percent in 1978. This change was primarily due to a drop in imports from 13.3 percent to 7.9 percent of GDP. Although the level of exports remained relatively steady at around 7 percent of GDP, export composition changed dramatically, as manufactured goods rose from 25 percent of total exports in 1973 to 40 percent in 1978.

---

[1] Inflation has traditionally been high in Brazil, with annual rates hovering above 10 percent dating back at least to World War II.

Table 2.1. Brazil: National Accounts, 1970-90

Year	GDP 1980 prices (Cr$1000)[1]	Growth rate[1]	GDP per capita[1]	Growth rate[1]	Imports (% GDP)[2]	Exports (% GDP)[2]	Investment (% GDP)[1]	External debt (US$ billions) Gross	External debt (US$ billions) Net	Int. on ext. debt. (US$ millions)[2]	Public savings (% GDP)[1]	Private savings (% GDP)[1]	Total savings (% GDP)[1]
1970	5,419	n.a.	0.057	n.a.	7.4	7.0	18.83	5.30	4.10	234.00	8.12	11.11	20.54
1971	6,037	11.41	0.061	8.71	8.2	6.5	19.91	6.62	4.90	302.00	7.57	11.03	21.26
1972	6,758	11.95	0.067	9.28	8.9	7.3	20.33	9.52	5.34	359.00	8.69	9.98	21.21
1973	7,700	13.94	0.075	11.26	9.0	7.8	20.37	12.57	6.16	514.00	8.70	11.34	22.04
1974	8,336	8.25	0.079	5.72	13.3	7.7	21.84	17.17	11.90	652.40	6.91	10.95	24.31
1975	8,763	5.12	0.081	2.67	11.0	7.2	23.33	21.17	17.13	1,498.00	6.34	14.20	25.70
1976	9,654	10.17	0.087	7.62	9.4	7.0	22.41	25.99	19.44	1,809.50	7.35	11.78	23.03
1977	10,130	4.93	0.089	2.51	7.9	7.2	21.32	32.04	24.78	2,103.50	7.60	12.15	22.03
1978	10,629	4.93	0.092	2.53	7.9	6.7	22.26	43.51	31.62	2,696.40	5.06	14.49	23.03
1979	11,348	6.77	0.096	4.34	9.3	7.2	23.35	49.90	40.22	4,185.50	3.47	14.85	23.13
1980	12,382	9.11	0.102	6.65	11.3	9.1	22.90	53.85	46.94	6,311.10	4.67	13.22	23.34
1981	11,838	-4.39	0.095	-6.54	9.8	9.4	22.94	61.41	53.90	9,161.00	4.28	14.36	23.08
1982	11,906	0.57	0.094	-1.67	8.3	7.6	21.44	70.20	66.20	11,353.30	1.40	13.90	21.09
1983	11,500	-3.41	0.089	-5.54	9.0	11.4	18.13	81.32	76.76	9,555.40	0.46	12.86	16.68
1984	12,107	5.28	0.091	2.98	7.9	13.5	16.89	90.09	79.10	10,202.70	0.26	15.50	15.74
1985	13,069	7.95	0.096	5.63	7.1	12.2	16.95	95.86	84.25	9,659.40	-0.22	19.31	19.20
1986	14,060	7.58	0.102	5.31	6.4	8.8	19.09	101.76	95.00	9,327.00	2.78	14.35	19.09
1987	14,569	3.62	0.103	1.45	6.2	9.5	22.30	107.51	100.06	8,792.20	2.72	19.10	22.30
1988	14,557	-0.08	0.101	-2.14	5.7	10.9	22.81	102.56	93.41	9,831.90	1.80	22.29	22.81
1989	15,037	3.30	0.102	1.21	5.0	8.3	24.86	99.29	89.61	9,632.90	-1.31	26.40	24.86
1990	14,430	-4.04	0.096	-5.93	5.5	7.2	21.67	96.55	86.57	9,009.00	n.a.	21.00	21.67

Sources:
[1] IBGE: National Accounting Department.
[2] BACEN: (Central Bank) Newsletters.

Table 2.2. Brazil: Macroeconomic Indicators, 1970-90

Year	Real exchange rate[1,2] (%)	WPI inflation[3] (%)	CPI-FIPE inflation[4]	Interest rate[4]	Terms of trade[5]	Prime rate	Real wages (industrial/ rate)[6,7]
1970	86.48	18.50	—	—	100.00	—	—
1971	84.85	21.40	—	—	92.82	5.67	—
1972	85.15	15.90	—	—	98.37	5.33	—
1973	85.54	15.50	—	—	107.03	8.21	—
1974	87.25	35.40	—	17.32	87.98	10.83	—
1975	89.28	29.30	—	21.84	85.17	7.85	—
1976	87.50	44.90	38.01	41.09	96.32	6.85	100.00
1977	87.50	35.50	41.18	41.91	112.77	6.90	131.80
1978	86.73	43.00	39.93	46.44	96.96	9.21	165.30
1979	93.69	80.10	67.14	42.58	88.98	12.73	143.60
1980	100.00	121.40	84.77	46.44	73.57	15.46	181.40
1981	90.45	94.30	90.86	89.26	62.58	18.69	210.10
1982	91.67	97.70	94.63	119.48	60.87	14.60	234.10
1983	112.62	234.00	164.06	200.09	60.10	10.75	143.50
1984	111.00	230.30	178.58	255.56	64.95	12.00	136.40
1985	114.61	225.70	228.21	276.85	65.09	9.88	155.80
1986	102.65	62.60	68.08	68.81	87.92	8.25	197.10
1987	96.61	407.20	367.12	358.00	80.42	8.21	206.30
1988	84.42	1,050.00	900.78	1,067.91	80.78	9.35	253.60
1989	68.56	1,748.80	1,635.85	2,617.93	73.70	10.91	356.50
1990	60.37	1,449.52	1,639.08	1,412.06	70.21	—	295.25

Sources:
[1] (CR$/US$)
[2] Carneiro y Werneck (1992).
[3] FGV - Fundación Getulio Vargas.
[4] FIPE - University of São Paulo.
[5] BACEN (Central Bank) Newsletter.
[6] Wages - PIM (FGV).
[7] Exchange Rate - FGV

One negative outcome of the growth strategy based on foreign borrowing was an external debt that tripled from US$13 billion (8 percent of GDP) in 1973 to US$44 billion (21 percent of GDP) in 1978. Although the cruzeiro was not devalued, inflation rose from 15 percent in 1973 to 43 percent in 1978 because of increased oil prices and a high price indexation. Despite increased inflation, however, uncertainty was kept under control by introducing a general indexing scheme that helped keep investment levels steady at 22 percent of GDP and growth rates high during the entire period (GDP grew at an annual rate of 6.7 percent from 1974 to 1979).

The Second Oil Crisis and Increased Interest Rates: 1979-82

The second oil crisis in the late 1970s increased the trade deficit and raised imports from 7.9 percent of GDP in 1978 to 11.3 percent in 1980. At about the same time, the steady rise in interest rates between 1978 and 1980 and the related debt increase raised debt service obligations from US$2.7 billion in 1978 to US$11.3 billion in 1982. These events raised doubts about the viability of Brazil's growth strategy based on foreign borrowing.

A more expeditious approach was needed to alleviate the current account deficit. The policy that was adopted involved a devaluation in the real exchange rate of the cruzeiro, which increased export levels from 6.7 percent of GDP in 1978 to 9.4 percent in 1981. However, because the devaluation was short-lived, in 1982 exports reverted to their 1979 levels. At the same time, the devaluation of the cruzeiro in an indexed economy led to inflation which rose from 43 percent in 1978 to 121 percent in 1980. Moreover, despite the devaluation of the cruzeiro and an increase in exports, the trade account still showed a deficit of 2 percent of GDP in 1980.

By 1981, the persistent and substantial current account deficit and unattractive interest rates led to import restrictions. The country adopted a policy of contraction that included a reduction in domestic credit. This policy brought an end to the growth that had characterized the 1970s, and reduced imports from 11.3 percent of GDP in 1980 to 8.3 percent in 1982. Despite an appreciation of the cruzeiro and a subsequent drop in exports, trade was almost brought into balance thanks to a drastic reduction in imports.

The Debt Crisis: 1982-84

By 1984 the flow of private foreign capital to Brazil had stopped completely. The lack of foreign credit constrained economic growth and required an immediate solution to the current account deficit problem. The response of the economic team was to again devalue the cruzeiro and restrict credit and imports. These policies were highly successful in balancing trade. Higher export and lower import levels led to a trade surplus, which in 1984 was large enough to balance the current account. Devaluation in the real exchange rate of the cruzeiro and a series of fiscal incentives had a significant impact on exports, which increased from 7.6 percent of GDP in 1982 to 13.5 percent in 1984. Import restrictions achieved, through steep tariff increases and nontariff barriers, a decline in domestic consumption induced by the 1981-83 recession, and the development of import substitution programs in the late 1970s, led to a new drop in imports which accounted for 7.9 percent of GDP in 1984.

The current account adjustment measures had a profound impact on the country's economy. The GDP dropped by more than 7 percent during the 1981-83 recession, and as a result of the devaluation of the cruzeiro, inflation doubled from 98 percent in 1982 to 230 percent in 1984. Moreover, since more than 80 percent of Brazil's foreign debt is held by the government,[2] its inability to obtain foreign loans forced the government to purchase hard currency from exporters to pay interest on foreign debt. This increased both inflation and the domestic debt.

Democratization and Inflation: 1985-90

Between 1985 and 1990 the cruzeiro underwent a significant appreciation in its real exchange rate which led to a sharp drop in exports from 12.2 percent of GDP in 1985 to 7.2 percent in 1990. At the same time, a systematic policy of import restriction and substitution brought about a decline in imports from 7.1 percent of GDP in 1985 to 5.5 percent in 1990. The net result was a sizable trade surplus which balanced the current account.

Restrictive monetary policies and the allocation of trade surpluses to service foreign debt obligations increased internal debt. Also contributing to the increase in internal debt during this period was significant government spending, which increased from 9.9 percent of GDP in 1985 to 15.6 percent in 1990. The increase in government spending was linked to expanded subsidies and government hiring at all levels.

Moreover, while the economy embarked on a period of renewed growth by 1984, the annual rate of inflation had climbed to 230 percent. Attempts to curb inflation failed, and rates doubled between 1984 and 1987, and then again between 1988 and 1989, peaking at an annual rate of 2,000 percent in 1989.

Conclusion and Outlook

During the last 20 years, Brazil's economy has been buffeted by severe external economic shocks which compelled it to generate trade surpluses. These were

---

2 The increase in the official foreign debt was the result of state enterprise and state governments' borrowing, and the central bank's absorption of private debt.

achieved mainly by restricting imports. While imports dropped from 13.3 percent of GDP in 1973 to 5.5 percent in 1990, export levels during the same period fell slightly as a percent of GDP. The composition of exports also changed significantly: in 1973 manufactured goods represented less than 25 percent of total exports, while in 1990 they represented almost 60 percent. Despite this important qualitative change, the Brazilian economy became more self-sufficient during these last two decades. Total import and export volumes in 1990 (12.7 percent of GDP) were not only low but had also fallen 2 percent below their 1970 level (14.4 percent of GDP).

In regard to economic growth, Brazil's performance during the 1980s was the worst since World War II. However, the current recession has been more severe than that in the early 1980s, and consequently GDP growth has not only been small, but also highly unstable.

In conclusion, the Brazilian economy has been successful in erasing the current account deficit brought about by the oil crises and higher international interest rates. The strategies that were adopted led first to a large increase in external debt and then, when external capital flows stopped, to growing inflation rates, higher fiscal deficits, and greater economic inefficiencies. Policies to counterbalance the external impacts have hampered Brazil's return to sustained growth. Thus, although Brazil was able to generate a trade surplus, the country's economic evolution since the mid-1970s can best be described as an example of failed economic adjustments rather than a structural adjustment.

Size and Cost of Structural Adjustment

Structural changes or cyclical economic fluctuations generate by necessity the loss and creation of jobs. Therefore, adjustment to these changes requires time and implies financial losses for workers as they change jobs, retrain, and acquire new skills and abilities. Generally, the costs of the adjustment process involve: (a) losses in production during the transition; (b) higher than "traditional" unemployment levels; (c) salary reductions resulting from loss of human capital in private firms or in the productive sector as a whole; and (d) higher wage disparities due to disequilibria prevailing in the labor market during the adjustment period.

Despite the fact that all types of structural reforms and cyclical economic fluctuations impose adjustment costs on the labor force, the nature of the costs and their impact can differ significantly depending on whether the change is a structural adjustment or a cyclical fluctuation. For example, adjustments to aggregate cyclical fluctuations tend to have a lesser impact on those workers whose human capital matches the specific needs of a company. However, structural adjustments requiring sectoral labor reassignments result in greater costs for the workers affected. This is highly relevant to the Brazilian case. While it is clear that adjustments intended to restore equilibrium to the external sector are cyclical, it is not certain whether the magnitude and impact of the changes would be the same if the economy were to become open to outside competition and state intervention in the market were reduced.

Gross Domestic Product

The annual GDP growth rate in the 1980s was small, both in absolute terms and in comparison with previous decades. GDP grew at an average annual rate of 6.5 percent in the 1950s and 1960s, 8.6 percent in the 1970s, and only 1.5 percent in the 1980s (Table 2.1). In the 1980s, GDP growth was not only small but also unstable, changing from almost 8 percent in 1985 and 1986 to less than 4 percent in 1981 and 1990. In general, growth was more rapid in the mid-1980s (1984-87) and negative at the beginning and end of the decade.

Brazil's population grew at an annual rate of 2.1 percent in the 1980s, while the per capita GDP annual growth for the decade was -0.6 percent. Because the population growth rate remained constant during the decade, the per capita GDP growth and the GDP growth profiles track each other. To be exact, per capita GDP growth rates fluctuated from negative values in the early and late 1980s (-6.5 percent in 1981 and -5.9 percent in 1990) to highly positive values in the mid-1980s (5.6 percent in 1985 and 5.3 percent in 1986) (Table 2.1).

Employment and Unemployment

Despite limited economic growth during the 1980s, job creation did not present a significant problem. Surprisingly, employment levels grew at a steady pace throughout the decade, producing more than 15 million jobs (Table 2.3). At the same time, the population's rate of participation in the work force increased almost steadily from 1979 to 1987, being 3.5 percent higher in 1987 than in 1979. Beginning in 1987, however, participation in the work force declined by 0.5 percent.

Unemployment rates increased during recessions and declined during periods of economic growth, but never exceeded 5 percent. During the 1981-83 recession, unemployment peaked at 4.9 percent in 1983, and quickly declined to 2.5 percent during the 1986 Cruzado Plan. After 1986, unemployment rates rose slightly, reaching almost 3.9 percent between 1987 and 1990. In relation to the size of GDP growth fluctuations, unemployment rates remained quite low and stable even during the recessions of 1981-83 and 1990-92 (Table 2.3).

Sectoral Structure of Employment

Table 2.4 shows that, from 1981 to 1989, the proportion of employment in the service and trade sectors increased by 6 percent, while the proportion of employ-

Table 2.3. Brazil: Demographic and Employment Indicators, 1979-90

Year	Economically active population (millions)	Rate of participation %	Trend of the unemployment rate %
1979	43.90	53.60	—
1980	—	—	—
1981	47.50	53.40	4.30
1982	49.90	54.90	3.90
1983	50.90	54.80	4.90
1984	52.40	54.80	4.30
1985	55.50	56.00	3.40
1986	56.80	55.80	2.40
1987	59.50	57.10	3.60
1988	61.00	58.80	3.80
1989	62.50	56.70	3.00
1990	64.50	56.70	3.70

Sources: Demographic Census and PNAD, 1980.

ment in the agricultural sector declined by almost the same figure. In absolute terms, this means that employment in the service and trade sectors increased by almost 50 percent between 1981 and 1989, generating more than 9 million new jobs. However, employment in the agricultural sector increased by only 6 percent.

The proportion of employment in manufacturing remained relatively constant in the 1980s, which implied an increase of 30 percent in absolute terms. Employment in public administration and defense increased by 0.7 percent from 1981 to 1989, most of this increase taking place during 1984-88. In absolute terms, the 53 percent employment increase from 1981 to 1989 corresponds to the creation of 1.1 million new government jobs.

The preceding data indicate a clear production shift from tradable to nontradable goods, a shift which actually counters the import substitution and export promotion programs enacted by Brazil during this decade. Also evident is that Brazil's effort to generate a trade surplus did not necessitate a labor shift to the tradable goods production sector. The contribution of manufactured goods to exports increased by less than 10 percent between 1981 and 1989 and represented only 3 percent of total manufacturing production. Since employment in manufacturing increased by 30 percent in the 1980s, it is not surprising that a shift in labor was not needed to balance Brazil's current account.

In conclusion, the adjustment of the current account was achieved without requiring intersectoral reallocation of labor, while employment grew because of strong growth in the tertiary sector, more specifically increased employment in the trade, service, and public sectors.

Table 2.4. Brazil: Trend of the Sectoral Structure of Labor, 1981-89
(Percentages)

Sector	1981	1982	1983	1984	1985	1986	1987	1988	1989
Nontradable	55.60	55.60	58.30	55.40	56.40	57.40	58.80	59.70	60.20
Construction	8.40	7.50	9.70	6.10	6.10	6.70	6.90	6.60	6.50
Trade	10.90	10.80	11.10	11.20	11.50	11.90	12.10	12.10	12.80
Transportation	3.90	3.80	3.60	3.60	3.60	3.60	3.70	3.80	3.80
Insurance and credit	2.20	2.20	2.40	2.40	2.60	2.20	2.20	2.20	2.20
Services	26.00	26.90	27.10	27.60	27.90	28.10	29.10	29.90	30.00
Public admin. and defense	4.30	4.50	4.40	4.50	4.60	4.90	4.90	5.10	5.00
Agriculture and mining	27.90	28.20	26.30	28.90	27.20	25.00	23.70	23.50	22.40
Manufacturing	15.40	15.20	14.40	14.60	15.20	16.50	16.10	15.60	16.20

Sources: Barros and Ramos (1991). PNADs.
Note: All individuals are 15 years of age or older and are employed.

As to the distribution of employment within different labor categories, Table 2.5 shows considerable stability during the period. Self-employment remained constant at approximately 26 percent. However, the number of employees working without formal agreements and non-paid family workers declined slightly, while the number of employees with formal agreements and government employees increased slightly, providing evidence of a growing formal labor sector. These changes, however, are clearly overshadowed by a decline in agricultural employment, as farm workers generally tend to be non-paid family workers or

Table 2.5. Brazil: Trend of Employment in Various Types of Labor Relationships, 1981-89
(Percentages)

Sector	1981	1982	1983	1984	1985	1986	1987	1988	1989
Self-employed	26.60	27.30	26.20	27.00	26.40	26.70	26.30	26.80	26.60
Formal employee	32.90	31.90	30.20	30.50	31.90	33.00	33.20	33.20	34.00
Public employee	10.30	10.40	10.50	10.70	10.90	11.30	11.30	11.90	11.70
Informal workers[1]	21.60	21.60	24.90	23.30	22.30	21.90	21.70	21.10	20.50
Non-paid	7.50	7.70	7.10	7.40	7.30	5.90	6.10	5.80	6.00
Others	1.10	1.00	1.00	1.10	1.20	1.10	1.40	1.20	1.10

Sources: Barros and Ramos (1991). PNADs.
Note: All individuals are 15 years of age or older and are employed.
[1] Employees without formal labor agreements.

informal employees. If the analysis had been restricted to urban areas, an opposite conclusion would have been reached. Indeed, in this case, a growing employment shift from the formal to the informal sector (the "informalization" of the labor force) was noted. Thus, the shift from agricultural to urban activities did imply a decline in the quality of employment, as measured by the degree of "formalization" in labor relationships.

Two conclusions can, therefore, be drawn. On the one hand, the current account adjustment program did not have a marked effect on structural employment. On the other, failure to achieve a reasonable level of growth led to deterioration of the quality of urban jobs with an increase in service employment and the informal urban work force.

Real Labor Income

GDP increased by 17 percent from 1980 to 1990, while the labor force increased by 40 percent. This implies that mean output declined by 17 percent. Therefore, if competitive conditions had prevailed in the labor market, real wages would have had to decline in order to allow for the absorption of the labor force. In fact, average labor income for each worker declined during this period, decreasing by 11 percent between 1980 and 1990.

However, the decline in labor income during the decade was not constant. It closely tracked the fluctuations in growth, but with a significantly wider spread. Wages declined during the recession of the early 1980s and later increased significantly during the recovery period of the mid-1980s, particularly in 1985 and 1986. At their highest in 1986, wages were 60 percent above their 1983 and 1984 levels. Except for a brief recovery in 1989, wages have been steadily declining since 1987. In 1990 the average labor income of the work force was 27 percent lower than in 1986.

Table 2.6 shows manufacturing wage trends in São Paulo. The figures reveal patterns that are radically different from average work wages. Wages in this industry did not decline in step with the average work income of the labor force during the 1981 recession. While wages increased at the same rate as that of the average work income, exhibiting a growth in mid-decade, they did not decline between 1986 and 1989. As a result, manufacturing wages in 1990 were 43 percent higher than in 1980 despite a sluggish growth of just 10 percent in manufacturing. The fact that manufacturing wages increased 43 percent despite a decline in average productivity of at least 15 percent suggests, therefore, that they were not awarded on a competitive basis. Stronger labor unions seem to have played an important role.

Table 2.6. Manufacturing Wage Index, São Paulo, 1979-90
(1979 = 100)

Year	Real income	Real manufacturing wages (São Paulo)	Income disparity (Gini)
1979	1.00	100.00	0.58
1980	1.21	108.00	0.59
1981	1.09	113.00	0.57
1982	1.07	116.00	0.58
1983	0.81	102.00	0.59
1984	0.80	105.00	0.59
1985	0.95	130.00	0.60
1986	1.48	163.00	0.59
1987	1.02	155.00	0.60
1988	0.88	165.00	0.62
1989	0.96	179.00	0.63
1990	0.94	154.00	0.61

Sources: Economic Trends (December 1979); PNAD and Demographic Census, 1980.

Income Inequality

Income inequality in Brazil is among the highest in the world. During the period of rapid growth (1968-80) and until the mid-1970s, income inequality rose considerably. Langoni (1973), for example, has argued that increasing inequality was one of the necessary costs of rapid economic growth and in-depth structural change. However, between the mid-1970s and the early 1980s, this inequality decreased moderately.

Table 2.6 shows the inequality measured by the Gini coefficient for the economically active population with positive incomes (from all sources). The table shows that the level of inequality increased significantly during the 1980s, especially between 1986 and 1989. During the recession of the early 1980s, inequality grew steadily but moderately. In 1986 the Cruzado Plan induced a modest reduction in inequality, but because of the failed economic plan and the growth of inflation, income inequality began to rise again. In 1989 the Gini coefficient reached a value of 0.63, a record for Brazil. The reasons for the drastic reduction in income inequality in 1990 are still unexplained.

The Impact of Adjustment Costs

The preceding section showed that the greatest cost stemming from the economic fluctuations of the 1980s was not high levels of unemployment, but rather losses in job quality and lower real wages. This section assesses whether the same holds true for each socioeconomic group taken independently. It first examines whether unemployment rates actually remained low for all of the groups during the recessions in the early and latter part of the decade, and then analyzes the relative wage losses for each group during these two recessions.

Unemployment

Unemployment rates for men and women remained low during the 1980s (Table 2.7), with rates for men generally lower than those for women. Comparing unemployment rates for 1986 (when unemployment was very low) with those for 1983 and 1990 (the two years when the recession was at its highest), the figures show that, during the two recessions, the unemployment rate for women was slightly lower than that for men, with the opposite occurring during recovery periods. In other words, the unemployment rate for men is more sensitive to economic fluctuations, indicating that recession costs are higher for men than for women. This may also indicate that women have a greater propensity to leave the work force during recessions (the effect of the discouraged worker). However, the participation of women in the work force is totally noncyclical, which leads to the conclusion that, at least as far as unemployment is concerned, economic fluctuations impose higher costs on men than on women.

Moreover, Brazil's most industrialized region, the southeast, has the highest and most sensitive unemployment rate of all of the country's regions (Table 2.7). The figures also show that regional differences in unemployment rates are insignificant. Even in the southeast, the unemployment rate exceeded 5.5 percent only in 1983, when it reached 6.1 percent.

Unemployment mostly affects the youngest members of the work force. Table 2.7 shows that unemployment rates for workers over 24 are considerably lower and less sensitive to economic fluctuations. Unemployment rates for workers under 25 exceeded 8 percent in 1983, and fluctuated considerably during the 1980s. The lower sensitivity of the older workers' rate might be due to their cyclical participation in the work force, though this has not been proven empirically.

The unemployment curve based on educational level is in the shape of an inverted U. Unemployment is higher for workers with five to eight years of education than it is for illiterates, with the rate declining again for those with university education. As the figures show, the differences in the unemployment rate among educational groups during periods of recession tend to rise significantly. In 1983, for example, the unemployment rate for workers with 5 to 11 years of education was between 7 and 8 percent, while the unemployment rate for all other groups during that year was less than 4.5 percent. This, then, provides evidence that workers with 5 to 11 years of education are subject to higher unemployment rates and are more sensitive to cyclical fluctuations.

Table 2.7. Unemployment Rate in Brazil, 1981-90
(Percentages)

	1981	1982	1983	1984	1985	1986	1987	1988	1989	1990
Men	4.2	3.9	4.9	4.1	3.2	2.3	3.4	3.6	3.1	3.8
Women	4.4	4.1	4.8	4.6	3.8	2.7	4.0	4.3	3.0	3.5
Region:										
SW	2.9	2.7	3.9	3.4	2.7	1.7	2.7	3.4	2.4	3.0
SE	5.4	5.0	6.1	5.4	4.3	2.8	4.2	4.1	3.2	4.3
ME	3.4	2.9	3.3	3.0	2.4	2.1	2.9	3.1	2.5	3.0
NE	3.5	3.1	3.8	3.3	2.5	2.3	3.5	3.8	3.3	3.4
NW	3.6	4.3	4.4	3.9	3.1	2.8	3.0	4.5	3.1	3.7
Age:										
less than 25	7.5	6.9	8.1	7.6	6.0	4.4	6.4	6.8	5.3	6.4
25 - 34	3.6	3.5	4.6	3.9	3.1	2.2	3.3	3.6	3.0	3.8
35 - 44	2.1	1.8	2.6	1.9	1.6	1.1	1.8	1.9	1.6	2.1
45 - 54	1.7	1.3	2.0	1.5	1.2	0.7	1.3	1.4	1.0	1.4
55 and over	1.0	0.9	1.0	0.9	0.7	0.4	0.6	0.7	0.6	0.8
Education:										
0	2.0	1.9	2.3	1.7	1.2	1.0	1.5	1.7	1.5	1.6
1 - 4	4.0	3.6	4.2	3.6	2.8	2.0	3.1	3.3	2.6	3.2
5 - 8	7.1	6.6	8.0	7.2	5.8	3.9	5.6	6.2	4.8	5.8
9 - 11	5.8	5.4	7.1	6.4	5.1	3.5	4.9	5.2	3.8	4.7
12 or more	2.7	2.6	3.4	2.9	2.1	1.7	2.1	1.9	1.5	2.1

Source: PNAD.

Figure 2.1. Unemployment Rate by Educational Level, Metropolitan Brazil, 1981-90
(Percentages)

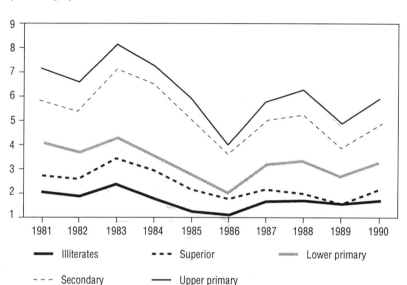

The inference that unemployment rates for less educated workers are not the highest and most sensitive is so central to this study that more evidence was sought. Two factors cloud the validity of the data in Table 2.7: the data are based on annual surveys taken in September and, therefore, do not represent an annual average; and less educated workers register lower rates of unemployment because they tend to be a majority. To deal with these problems, use was made of a Monthly Employment Survey which allowed for unemployment estimates grouped by educational level, region, sex, and age.

Figure 2.1 shows that grouping the unemployment rate by region, sex, and age, and restricting the universe to metropolitan Brazil, the rate for workers with fewer than four years of education (illiterates and those with basic elementary education) is higher and becomes more sensitive to economic fluctuations. The figure also confirms that the unemployment rate for workers with university education is lower and less sensitive to economic fluctuations than the rate for workers with average levels of education (5 to 11 years).

In summary, the impact of unemployment in the 1980s was not evenly distributed among socio-demographic groups. Unemployment was higher and had a stronger impact on the economic conditions of young people (under 25 years of age), workers with average levels of education (5 to 11 years of education), and the southwestern region. Therefore, during the 1980s recessions, unemployment did not particularly affect the poorest segments of society.

Table 2.8. Wage Differentials in Brazil, 1981-90
(As a percentage of the average wage of the highest income group)

	1981	1982	1983	1984	1985	1986	1987	1988	1989	1990
Men	4.2	3.9	4.9	4.1	3.2	2.3	3.4	3.6	3.1	3.8
Women	4.4	4.1	4.8	4.6	3.8	2.7	4.0	4.3	3.0	3.5
Region:										
SW	2.9	2.7	3.9	3.4	2.7	1.7	2.7	3.4	2.4	3.0
SE	5.4	5.0	6.1	5.4	4.3	2.8	4.2	4.1	3.2	4.3
MW	3.4	2.9	3.3	3.0	2.4	2.1	2.9	3.1	2.5	3.0
NE	3.5	3.1	3.8	3.3	2.5	2.3	3.5	3.8	3.3	3.4
NW	3.6	4.3	4.4	3.9	3.1	2.8	3.0	4.5	3.1	3.7
Age:										
less than 25	7.5	6.9	8.1	7.6	6.0	4.4	6.4	6.8	5.3	6.4
25 - 34	3.6	3.5	4.6	3.9	3.1	2.2	3.3	3.6	3.0	3.8
35 - 44	2.1	1.8	2.6	1.9	1.6	1.1	1.8	1.9	1.6	2.1
45 - 54	1.7	1.3	2.0	1.5	1.2	0.7	1.3	1.4	1.0	1.4
55 and over	1.0	0.9	1.0	0.9	0.7	0.4	0.6	0.7	0.6	0.8
Education:										
0	2.0	1.9	2.3	1.7	1.2	1.0	1.5	1.7	1.5	1.6
1 - 4	4.0	3.6	4.2	3.6	2.8	2.0	3.1	3.3	2.6	3.2
5 - 8	7.1	6.6	8.0	7.2	5.8	3.9	5.6	6.2	4.8	5.8
9 - 11	5.8	5.4	7.1	6.4	5.1	3.5	4.9	5.2	3.8	4.7
12 and over	2.7	2.6	3.4	2.9	2.1	1.7	2.1	1.9	1.5	2.1

Source: PNAD.

Table 2.9. Wage Differentials in Brazil. Selected Years
(As a percent of the average wage of the highest income group)

	1983 (1)	1986 (2)	1990 (3)	{[(1)+(3)]/2}-2
Women/Men	0.48	0.46	0.40	0.98
Region				
SW/SE	0.13	0.12	0.13	1.01
NE/SE	0.51	0.50	0.51	1.02
Age:				
Less than 25/25-54	0.63	0.62	0.63	1.01
55 and over/25-54	0.15	0.12	0.16	1.03
Education:				
0/12 and	0.89	0.88	0.90	1.01
1-4/12 and more	0.80	0.79	0.81	1.01
5-8/12 and more	0.74	0.75	0.76	1.00
9-11/12 and more	0.58	0.61	0.60	0.98

Source: PNAD.

Wage Structure

Table 2.8 shows trends in the Brazilian labor wage structure during the 1980s. Table 2.9 shows the same structure for selected periods during the decade. All figures shown are wage differentials calculated as a percent of the average wage of the highest income group. Comparison of the wage structure for the recession years (1983 and 1990) with that for 1986 (a year when labor unemployment was very low) allows identification of those groups most affected by the recession. In order to identify cyclical movements and to remove any trend component, the last column in Table 2.9 is a measure of the contrast in the predominant wage structure for 1986 and that for 1990 and 1983.

The evidence clearly shows a cyclical behavior in the man-woman wage differential. This differential increased during the recession of 1981-83, but decreased during the 1992-93 recession when the wage adjustment for men was more drastic than for women.

Salaries in the southeast are somewhat more sensitive to economic fluctuations than salaries in the southern and northeastern regions.[3] Moreover, since economic fluctuations tend to be greater in the southeast than in the northeast

[3] The northeast is the country's poorest region.

and south, the data in Table 2.9 indicates that, for a constant economic fluctuation amplitude, wage fluctuations in the northeast and south can be considerably
greater. The greater sensitivity to wages in the south and northeastern regions
might also be evidence that the job markets in these regions operate on a more
competitive basis than the southeast.

Wages of young workers tend to be more sensitive to economic fluctuations
than wages of workers at the peak of their careers (Table 2.9). At the same time,
wages of older workers tend to be considerably more sensitive. Likewise, wages
of the least educated (for example, illiterates and workers with up to 4 years of
education) are more sensitive to economic fluctuations than wages of better educated workers.

Brazil's Education System

Structure of the Formal Education System

Like most countries, formal education in Brazil consists of three levels: elementary, secondary, and post-secondary. As a result of the 1972 reform in education,
elementary education consists of eight sublevels. Brazil's constitution stipulates
that the government is responsible for providing free elementary education to all
young people, and that parents must keep young children in school from the age
of 7 (when elementary school begins) until the age of 14. Secondary education
consists of three sublevels. Finally, higher education lasts between two and six
years, depending on the type of program involved.

Two supplementary systems of education exist alongside the formal system. First, there are two programs, known as "Supletivo Primeiro Grau" and
"Supletivo Segundo Grau," which provide elementary and secondary education for young people and adults. The purpose of these programs, which are
shorter than the formal ones, is to upgrade the educational level of young
adults. The programs are restricted to individuals between the ages of 15 and
18. Second, given the country's high rate of adult illiteracy (currently exceeding 20 percent of the adult population), Brazil has enacted several programs
since 1960 to eradicate the problem. In 1967, the Ministry of Education
launched an ambitious program aimed at all of the country's regions. Achieved
results were insignificant, however. For example, in 1980 only 4 percent of
the illiterate population over 15 years of age participated in the programs
(Borba, 1976).

Responsibility for providing public education in Brazil is divided among the
federal, state, and municipal governments. While the federal government is responsible for providing post-secondary education, the state is responsible for
providing secondary education, and local governments are responsible for pro-

Table 2.10. Public Spending on Education (Federal, State and Municipal) in Selected Countries, 1989

Country	Per capita GDP (US$)	Public spending on education (% of GDP)
Argentina	2,160	3.10
Brazil	2,540	3.70
Chile	1,770	3.60
Costa Rica	1,780	4.40
Mexico	2,010	3.80
Uruguay	2,620	3.10
Venezuela	2,450	4.20

Source: United Nations (1990).

viding elementary education. However, states must help municipalities whenever the latter lack the necessary resources.

Public Spending on Education

The percentage of GDP Brazil has spent on education is the same as that of Latin American countries with similar per capita income levels; that is, Chile, Mexico, and Venezuela (Table 2.10). Moreover, the trend in public spending on education, as a percentage of GDP, shows progressive growth from 1.62 percent in 1960 to 4.5 percent in 1988.

Most of Brazil's problems in public education are found at the elementary level, thus making it important to examine this sector separately. For example, since spending on education may be unevenly distributed among different levels, aggregate estimates of government spending might not be a true indication of the effectiveness of spending on elementary education. Allocation data reveal that in 1988 elementary education accounted for 50 percent of total spending, with 40 and 10 percent of the allocations being channeled to the secondary and post-secondary education levels, respectively (Table 2.11). The data also show that 88 percent of all students in the public system were enrolled at the elementary level, with 8.3 and 3.5 percent at the secondary and post-secondary levels, respectively. This comparison leads to the conclusion that much of the spending is concentrated at the post-secondary level, where cost per student is approximately 20 times that at the elementary level.

The distribution of spending on education by federal, state, and municipal governments reveals that spending by local governments represents less than 15 percent of total public spending on education. The elementary level

Table 2.11. Brazil: Distribution of Public Spending and Enrollment According to Educational Level, 1988
(Percentages)

	Elementary	Secondary	Post-secondary	Total
Public Spending				
Federal	0.09	0.04	0.31	0.43
State	0.32	0.05	0.08	0.44
Municipal	0.12	0.00	0.00	0.12
Total	0.52	0.09	0.39	1.00
Enrollment				
Federal	0.00	0.00	0.02	0.03
State	0.57	0.07	0.01	0.66
Municipal	0.31	0.01	0.00	0.32
Total	0.88	0.08	0.03	1.00

Sources: Marques (1991) and IBGE (1990).

accounts for nearly 90 percent of enrollments and 50 percent of public spending. Thus, the conclusion can be drawn that local governments are incapable of fulfilling their role as the main providers of universal elementary education. In this respect, two-thirds of the total offering of public elementary education is provided by state public schools.

Regional Disparities

The regional distribution of public education is as important as the level of government spending. Indices of per capita spending on education and the cost per student in state and municipal elementary schools reveal extremely high regional disparities (Table 2.12). Indeed, the cost per student in Rio de Janeiro is almost 10 times higher than that in the State of Piau. A simple statistical analysis yields a correlation coefficient between per capita costs in education and per capita income for each region that exceeds 0.8.[4]

The data also show that state public schools spend almost three times more per student than municipal public schools. Unlike in the southeast, a large proportion of young people in the northeast are in municipal schools. Thus, a comparison of the cost per student in state and municipal schools in these two regions would tend to underestimate the extent of the disparity between the regions.

---

[4] Similar results were found by Mello e Souza (1979), who shows that regional disparities in spending on education have been decreasing over time.

Another important issue relates to the way in which the central government is strengthening or reducing regional disparities in public spending through resource transfers to states and municipalities. Since a significant part of state and municipal revenues come from central government transfers, these transfers could be used to reduce regional disparities. If the central government were to adopt a redistribution policy, the overall per capita central government transfers would correlate negatively with the state per capita income. However, the correlation estimates are positive. Mello e Souza (1979) arrived at a similar conclusion, further showing that if the analysis were limited to transfers specifically geared to education, then the correlation with the state per capita income would disappear.

Educational Results

Brazil's performance in education is evaluated through two comparisons. First, a series of educational results are compared with the average for seven high-income Latin American countries.[5] Second, a series of relationships between educational results and per capita GDP are estimated for all Latin American countries. Based on these estimated relationships, the real value of each educational achievement in Brazil is compared with the estimated or projected value for each relationship. These estimates are shown in Table 2.13 and in Figures 2.2 and 2.3.

Illiteracy Rate.   Brazil's illiteracy rate for the population over 15 years of age was approximately 20 percent in 1990 (Table 2.13). This level is almost 10 percentage points higher than that for other high-income Latin American countries, and higher than the level projected for Brazil by the Latin American regression line. This clearly indicates a much weaker performance for Brazil, as evidenced by an illiteracy rate that is higher than in any other high- and middle-income Latin American country, except Guatemala.[6]

Years of Schooling.   The mean years of schooling completed by Brazilians over 25 years of age is approximately four (Figure 2.2). This level is approximately three years below the average level for high-income Latin American countries and below the level projected by Latin America's regression line. The mean years of schooling completed in Brazil is lower than that for all other high- and middle-income Latin American countries.

---

[5] The countries are Argentina, Chile, Colombia, Costa Rica, Mexico, Uruguay, and Venezuela.

[6] Middle-income countries are those with a per capita GDP between $2,500 and $3,500. Besides Guatemala, these countries include Cuba, the Dominican Republic, Ecuador, Panama, Paraguay, and Peru.

Table 2.12. Brazil: Regional Disparities in Public Spending on Education by Government Level
(1988 US$)

State	Cost per student		Average income	Per capita transfers
	State	Municipal		
Brazil	146.3	52.2	2,241	n.a.
North	62.6	34.5	1,401	n.a.
Acre	48.6	49.2	n.a.	1.05
Amazonas	81.3	44.1	2,035	0.27
Amapá	98.3	31.7	n.a.	1.64
Roraima	143.7	n.a.	n.a.	2.40
Rondônia	207.8	n.a.	n.a.	0.34
Pará	53.1	27.4	1,199	0.16
Northeast	67.3	28.6	918	n.a
Maranhão	33.2	22.6	564	0.15
Piauí	32.6	22.4	472	0.19
Ceará	67.2	21.6	778	0.13
R.G.do Norte	97.7	42.0	585	0.20
Paraíba	74.3	36.4	628	0.17
Pernambuco	76.5	36.9	1,102	0.12
Alagoas	66.9	21.2	895	0.18
Sergipe	56.7	32.0	943	0.30
Bahia	62.0	27.5	1,226	0.11
Southeast	194.1	209.8	3,271	n.a.
Minas Gerais	n.a.	n.a.	1,850	0.08
Espírito Santo	89.1	106.6	1,914	0.10
Rio de Janeiro	306.1	266.1	3,352	0.04
São Paulo	202.7	138.0	3,993	0.03
South	142.8	109.0	2,382	n.a.
Paraná	106.7	62.7	2,037	0.05
Santa Catarina	106.1	139.4	2,344	0.06
R.G.do Sul	227.2	138.3	2,738	0.05
West-Central	83.7	39.7	1,949	n.a.
Mato Grosso	91.4	39.4	1,788	0.18
Mato G. do Sul	74.7	44.5	n.a.	0.11
Goiás	84.0	37.5	1,277	0.09
Federal District	308.2	n.a.	4,498	0.05

Sources: Ministry of Education (1989, 1990); Ministry of Finance (1986); and Albuquerque and Villela (1991).

Table 2.13. Educational Results for Brazil and Comparison Groups, 1990

Results	Brazil	High-income Latin American countries	Projection by regression
Adult population			
Illiteracy rate			
(15 or more years old)	18.90	8.60	8.60
Years of education	3.90	6.80	6.60
School-age population			
% in school			
(6-11 years old)	74.30	88.70	91.40
% repeating in:			
Elementary level	20.00	6.1	11.70
First grade	29.00	18.20	19.50

Sources: United Nations (1992), Statistical Yearbook (1991), and World Bank (1991).

Attendance Rates.   Less than 75 percent of Brazil's population between the ages of 6 and 11 attend an educational institution. This attendance rate is almost 15 percentage points below the average level for the other seven high-income Latin American countries. The attendance rate in Brazil is also 17 percentage points below the level projected by the regression line for attendance and per capita income for Latin America. Furthermore, the attendance rate in Brazil is lower than that in all other high- and middle-income Latin American countries, except Guatemala. These results categorically demonstrate that Brazil's current investment in education is quite low.

Repetition Rates.   Attendance rates might not be accurate indicators of the real investment in education whenever class repetition rates are high. Indeed, when faced with high repetition rates, attendance rates merely indicate an attempt at investment. Approximately 30 percent of Brazilian students in the first grade are repeaters (Figure 2.3), a rate which is 10 percentage points higher than the average level for high-income Latin American countries, and 10 percentage points higher than the level projected for Brazil by the corresponding regression line. Therefore, the percentage of repeaters among first grade students is higher in Brazil than in any other Latin American country. This would suggest that attendance rates in Brazil categorically overestimate the actual investment in education.

In summary, all of the indicators analyzed in this study lead to the conclusion that Brazil's investment in education is minimal. This poor qualitative and quantitative performance has important consequences on the ability of the work

Figure 2.2. Average Years of Schooling in Latin America

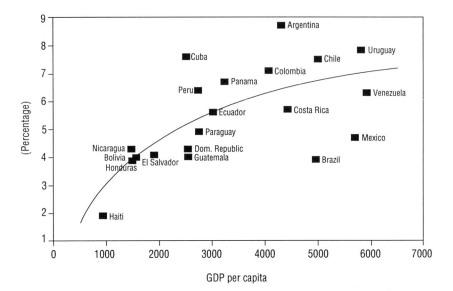

force to become technically proficient. For example, while major training institutions such as the National Service of Industrial Training (SENAI) require a minimum of four years of education, the average education prevailing in Brazil is 3.9 years. In 1990, 36 percent of the Brazilian labor force over 24 years of age had less than four years of schooling. Thus, it can be inferred that more than a third of this labor force will never have the opportunity to acquire training in a major public institution.

Vocational Education in Brazil

Training is clearly a key element for creating a flexible work force and for increasing its productivity. In this context, the concept of flexibility has two aspects. One is associated with the worker's ability to learn and to adapt himself to a changing environment, and the other is related to the knowledge of specific, productive skills. An effective training system should include both aspects.

The training process takes place both within and outside a company. It is assumed that training institutions in Brazil will have to provide both general education and vocational training, thereby satisfying the demand by different types of firms. For this reason, individual companies have no incentive to finance general and vocational education. However, on-the-job training which takes place within

Figure 2.3. First Grade Repetition Rate in Latin America

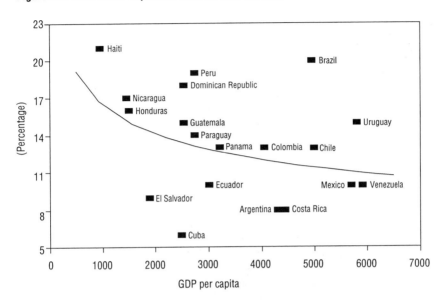

companies is an essential counterpart to the effort of training institutions and can be considered an asset companies are more prone to supply and fund.

This section lists tenets and concepts derived from the theory and practice of other countries:

- The success and cost of vocational training is largely affected by the quality of basic education. Dougherty, for example, (in Tuijnman, 1992, p. 559) points out that the better the quality of a worker's basic education, the greater his potential to be trained and to learn a specific skill. In any case, since making continuous education and training available to an employee would prove to be a cost-effective decision, the employer's incentive to do so will be high.
- In the realm of vocational education, there is a difference between the objectives one hopes to accomplish through formative and extended education programs and through specialized, short training courses. The latter usually involve curricula that are germane to the company's operations and, therefore, are best suited to workers already hired for specialized tasks. Formative courses, on the other hand, provide the worker with general skills and, therefore, improve his ability to learn and communicate.
- Formative courses are like public services that benefit all companies, while specialized training represents a private asset that benefits individual com-

panies. Since there are no incentives for companies to provide formative courses, these should, therefore, be provided by public institutions. Specialized training, on the other hand, should be the responsibility of the companies.

- The human capital of unemployed workers tends to depreciate, as they may find it difficult to pay for training. On the other hand, employed workers are trained by the companies for which they work. Therefore, it makes sense to provide general training to unemployed workers in order to compensate them for the natural depreciation of their skills. When trends in the labor market are uncertain, it is particularly inappropriate to provide specialized training to the unemployed. Rather, the unemployed should receive general training that strengthens their overall human capital.

National Industrial Training Service (SENAI)

SENAI was created in the early 1940s to provide vocational education and training to Brazilian industry. The service plays an important role in training qualified workers. SENAI is administered by the National Confederation of Industries and by the Federation of Industries in each state.

SENAI maintains close ties with companies and employer associations. Some of the courses offered are provided within the company, and some of them are specialized. A major part of SENAI's funding comes from a 1 percent corporate tax on company salaries. Companies with more than 500 workers pay 1.2 percent in tax. Companies are exempt from the tax if they contract SENAI to provide specialized training services.

Much of the information available on SENAI students and their performance in the labor market comes from surveys covering alumni activities in São Paulo, where more than 50 percent of SENAI activities are concentrated. The main SENAI courses fall within the following categories:

- Industrial Training Course (CAI). Designed to provide basic training for students between the ages of 14 and 18 who have completed at least four years of elementary school. The course provides general education and consists of 880 hours per year, lasting from one to one and a half years.
- Professional Skills Training (HP). Provides training for specific skills to young workers. Participants must have completed elementary school. Course work consists of 960 hours per year over a period of one to two years.
- Professional Specialization Course (CEP). Provides specialization programs to students between the ages of 14 and 18 who have completed at least four years of elementary education. Consists of relatively short (approximately 45 hours) courses.
- Professional Qualifications Course (CCP-I). Teaches specific skills to

adults. Enrollment is free of charge. Participants are required to have completed elementary school. Program consists of 100 hours of daytime courses.
- Professional Qualification Course (CCP-IV). Teaches specific skills to employed adults sent by their respective companies. Participants must have completed elementary school. Program consists of 180 hours of daytime courses.

SENAI Students

Except for CAI and HP students, most SENAI students are employed. About 90 percent of CCP students have jobs and are trying to improve their skills or learn a new profession. Admission for CAI and HP students is demand-driven, in the sense that SENAI estimates the size of its enrollment based on the prevailing demand for trained individuals. Only 35 percent of CAI students are employed when they begin the course, but most (approximately 70 percent) work as apprentices during the course of the program. With respect to the students' family background, it is worth mentioning that their parents are generally better educated than the average population (Table 2.14).

Moreover, the educational level of SENAI students is quite high when compared with that of the population 40 years of age and older. In Brazil, the average number of years of schooling for individuals between the ages of 15 and 19 is 5.2, and only 22 percent of those entering first grade ever reach seventh grade. The figures clearly show that SENAI trains individuals who are already educated, rather than the uneducated (Tables 2.15 and 2.16).

The data also show that 70 percent of CAI graduates in 1985 pursued an additional year of study after completing the course. Similarly, 40 percent of HP graduates continued with their studies. The proportion of graduates who attend university preparatory courses or who enroll in a university is 72 percent. These figures indicate that two years after graduating from the HP course, approximately 30 percent of the graduates are already enrolled, or are preparing to enroll, in a university.

In the CCP-IV group, the proportion of graduates who continue their studies one year after completing the SENAI course is 31 percent. Among these graduates, 49.1 percent enroll in university preparatory courses or are already enrolled in a university. These figures indicate that 25 percent of SENAI CCP-IV students are enrolled, or are preparing to enroll, in a university one to two years after graduation.

Employment Level of Graduates

SENAI graduates show approximately the same employment level as the average work force population between 19 and 24 years of age. The only exceptions

Table 2.14. Educational Level of Parents of SENAI Students, São Paulo, 1975-85
(Percentages)

	CAI	HP	CCP-IV	CEP	CCP-I	Population[1]
Illiterate	7	3	10	5	26	25
Elementary (incomplete)	27	15	34	26	31	28
Elementary (complete) and Secondary (incomplete)	61	57	49	63	31	41
Secondary (complete) or more	5	25	7	4	1	6

Source: SENAI.
[1] Male population, 40 years or older in São Paulo, 1985.

Table 2.15. Educational Level of Students Entering SENAI, São Paulo, 1975-85
(Percentages)

	CAI	CEP 1975-85	CEP 1985	CCP-I 1985
Elementary				
(Up to 4th grade)	26	0.7	1	30
5th-7th grade	65	84	27	36
Elementary (complete)	13	15	48	21
Secondary (incomplete)	4	0	20	8
Secondary (complete)	0	0	5	4

Source: SENAI.

Table 2.16. Educational Level of Students Entering SENAI in 1985, São Paulo
(Percentages)

	HP	CCP-IV
Elementary (complete)	90	50
Secondary (incomplete)	10	22
Secondary (complete)	0	22
University (incomplete and complete)	0	4

Source: SENAI.

are CAI students whose educational level is below average, probably because they are fulfilling their military obligation.

Surveys taken between 1975 and 1985 indicate that for all courses the majority of students held higher positions (i.e. executive or supervisor) when the survey was taken than those they found directly after finishing the course. The trend was especially pertinent to students from CAI and CEP (day students). The

Table 2.17. Trend of Wages in Minimum Wages (MW) One, Two and Three Years After Graduation, São Paulo

	Number of minimum wages	One year	Two years	Three years
	1-3 MW	69	63	51
CAI	3-5 MW	17	24	28
	5 or more MW	3	5	10
	2-5 MW	52	48	21
HP	5-7 MW	15	24	23
	7 or more MW	9	19	49
	3-5 MW	29	26	9
CCP-IV	5-7 MW	21	16	13
	7 or more MW	42	47	66

Source: SENAI.

exception is students in CEP night courses. Likewise, information on students from CAI (1985), CCP-IV (1986), and CCP-I (1987) in São Paulo (Table 2.17), indicates that a high proportion of workers earn higher wages between the first and third year after graduation.

Among the CAI students who found employment one month after finishing the program (1975-85), 60 percent were using the skills they learned at SENAI. By the time the survey was taken, shortly after the first month, this figure had dropped to 42 percent. In the HP group, 55 percent were using their skills at the time of the survey. As for students from CCP-IV (1975-85), 66 percent were using their acquired skills, a remarkable performance when compared to the other groups. The worst performance involved the short courses: among CCP-I graduates, 18 percent were using their acquired skills after one month, but only 15 percent were using them when the survey was taken. For the CEP group, 50 percent were using the skills they learned one month after completing the course. However, when the survey was taken, the percentage had dropped to 35 percent.

Industries and Companies that Hire SENAI Students

About 60 percent of CAI graduates are hired by three industries: metallurgy, heavy equipment (mechanical and electronic), and electronics. Together these industries provide work for 32 percent of Brazil's industrial labor force. The other industries employ 69 percent of the labor force, but hire only 19 percent of CAI graduates. The mechanical and transportation industries provide employment for more than 30 percent of SENAI graduates from HP, CCP-IV, and CCP-I courses, and for approximately 16 percent of the total work force.

Table 2.18. Hiring of SENAI Graduates by Size of Firm, Saõ Paulo 1986-88, One Year After Graduation
(Percentages)

	Small firm	Medium-and large-sized firm
HP	19	81
CCP-IV	8	92
CAI	39	61
CCP-I	29	48

Source: SENAI.

Middle-sized companies and large companies with more than 99 workers provide employment for 61 percent of CAI graduates, 81 percent of HP graduates, and 92 percent of CCP-IV graduates (Table 2.18). The proportion of the total number of industrial workers hired by medium and large companies is approximately 58 percent. This obviously implies that SENAI graduates (especially the most qualified) tend to work for large companies.

Figure 2.4 clearly shows a positive correlation between the level of industrial concentration and relative wages. Industrial sectors where large companies control the market (oligopolic markets) are the ones that pay higher wages. The industries that attract SENAI graduates (machinery, metallurgy, electronic equipment, and transportation) are among those that pay better wages and, except for the machinery industry, enjoy the highest industrial concentration.

Course Structure

The structure of SENAI courses has changed dramatically in the last 10 to 20 years. The total number of enrollees, graduates, and hours dedicated to short courses (training) has grown considerably between 1970 and 1990. The ratio of training enrollments (equivalent to CEP and CCP-I courses in São Paulo) to the total number of enrollments grew from 38 percent in 1970 to 85 percent in 1990 (Figure 2.5). Moreover, the proportion of graduates increased from 49 to 90 percent, and the proportion of hours devoted to these courses increased from 11 to 31 percent, while the proportion of hours for vocational courses dropped from 75 to 49 percent.

Course Program Funding

Companies can gain an exemption from the 1 percent wage tax if they enter into a cooperation agreement with SENAI and, as part of the agreement, contract services directly. With the tax rebate, companies have preferred to contract with

Figure 2.4. Relative Wages and Level of Industrial Concentration
(Percentages)

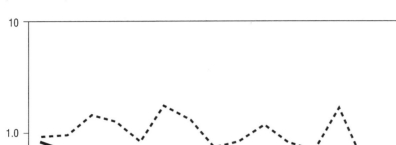

1. Tobacco	2. Rubber	3. Transportation	4. Electronics	5. Perfumes,Wax, etc
6. Chemicals	7. Metallurgy	8. Liquors	9. Papers	10. Pharmaceuticals
11. Plastic	12. Textiles	13. Mechanics	14. Clothing	15. Food

- - - Relative Wages   ▬▬ Level of Ind. Conc.

SENAI for short, specialized training courses. Thus, a tax whose purpose is funding the provision of a public service—specifically, general vocational education—is transformed into a tariff that finances a private service like specialized training.

The total number of students enrolled in SENAI increased by 52 percent between 1986 and 1990. Direct action (operations carried out by SENAI on its own) increased by 24 percent, and indirect action (through cooperation agreements with companies) increased by 88 percent. The total number of hours dedicated to direct action increased by 11 percent, while the number of indirect actions declined by 12 percent.

National Commercial Training Service (SENAC)

SENAC is SENAI's counterpart in the service and trade sectors. The data for SENAC, unlike those for SENAI, are scarce and highly unreliable, mainly because related terminologies originating in field agencies are not standard. For this reason, the evaluation of SENAC is much less complete than that for SENAI, and

Figure 2.5. SENAI Enrollments by Type of Course, 1970-91
(Percentages)

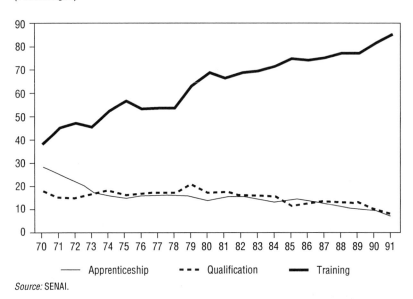

Source: SENAI.

caution must be exercised when interpreting the data pertaining to the former service.

SENAC relies on a 1 percent tax on corporate salaries of service companies for its funding. Unlike SENAI, tax exemptions for SENAC are not common. The relationship between the field agencies and the trade federations is quite strong—particularly because the organization's administration is totally controlled by the federations. The relationship with private companies is, however, quite weak. The result is that most of SENAC's clients are students, not companies and their workers.

SENAC provides many types of courses, but four of these account for 93 percent of enrollments:

- Introduction. Designed to introduce young students to the acquisition of basic skills geared to a specific occupation. In 1990, these courses accounted for 22.2 percent of SENAC's income and 15 percent of its hours. Most courses last from 30 to 120 hours.
- Qualification. Provide the student with general education and job-related skills. In 1990, these courses accounted for 34 percent of SENAC's income and 62 percent of its hours. Courses typically last from 40 to 250 hours.

- Skills Improvement. Extension courses designed to improve the skills of employed students who have work experience. In 1990, these courses accounted for 25 percent of SENAC's income and 12 percent of its hours. The courses are generally short (between 15 and 60 hours).
- Tools. Education courses in subjects such as Portuguese, mathematics, English, and drafting. In 1990, these courses accounted for 11 percent of SENAC's income and 6 percent of its hours.

In 1984, 61 percent of students registered in the SENAC were women, 56 percent were under the age of 20, and only 3.3 percent were over the age of 40. Furthermore, the students' educational level was surprisingly high. More than 60 percent had completed elementary school, and 23 percent had completed secondary school. In 1989, 88 percent had completed elementary school and 54 percent had completed secondary school. Since most students are young, it is reasonable to presume a significant proportion will continue their formal education.

Unlike SENAI, whose students are mostly employed, only 29 percent (in 1984) and 46 percent (in 1989) of SENAC's students held outside jobs during the course program. In 1984, the percentage of students who had never before held a job was 47 percent, indicating that SENAC's students are seldom affiliated with companies. Furthermore, among the students who did not hold jobs in 1984, 29 percent were looking for their first jobs, 28 percent found employment, and 25 percent decided to continue studying. Among those who were not working (70 percent in 1984), 65 percent had no job experience. Among those who had worked before, 11 percent were unemployed for less than three months, 22 percent were unemployed for three to six months, 14 percent for six to 11 months, 21 percent for one to two years, and 22 percent for more than two years.

Among the 1984 graduates, 69 percent were earning a salary in the formal sector, 15 percent in the informal sector, and 9 percent were self-employed. The salaries of graduates were considerably low when compared to their educational levels, which were high by Brazilian standards. Only 23 percent received more than three times the minimum salary.[7] Among those who earned wages in the informal sector, 55 percent received less than the minimum salary, and among those who were self-employed, 32 percent received less than the minimum salary.

The number of enrollees in skills improvement courses remained relatively stable during the 1980s, while those enrolled in qualification and introduction programs increased. The total number of hours for qualification courses, particularly those involving training, increased significantly. In this regard, SENAI and SENAC have been moving in different directions: while the number of SENAI hours devoted to educational courses has declined, the same number for SENAC has increased.

---

7 The minimum salary in 1984 was approximately $80 per month.

Evaluation of the Policies for Reducing the Adjustment Cost

This section's main objective is to evaluate the educational system, public professional, and technical training programs (particularly the SENAI and SENAC systems), and the linkages between the formal and vocational education systems. In this regard, there is also a discussion of the policies that influence labor market performance and which, as a result, can be used to reduce adjustment costs.

The Role of the Educational System

Workers are endowed with two types of human capital: general and specialized. Specialized human capital is directly related to productivity increases in particular activities. Since it is likely that a worker's specialized human capital can be lost during the adjustment process, the cost of adjustment will rise in relation to the range of workers' specialized human capital.

While workers with relatively high levels of general education can be trained cheaper and faster, the amount of retraining needed for highly skilled workers to recuperate their original levels of human capital and productivity is quite high.

General human capital and adjustment cost interrelate at three levels. First, during periods of adjustment, labor market conditions tend to change in predictable and rapid ways. Workers endowed with greater general human capital have a greater capacity to understand and correctly interpret economic changes (Schultz, 1975). Although these workers may not adjust rapidly, they will be the ones who, *ceteris paribus*, will benefit most from the creation of new opportunities.

Second, general human capital can enhance learning abilities, enabling workers to learn new techniques faster while reducing the cost of training. Therefore, since companies pay part of the training cost, they prefer to train better educated workers. As a result, workers with greater general human capital also tend to be endowed with more specialized human capital. This has contradictory effects on adjustment costs. On the one hand, the fact that these workers require less training reduces the cost of rebuilding, whenever necessary, their specialized human capital. On the other, the retraining required by skilled workers in order to recuperate their original levels of productivity is greater, increasing training periods and entailing higher adjustment costs. At the same time, the fact that skilled workers have more specialized training provides them with higher job security during periods of change and uncertainty. This occurs because companies cannot predict market changes with absolute certainty, and therefore delay adjustment steps in order to avoid the extra training costs they would incur if they mistakenly dismissed trained workers.

Finally, since workers with greater general human capital can be retrained faster and at a lower cost, they will be the first to receive training, thereby reducing their adjustment period and costs.

In conclusion, adjustment costs increase when dealing with specialized human capital, and decrease when dealing with general human capital, at least when the amount of specialized human capital is constant. Since workers with less general human capital also tend to be endowed with less specialized human capital, they will face lower adjustment costs because of lower losses in specialized human capital during the adjustment process. Workers highly endowed with both types of human capital will also face lower costs. Despite the fact that they may stand to lose considerable specialized human capital, their cost for reestablishing it will be low, thanks to the large amount of general human capital they possess.

As a result, general human capital and the cost of adjustment are not necessarily inversely related, nor is the relationship unstable. Workers with higher general human capital do not necessarily face lower costs and more rapid adjustment periods. Everything will depend on their degree of specialized and general human capital. The greater the gap between specialized and general human capital, the greater the retraining cost required to recuperate productivity after a structural adjustment. However, when specialized human capital is held constant, increases in general human capital will always bridge the gap, and will therefore help to reduce the adjustment cost.

In summary, it should be pointed out that SENAI does not have special programs for the unemployed, evidence that the institution is not prepared to facilitate the adjustment processes required by job reassignments. It is pointless to provide unemployed individuals who have specialized training with new specialized training as long as future market requirements remain uncertain. Responsibility for specialized training resides in the company that will eventually hire the unemployed individual. However, it is the government's responsibility to provide general education to unemployed workers who meet minimum requirements, in order to improve their abilities and help them acquire new skills. This should hold true particularly during an adjustment period when the educational vocational system can play an important role in increasing labor mobility. This also provides an important contribution to an environment that undergoes technological change, wherein work flexibility and adaptability are extremely important factors.

A highly controversial argument holds that there already exists an adequate supply of "educated" students trying to enter vocational schools, and that providing education and training to the uneducated would be costly. The cost of professional education and training for the uneducated is clearly higher than that for students of a certain educational level. SENAI's costs are reduced by the demand for qualified labor. The institution should consider lowering its admission standards only if the supply of candidates would be lower than the demand by qualified students. According to this argument, SENAI should not function as an academic school, providing formal education to the less educated. Public schools should be the vehicle for a comprehensive education that provides equal opportunity to the poor and allows them to compete with the wealthy on SENAI admission exams or in the labor market. Improving equality standards should not be the obligation of an institution like SENAI, which is specifically oriented to the labor market.

A second argument is less favorable to SENAI. It maintains that SENAI acts as an academic school for students whose parents are better educated than the average population, and who, therefore, most likely come from a wealthier class. These students continue their education after graduating from SENAI, and a significant number of them enter a university. The goal of these students is to become engineers, not technicians.

The fact that small companies do not hire SENAI graduates can be viewed as evidence that, unlike larger companies, small businesses do not value qualified workers. Large companies, however, do not complain about a lack of qualified workers. Small companies may not be drawn to SENAI graduates because their wage expectations are quite high compared to what companies can afford. There is evidence that SENAI graduates are attracted to industries that pay higher wages.

The main recommendation that can be derived from this interpretation is that SENAI funding criteria should be revised. Large companies that can finance in-house training should be exempt from paying their contribution. Also, students able to pay for their studies should be required to do so. Finally, as the World Bank has recommended in its studies on secondary education in Brazil, extra funding should be used to increase education and general courses, and to provide more opportunities to the less educated. As a result, there should be an increase in the supply of qualified workers with general education, which would possibly reduce the salary differential between qualified and unqualified workers and could open the possibility for small companies to improve the quality of their human resources.

Several comparisons could be made. First, it should be pointed out that SENAC trains and educates young, unemployed students, while SENAI trains and educates employed students. Second, the educational level of students in both institutions is high when compared with Brazilian standards, but it seems to be higher in SENAC than in SENAI. Third, salary levels for SENAC graduates are rather low if one considers their level of education. This can be explained by their age and lack of experience. Fourth, despite the fact that very little can be verified from aggregate information on the SENAC course structure, it seems that neither the total number of hours nor the average number of hours per student enrolled in the training courses has declined in the 1980s.

Regional Integration of Labor Markets

Huge disparities exist in the composition of Brazil's production and employment sectors. Agriculture continues to be the main economic sector in the northeast and the south. Most manufacturing is still located in the southeast. Furthermore, while in the northeast subsistence farming is the main source of employment, in the south most agricultural labor is engaged in the production of exportable goods. Therefore, it is hoped that structural changes, particularly those related to changes in trade policy, will have important effects on regional differences. Thus, rapid redeployment of the labor force is an essential requirement for reducing adjustment costs. The degree to which labor will respond to redeployment pressures resulting from regional changes will depend on how integrated regional labor markets are.

Regional integration has been a constant policy objective for the government. The steps required for implementing this objective are not easy or beyond scrutiny. Figure 2.6 illustrates one of these steps: the degree of regional disparity in wages for metropolitan Brazil (Savedoff, 1991).[8] The data show a significant level of disparity in regional wages, thus questioning the degree of success attained by a longstanding history of policies aimed at regional integration.

In conclusion, the expected structural changes should have different impacts on Brazil's regions. Regional labor markets are far from being totally integrated, and the enactment of policies designed to accelerate the integration process is essential for reducing adjustment costs associated with structural changes, particularly those changes which stem from reductions in trade barriers.

The Informal Sector and the Cost of Adjustment

The Brazilian labor market is characterized by a low rate of unemployment and a high level of informality (approximately 60 percent of the labor force). Under some circumstances, informality can considerably reduce adjustment costs. Thus, if informality acts as an alternative to unemployment, the proportion of workers in the informal sector should increase when the rates of unemployment increase. As can be observed in Table 2.19, the rate of unemployment increased during two periods: from 1983 to 1984 and from 1989 to 1991. In the second period, the increase in the level of informality was small in relation to the increase in unemployment, thus providing insufficient evidence in favor of the cited hypothesis. However, during the first period, the level of informality increased more than the unemployment rate, providing an extremely clear example in support of the ar-

---

[8] These data have been adjusted for regional differences in cost of living. The data relate to workers who have identical observable characteristics and who hold the same jobs and work in identical sectors.

Figure 2.6. Brazil: Regional Disparities in Real Wages

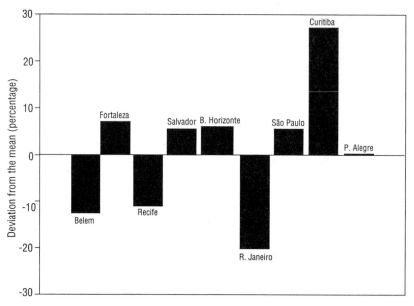

Source: Savedoff (1991).

gument that informal employment is an alternative to unemployment in periods of declining levels of economic activity.

The informal sector would not have an important role in reducing adjustment costs if income losses related to employment shifts from the formal to the informal sector were very high. Thus, a second condition needed in order for the informal sector to reduce adjustment costs is that the salary differential among equally productive workers engaged in formal and informal activities be small. It should be noted that this condition ought to prevail mainly during times of high or growing unemployment rates, and for those workers in the formal sector who are in danger of losing their jobs. To study this problem, an analysis was undertaken on wage differences between formal and informal workers and between formal and self-employed workers, by education, age, sex, and regional groups for the periods 1983-84 and 1990-91. The results show that both alternatives to formal employment are costly (Table 2.20), informal jobs being less attractive than self-employment. The decline in the income logarithm associated with shifts from formal to informal jobs is on the average 0.50 between 1983 and 1984, and 0.36 between 1990 and 1991. As to the shift from formal employment to self-employment, the loss in the income logarithm is estimated at between 0.5 and 0.26 for the first and second periods, respectively. It is important to note that

Table 2.19. Temporal Trend of the Unemployment Rate, Segment of Workers with and without Formal Labor Agreement, and Self-employed Workers in Metropolitan Brazil *(Percentages)*

Periods	Unemployment rate	Degree of formality	Degree of informality	
			Informal	Self-employed
1982	3.80	57.70	14.20	17.70
1983	4.80	55.70	13.40	18.00
1984	5.40	54.30	14.20	19.00
1985	4.00	55.60	13.90	18.60
1986	2.90	56.50	13.50	18.20
1987	3.10	56.30	13.40	18.60
1988	3.20	55.80	13.50	19.50
1989	2.80	56.10	13.00	19.80
1990	3.60	55.10	13.30	21.10
1991	4.10	51.60	15.40	22.80
Average	3.77	55.47	13.78	19.33
STD	0.008	0.015	0.007	0.015

Source: EME.

income losses were less during the second period, when informal employment did not act as an alternative to unemployment. On calculating the wage differential by education level, sex, and region, it can be seen that in relative terms the loss of income is higher for lower income groups.

A third condition needed for the informal sector to contribute significantly to the reduction of adjustment costs is the existence of a substantial universe of formal sector workers during periods of declining unemployment. It is important to point out that, in seeking employment in the formal sector during an economic recovery, informal workers do not enjoy special advantages over the unemployed.

Finally, it should be mentioned that workers who persevere in the informal sector over extended periods face much more than just a loss in formal income. If work experience is accumulated more rapidly in formal activities, or if the experience accumulated in informal activities cannot be transferred to formal jobs, workers who are obliged to engage in informal activities over extended periods will be subject to lower rates of wage growth and, therefore, will derive less income benefits. This represents a dynamic loss in income, due to the fact that the workers remain in the informal sector. As a result, a fourth condition needed for the private sector to contribute to a reduction in adjustment costs is that these dynamic income losses be small. The size of dynamic losses depends on two factors: the differential between the rates of accumulation in experience in formal and informal activities, and the degree to which accumulated experience in

Table 2.20. Wage Differences in Brazil

	1983-84 Period			1990-91 Period		
	Wage differential		Average formal wages	Wage differential		Average formal wages
	Formal/ informal	Formal/ self-emp.		Formal/ informal	Formal/ self-emp.	
Average	0.50	0.51	1.00	0.36	0.26	1.00
Illiterate	0.52	0.39	0.29	0.26	0.06	0.30
Lower elementary	0.51	0.39	0.46	0.29	0.05	0.43
Upper elementary	0.47	0.48	0.79	0.28	0.12	0.65
Secondary	0.55	0.59	1.34	0.32	0.33	1.12
Higher	0.49	0.55	2.45	0.44	0.37	2.68
Correlation	0	0.80		0.99	0.86	
States						
Belo Horizonte	0.60	0.59	1.01	0.40	0.36	1.01
Porto Alegre	0.31	0.44	1.01	0.28	0.21	0.98
Recife	0.51	0.63	0.75	0.32	0.27	0.80
Rio de Janeiro	0.51	0.48	0.95	0.38	0.25	0.87
Salvador	0.56	0.44	0.99	0.45	0.26	0.98
São Paulo	0.56	0.56	1.28	0.37	0.26	1.36
Correlation	0	0		0	0	
Women	0.45	0.62	0.63	0.31	0.19	0.70
Men	0.52	0.48	1.25	0.38	0.30	1.19
Correlation	1.00	-1.00		1.00	1.00	

Source: EME.

informal activities can be transferred to formal activities. To study the magnitude of the first factor, a comparison is made between the age-wage profile pertaining to formal activities with that pertaining to informal activities. The figures show that formal and informal employees have almost parallel age-logarithm wage profiles, while the profile for self-employed workers is considerably flatter (Figure 2.7). As a result, self-employment represents an option that yields smaller immediate income losses but increased losses over the duration of workers holding jobs in the sector. A job in the informal sector, on the other hand, implies an immediate larger income loss, but not a dynamic one, at least while the accumulated labor experience in informal jobs can be transferred to formal activities.

Figure 2.7. Brazil: Age-Log Wage Profile by Type of Worker

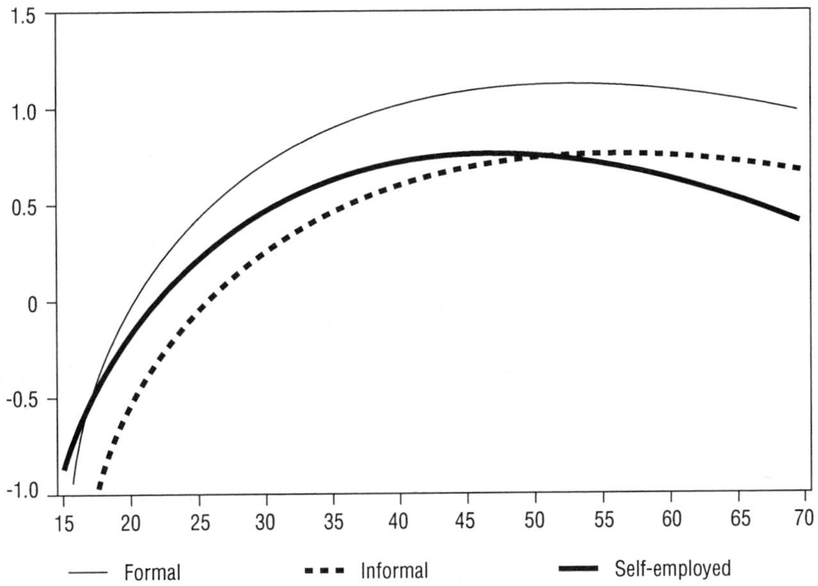

Source: Porcentaje Mensual de Empleo (PME).

Brazil's Labor Legislation and Assistance Programs

An important characteristic of Brazil's labor market relates to the complex institutional regulations which affect market behavior. These include: (a) the Labor Code, which is a complete set of laws dealing with individual and collective rights of employees and employers; (b) a compensation fund for laid-off workers; (c) an unemployment insurance law; and (d) wage adjustment clauses tied to inflation rates. The following is an analysis of the compensation fund for laid-off workers and the unemployment insurance program.

The cost of laying off a worker has two components: the "advance notice" and a premium assessed on the unemployment compensation fund. Under the "advance notice," companies are obliged to notify workers one month in advance of the layoff. During this month, the worker can legally take off two hours a day to look for another job. This represents a cost of at least 25 percent of the worker's salary. However, this cost is higher since during this period the worker's productivity will decline. On the other hand, if the company notifies the worker, pays his salary, and dismisses him immediately, which is normal procedure for most Brazilian companies, the company's cost will be one month's salary. Therefore, this cost varies between 25 and 100 percent of a worker's monthly salary.

The second component of dismissal costs is a premium assessed on the unemployment compensation fund. This fund is a capital formation fund set up by all companies for their employees. Each month the company deposits 8 percent of an employee's salary in a bank account set up in his name. These resources are adjusted according to inflation and earn a fixed interest rate of 3 percent per year. This fund can be used only when the employee has been dismissed without good cause, to purchase a home, or when the employee retires. When the employee is dismissed, aside from the amount accumulated in the fund, the company must pay the employee a premium of 40 percent of the monies deposited during the time of employment. Therefore, the amount of the premium depends on how long the employee was employed by the firm.[9]

Table 2.21 shows the costs of dismissal for different lengths (in months) of employment, if the companies pay the "advance notice" and dismiss the worker immediately, and if the salary amounts to $100 being constant during the time the contract is in effect.

These figures show that if the employee worked three years for the company, receives advance notice, and is dismissed immediately, the cost of dismissal is 2.15 times his salary. If the length of employment were 10 years, the cost of dismissal would amount to 4.84 times his salary.

A second important mechanism that impacts on employment flexibility in Brazil's labor market is the dismissal compensation fund. As previously mentioned, all companies must open a bank account for each registered employee and deposit 8 percent of the employee's salary into it each month. In the event that the employee is dismissed without good cause, he has the right to withdraw the funds accumulated in his name, and the company has to pay him a premium equivalent to 40 percent of the value of the fund accumulated during the employee's tenure. Therefore, when the employee is dismissed, in addition to receiving a month's salary because of the advance notice, he has access to the accumulated amount which corresponds to the salary of one year of employment, plus a premium. The size of the premium increases with the length of employment. The cost of dismissal without good cause after six months of employment is 1.67 times the employee's salary. For a four-year employment stint, it is 6.38 times the salary.

Poorly paid unskilled workers who also have fewer possibilities for receiving salary raises from their company face an additional problem. This mechanism, in effect, creates a strong incentive for such workers to seek dismissal

---

[9] Generally this amount can be represented by the equation:

$f = 100 \times 0.08 \times 0.40 \times n = (3.2 \times n)\%$ of the average salary where:

f = amount of the premium.

100 = average salary during the time the employee worked for the company.

n = number of months the employee worked for the company.

Table 2.21. Brazil: Costs of Dismissal with Advance Notice
(In number of wages)

Length of employment (months)	6	12	24	36	48	120	240	360
Advance notice	100	100	100	100	100	100	100	100
FGTS fine	19	38	77	115	154	384	768	1.152
Total cost	119	138	177	215	254	484	868	1.252

Source: Author's estimates.

when the economy is growing and the labor market is tight. While their salaries are low, the workers' rate of discount will be quite high as is the incentive for early withdrawals of the fund money. One year of employment in the company will give the employee 2.34 salaries, or real earnings of 18 percent (since every registered employee has 13 annual salaries) over his annual salary. In reality, the best strategy for this employee is to use his time judiciously, search for a new job, and find one while still employed. Such would be the case if the employee does not foresee a real possibility for advancement within the company. A likely consequence is a reduction in productivity.

As a result, these workers will not be motivated to make an investment in their jobs. This being the case, the company will have little incentive to invest in their training, since the probability of losing the investment is quite high. Therefore, only investment in specialized human capital would take place. The less skilled the worker is, the fewer opportunities he can expect should he remain with the company. From the company's point of view, the best strategy is to obtain the most from the worker while he is employed, but not to invest in his future. This incentive structure is as important as its counterpart—dismissal costs—which hampers the expansion of labor relations and reduces the investment that workers and companies make in training, and generates high labor turnovers among jobs. On the other hand, it creates low rates and short periods of unemployment. This argument is supported by the low open unemployment in Brazil during the 1980s which coincided with the lack of growth in per capita income.

The duration of unemployment in Brazil is quite short, when compared with that of other countries (Table 2.22). Brazil has the shortest duration of unemployment, 1.6 months on the average, and one of the highest frequencies of unemployment, 2.5 times per year on the average. Among the countries listed in the table, Brazil ranks just under Canada in terms of frequency of unemployment. Brazil enjoys a low rate as well as high frequency and short duration of unemployment which is a clear indication of job flexibility. Therefore, if the costs of dismissing employees in Brazil is high, they are offset by the incentives created by the dismissal fund.

Table 2.22. Frequency and Duration of Unemployment, 1990

Country	Frequency of unemployment[1]	Duration of unemployment (months)
Belgium	0.2	50
France	0.6	21
Germany	0.4	16
Ireland	0.7	30
Italy	0.2	36
Netherlands	0.4	25
Spain	0.2	105
United Kingdom	0.9	10
Canada	2.6	3
United States	2.2	3
Finland	1.1	5
Japan	0.5	3
Norway	1.1	3
Sweden	0.5	3
Brazil	2.5	1.6

Source: Bivar (1991) p. 86.
Note: The data for Brazil are from the state of São Paulo.
[1] How many times a worker loses his/her job, on average, within the year.

Conclusions

This study shows an important relationship between human resources and the cost of economic adjustment processes. An adjustment process implies job shifts by a large part of the work force. If work force flexibility is low, adjustment costs will be high. These costs can take the form of unemployment or salary losses, and are the result of constraints in human capital investments or of a fragmented labor market.

The degree of flexibility in the labor market will generally depend on how flexible the labor force is, which is a function of the type of human resource investment made. Workers with greater general human capital are better suited to perceive and interpret economic changes correctly and have a higher capacity for learning, which reduces the cost of specialized training. Therefore, firms give priority to these workers when training them. On the other hand, workers with little investment in human resources require small adjustment costs, since they lose little specific human capital during the adjustment process. As a result, adjustment costs tend to widen the differences between general human capital and specialized human capital.

The study shows that Brazil lags behind other Latin American countries with similar per capita incomes in the quality of general human capital. The illiteracy rate is high, the average years of education of the labor force is low, and there is an under-investment in general human capital, as evidenced by elevated school dropout and repeater rates. Regional disparities in educational performance and in levels of investment in education are significant. Furthermore, these regional disparities are not being offset by federal resource transfers to the education systems of the country's poorest regions.

This study also shows the importance of Brazil's vocational education system, SENAI and SENAC, in reducing the below-par investment in the country's general and specialized human capital. Thanks to the quality services provided by these two institutions, the industrial and services sectors were able somewhat to avoid the problems caused by the inferior quality of the human resources being turned out by the formal education system.

An important topic analyzed in this study relates to the trend of vocational schools, mainly SENAI, to provide more specialized and less general education. This trend tends to diminish labor force flexibility and, therefore, increases the cost of adjustment.

This study also analyzed the relationship between the formal and informal sectors of Brazil's labor market. It has been shown that, during the recession of the early 1980s, the informal sector reacted by reducing the cost of adjustment. For example, during this period, the informal sector was able to avoid the level of unemployment of workers in the formal sector. This phenomenon was not observed during the subsequent recession in the same decade. Furthermore, even when the informal sector reduces adjustment costs, these can still be quite high because of wage losses that workers experience in shifting between sectors. Given the high mobility between these two segments of Brazil's labor market, however, these wage losses temporarily reduce the work force's adjustment costs even further .

Finally, this study analyzed the degree of flexibility in the labor market, and how this flexibility is affected by different institutional regulations. It was shown that the rate and duration of unemployment in Brazil is relatively low. This is the result of the low costs involved in dismissing employees as compared to other countries, and also of the incentives created by the employee dismissal fund. In summary, Brazil's labor laws do not play an important role in setting constraints and, therefore, cannot be considered as an important factor in cost adjustments.

Bibliography

Adamsson-Macedo, Colin. 1992. Training and "New" Technology. International Labor Office, Geneva. Mimeo.

Albuquerque, Roberto C., and Renato Villela. 1991. A situacão social no Brasil: um balanção de duas décadas. In *A questão social no Brasil*. Rio de Janeiro: Editora Nobel.

Amadeo, Edward and José Márcio Camargo. 1991. Fiscal Asymmetries and the Educational System in Brazil. International Labor Office, Geneva. Mimeo.

Azeredo, Beatriz, and José Paulo Chanad. 1992. O programa brasileiro de seguro desemprego: Diagnósticos e sugestões para o seu aperfeicoamento. November. Rio de Janeiro. Mimeo.

BACEN - *Boletín del Banco Central de Brasil*, various issues. Central Bank of Brazil.

Barros, Ricardo P. 1993. Formal Education and Wage Sensitivity to Economic Conditions. IPEA, Rio de Janeiro. Mimeo.

Bivar, Wasmália Socorro. 1991. Aspectos da estrutura do desemprego no Brasil—composicão por sexo e duracão. Master's thesis, PUC, Rio de Janeiro.

Borba, Sergio da Costa. 1976. *A problematica do analfabetismo no Brasil*. Rio de Janeiro: Editora Vozes.

Cacciamali, María Cristina. 1992. Mudanças estruturais e na regulacão do mercado de trabalho no Brasil nos anos 80. Paper presented at the Seminarío desenvolvimento Económico, Investimento, Mercado de Trabalho e Distribuição da Renda, BNDES, Rio de Janeiro.

Carneiro, Tania Regina. 1990. O mercado de trabalho industrial em São Bernardo do Campo. August. SENAI-SP (DPEA), São Paulo. Mimeo.

Carneiro, D., and Rogério Werneck. 1992. Public Savings and Private Investments Requirements for Growth Resumption in the Brazilian Economy. PUC, Rio de Janeiro. Mimeo.

Caruso, Luiz Antonio. 1991. Difusão da tecnología microeletrónica e modificações nas relações de trabalho: implicações para a formação profissional. Master's thesis, IEI/UFRJ, Rio de Janeiro.

Castro, Claudio de Moura. 1991. SENAI: Ha vida depois dos 50? Servicio Nacional de Aprendizaje Industrial (SENAI), São Paulo. Mimeo.

Clementes, María de Lourdes Mendes. 1992. *Análise da trajetória profissional nos 3 anos pós-curso dos formandos do 2° semestre de 1987.* Working Paper (July). Servicio Nacional de Aprendizaje Industrial, SENAI-DOP (DEP), São Paulo, July.

CNI. 1992. *Estado atual da gestão pela qualidade e productiva de nas brasileiras.* Working Paper.

ECLAC. 1992. *Statistical Year Book for Latin America and the Caribbean-1991.* Santiago: ECLAC.

Guerra, Marcia Halben, and María Fernanda Soares. 1991. Tendencia da evolução profissional e escolar dos ex-alunos de Habilitação Profissional - HP, formados em dezembro/86; análise dos resultados de acompanhamento realizado de 1987 a 1989. December. SENAI-SP, São Paulo.

Guerra, Marcia Halben, and María Rosa Lombardi. 1989. Tendência da evolução profissional e escolar dos ex-alunos da Habilitação Profissional—HP, formados em dezembro/86; análise dos resultados do acompanhamento realizado de 1987 a 1989. April. SENAI-SP, São Paulo.

Guerra, Marcia Halben, María Fernanda Soares, and Noriko Ribeiro Iwamoto. 1991. Tendência da evolução profissional e escolar dos ex-alunos do Curso de Qualificação Profissional-CQP-IV, formados em dezembro/86: análise dos resultados do acompanhamento realizado de 1987 a 1989. December. SENAI-SP, São Paulo.

IBGE. 1990. *Anuário Estatístico do Brasil* 50:1-784. Rio de Janeiro.

_____. Censos Económicos de 1985. *Censo Industrial No. 1 - Dados Gerais, Brasil.*

_____. *Pesquisa Mensal de Emprego.* Various years.

_____. *Pesquisa Nacional por Amostra de Domicili.* 1979, 1981-90.

Keep, Ewart and K. Mayhew. 1988. Education, Training and Economic Performance. *Oxford Review of Economic Policy* 4 (no. 3).

Langoni, Carlos Geraldo. 1973. Distribuição de Renda e Desenvolvimento Económico no Brasil. *Ensayos Económicos* 8. IBRE/EPGE, Rio de Janeiro.

Leite, Elenice M. 1986. *SENAI-SP: Dez anos de avaliação.* Working Paper (April) SENAI, São Paulo.

Lockheed, Verspoor. 1991. Improving Primary Education in Brazil. World Bank, Washington, D.C. Mimeo.

Lombardi, María Rosa. 1989. *Resultados da 2a. mala direta com ex-alunos de Habilitação Profissional formados em diciembre 1986: situação profissional em 1988, dois anos após a formatura.* Working Paper (May). SENAI-SP (SAPES), São Paulo.

_____. 1987. *Respondente e não-respondentes 1a. mala direta com egressos do CAI diciembre, 1985: testes para identificação de diferenças entre os dois grupos.* Working Paper (September). SENAI-SP (SAPES), São Paulo.

Mancuso, María Inés, and Noriko Ribeiro Iwamoto. 1991. *Notas de seleção versus desempenho no mercado de trabalho.* Working Paper (July). SENAI-SP, São Paulo.

Marques, Antônio Emílio. 1991. Despesas governamentais com educação: 1986/1990. Mimeo.

Mello e Souza, Alberto. 1979. Financiamento da educação e acesso a escola no Brasil. *Coleção Relatório de Pesquisa* (no. 42). IPEA, Rio de Janeiro.

Ministério da Educação no Brasil na década de 80. MEC/SAG/CPS/CIP, Brasilia.

Revista de Conjuntura Económica. 1979. Encarte de Salário (no. 12, December).

Ribeiro, Noriko Iwamoto. 1991. *Caracterização dos alunos do último termo do Curso de Aprendizagem Industrial do SENAI-SP.* Working Paper (September). SENAI-SP, São Paulo.

_____. 1988. *Resultados da 2a. mala direta com ex-alunos do CAI formados em dezembro/85: situação profissional dos egressos em fins de 1987.* Working Paper (June). SENAI-SP (SAPES), São Paulo.

_____. 1987. *Resultados da 1a. mala direta com ex-alunos do CAI formados em dezembro/85: situação profissional dos egressos em fins de 1986.* Working Paper (April). SENAI-SP (SAPES), São Paulo.

Salm, Claudio, and Azuete Fogaça. 1992. *A nova relação entre competitividades e educação.* São Paulo: IEDI.

SAPES. 1985. *Sistema de acompanhamento permanente dos egressos do SENAI-SP (1985), por mala direta.* Working Paper (December). SENAI (DPEA).

Savedoff, William D. 1991. Regional Wage Differences in Brazil's Urban Labor Markets. Doctoral thesis, Boston University, Mass.

Schultz, T.W. 1975. The Ability to Deal with Disequilibria. *Journal of Economic Literature* 13:827-846.

Sistema SENAI. 1990. *Relatório.* São Paulo.

Tuijnman, A.C. 1992. Effectiveness Research into Continuing Education International. *Journal of Educational Research* 17 (no. 6).

United Nations. 1992. *Human Development Report.* New York: Oxford University Press.

_____. 1990. *Human Development Report.* New York: Oxford University Press.

Velloso, João Paulo dos Reis. 1991. A Questão Social no Brasil. *Fórum Nacional.* Editora Nobel, São Paulo.

World Bank. 1989. Brazil—Issues in Secondary Education. *Sector memorandum* 1. (November).

CHAPTER THREE

CHILE

Ricardo Paredes[1]
Luis A. Riveros

In 1974, Chile's economic performance and industrial structure underwent substantial changes as a result of policies fostering a radical change in relative prices. These policies were closely linked to foreign trade expansion, less state intervention, and a deregulated market. The process culminated in the late 1980s with the privatization of a large number of companies and public services, the administrative and financial readjustment of social policy, and the creation of privately managed social security pension funds. The overall results, evaluated almost two decades after the changes were introduced, reveal significant advances towards macroeconomic stability, a reemphasis on export activity, the consolidation of the private sector as a leader in the growth process, and a notable development of the financial and investment sectors.

Despite achieving significant changes in a relatively brief period, the process has not been sustained. As to the nature and impact of the changes during the two decades under study, two substantially different periods emerge. Profound structural changes were experienced between 1974 and 1978, while 1981 was characterized by a marked decline in economic activity. A recovery, which began in the mid-1980s, has since developed into sustained growth that continues today. The second period, despite a certain amount of production realignment, can best be described as a macroeconomic cycle rather than a structural adjustment.

A conclusion that can be derived when comparing the two periods is that their differences were crucial in explaining the institutional performance and the adjustment of human resources. Unemployment remained high during the 1970s, reaching an average rate of 13 percent, as compared to 6 percent in 1960. A

[1] The authors wish to thank Héctor Contardo, Juan José Rivas, Manuel Hidalgo, and Felipe Balmaceda for their contributions to this study. They are also grateful to Jere Behrman, Fred Jaspersen, and Robert Kestell for their comments, and to Enrique Manzur for his invaluable help.

production recovery in the late 1970s did not significantly help to reduce unemployment. Furthermore, although the recession shock between 1982 and 1984 brought open unemployment to more than 26 percent of the work force, employment levels began to decline considerably after 1987 in the wake of economic recovery from the debt crisis.

Part of the changes in the labor market can be explained by the employment realignments in the public and private sectors and in the tradable and nontradable goods sectors, the latter resulting from changes in relative prices and production activity. All of this took place in a framework in which government intervention in wage determination was minimal thanks to labor market reforms introduced in 1980. Labor policies seem to have helped significantly in achieving greater flexibility in useful employment and greater labor mobility among the different industries, and in creating the climate of confidence needed for investments to expand.

The transition process of Chile's economy, particularly during the 1970s, follows a classical model of macroeconomic adjustment involving employment realignment. The change in relative prices associated with lessened public sector intervention and an open trade policy spurred an increase in the relative price of tradable goods. In the first phase of the adjustment, this meant a significant decline in the traditional import substitution industry, as well as a drop in state services and companies. Diminished demand for work in those sectors and a sluggish economic recovery kept unemployment high. This study suggests that growth in the tradable goods production sector and among the more efficient import substitution companies was constrained because of the mismatch of skills existing in Chile's economy. One explanation for this is that the skills required in the shrinking sectors were not those required in the expanding sectors, which were highly competitive in their search for greater economic efficiency. It was in this context that the institutional training and retraining framework became particularly important.

As this study points out, economic policy took a reactive posture in dealing with labor market problems. Proactive policies, such as the design and operation of training programs, the development of small businesses and employment services generally played a less important role during the 1970s and most of the 1980s. Human resource training underwent major changes during the period and became more efficient. However, the goal of these changes was not to facilitate the movement of productive resources between sectors. Thus, the National Institute of Professional Training (INACAP) was changed from a public to a private institution of higher education, no longer fulfilling its original mission to train specific segments of the labor force. Programs enabling private companies to provide direct training were also created. The Ministry of Labor's Training and Employment Service was given the task of coordinating programs for on-the-job training. These programs resulted in the institutional changes of the 1970s. Vocational and technical education also changed dramatically after the administration of several training institutions was transferred to the private sector. The goal was to provide training that was more in tune with company needs. Although these reforms succeeded in enhancing the efficiency and flexibility in the labor market, the system was redirected to focus training on company-specific needs which, presumably, would be subject to fewer externalities justifying state intervention in training.

This chapter analyzes the way in which Chile's human resources have been able to adjust to productive needs over the last 20 years. It also confirms the existence of a real skills mismatch resulting from sectoral recomposition of job demand. Finally, it looks at the efficiency of training infrastructures and incentives during the adjustment period. The first section provides a description of Chile's adjustment periods and processes during the last two decades. The second section describes and analyzes the human resources that were most affected by the adjustment. The third section reviews the human resource training programs instituted during the adjustment period and in recent years, primarily by analyzing the structure and mission of training programs. The fourth section puts forth the main policy recommendations derived from the Chilean experience.

Structural Adjustment of Chile's Economy

The socialist experiment in the early 1970s diverted Chile's attention from its normal economic development path. Although Chile has traditionally had a relatively closed economy, with a high level of government intervention in the market and a strong public sector, state control intensified during the Allende period (1970-73). The policy of nationalizing companies and converting them to state-owned enterprises was accompanied by measures that further enhanced tariff and nontariff protection. A concurrent drop in international copper prices raised an already high balance of payments deficit and caused a dramatic drop in foreign exchange reserves. An expansive fiscal and monetary policy was concurrently adopted, in hopes that the demand stimulus and improvements in income distribution would decisively increase aggregate supply. The result was an enormous fiscal deficit which exceeded 20 percent of GDP and an annual inflation rate that approached 350 percent. By mid-1973, the economy was in a state of chaos and in 1973 a military junta deposed President Allende.

The new economic team reversed the government's interventionist policy, reducing the size of the state and integrating the economy into that of the rest of the world. The team implemented a dramatic stabilization program which caused a 1975 decline in GDP that exceeded 16 percent. The fiscal deficit also declined from 25 percent of GDP in 1973 to 2.6 percent in 1975. As a result of these policies, the annual rate of inflation dropped from 343 percent in 1975 to 84 percent in 1977. These stabilization policies were subsequently strengthened in 1979 by the nominal fixing of the exchange rate, which reduced inflation to 38.9 percent during that year and to 31.2 percent in the subsequent year (Table 3.1). The 1975 stabilization policy was accompanied by a policy whose aim was to shrink the public sector. As a result, companies illegally acquired between 1970 and 1973 were denationalized. By the end of 1974, 210 out of 259 companies were returned to their owners (Larraín, 1988). Steps were also taken to reduce state assets. These included the sale of several state-owned banks. This program was responsible for an almost 24 percent drop in public employment between 1973 and 1977, which represented about 3 percent of the country's labor force (Riveros, 1986).[2]

Another key economic initiative of those years was the enactment of a strong open trade policy. During 1973-79, the average tariff dropped from 103 percent to 10 percent. Quantitative restrictions were practically eliminated by 1975. This had serious consequences for employment in the import substitution industry, compounded by the shrinkage of the public sector and by the stabilization policy which resulted in a dramatic drop in economic activity.[3] Recovery in the industrial sector was also slow, perhaps because the tariff reduction policy implemented between 1974 and 1979 failed to establish clear objectives in terms of product specialization and export orientation, which are required by an internationally-oriented global policy. This becomes clear when one notes that exchange rate policies were used as a stabilizing factor between 1972 and 1979, adversely affecting the production of tradable goods and employment (Corbo, 1985; Edwards and Edwards, 1987).

The conditions that would intensify the effects of the subsequent financial crisis germinated during this period of transition. In the 1970s, the financial sector was liberalized by freeing interest rates and eliminating quantitative restrictions on capital market operations. Deregulation was excessive, however, since it allowed bank-related companies to incur higher debt levels, which, in turn, translated into high domestic and foreign borrowing (Harberger, 1985; Barandiarán, 1987; Edwards and Edwards, 1987). Also, the use of the exchange rate policy as a stabilizing factor generated an exchange overvaluation, which had a serious impact on foreign borrowing due to the inter-linked and liberal international financial market of those days. Last, but no less important, the wage indexation introduced in conjunction with the 1979 labor law constituted a decisive factor for making the exchange rate policy a destabilizing and harmful element for production. The international crisis of the early 1980s occurred, then, in

---

[2] Despite the extent of these changes, the size of the public sector in 1981 still accounted for 24 percent of GDP (Hachette and Lüders, 1987).

[3] This happened despite the fact that the industrial sector had already stopped contributing significantly to the elevation of the level of employment in the economy (Corbo and Meller, 1984)

Table 3.1. Chile: Macroeconomic Indicators, 1970-90
(Percentages)

Year	GDP[1]	Tradable sector[2]	Non-tradable sector[3]	Prices[4]	Gross investment [5]	Fiscal deficit [6]	Real exchange rate (1975=100)[7]
1970	2.1	1.4	2.9	32.5	16.4	2.7	38.5
1971	9.0	9.2	8.8	22.1	14.5	10.7	35.3
1972	1.2	-0.8	-1.1	260.5	12.2	13.0	36.7
1973	-5.6	-7.3	-3.7	605.1	7.8	24.7	56.7
1974	1.0	6.6	-0.4	369.2	21.2	10.5	83.8
1975	-12.9	-16.6	-8.4	343.3	13.1	2.6	100.0
1976	3.5	5.3	1.6	197.9	12.8	2.3	91.5
1977	9.9	7.8	9.4	84.2	14.4	1.8	83.5
1978	8.2	4.5	9.6	37.2	17.8	0.8	101.6
1979	8.3	7.0	10.0	38.9	17.8	-1.7	105.9
1980	7.8	5.0	10.0	31.2	21.0	-3.1	94.0
1981	5.5	3.8	5.4	9.5	22.7	-1.7	74.8
1982	-14.1	-11.2	-10.8	20.7	11.3	2.3	81.1
1983	-0.7	0.5	-6.1	23.1	9.8	3.8	98.1
1984	6.3	7.9	5.3	23.0	15.3	4.0	100.8
1985	2.4	2.5	2.4	26.4	13.9	6.3	123.0
1986	5.7	6.7	5.0	17.4	15.0	2.8	139.9
1987	5.7	3.5	6.6	21.5	17.9	0.1	143.5
1988	7.4	6.9	7.7	12.7	18.1	1.7	149.9
1989	10.0	8.4	11.0	21.4	21.8	0.4	147.3
1990	2.1	0.7	3.0	27.3	20.8	-0.3	150.8

Sources:
[1,2,3,5,6] Central Bank of Chile
[4] Cortázar and Marshall (1979) and Central Bank of Chile;
[7] Cottani (1987) and Central Bank of Chile.

an economic environment in which the Chilean economy was in a weak production and balance of payments position.

As a result of the crisis, the ratio of foreign debt to exports rose from 2.7 to 4.6 between 1979 and 1983. This represented an increase in GDP from 40 percent to 100 percent. GDP dropped in 1982 by more than 11 percent, mainly because shrinking the current account deficit was achieved by reducing imports. Also, the terms of trade declined rapidly from 119 in 1979 to 88 in 1983, while the interest rate (LIBOR) increased from 2.6 percent to 4.6 percent.

The impact of the crisis on the labor market was to increase unemployment significantly, which in 1983 exceeded 26 percent of the labor force.[4] The aver-

---

[4] This figure includes workers who participated in emergency employment programs.

age real wage, which in 1982 barely reached 1970 levels, declined between 1982 and 1983 by about 12 percent and continued to decline slowly until 1987. The deteriorated conditions in the labor market, which prevailed until the early 1980s, undoubtedly intensified the effects of the financial crisis on income distribution and employment.

Unemployment, which peaked in 1983, declined sharply as a result of a series of isolated reforms and a more coherent macroeconomic policy. The exchange rate policy was used consistently to stimulate nontraditional exports. The state also relied on other means, such as tax rebates and the promotion of information through state agencies.[5] Fiscal management became even more conservative, shrinking the consolidated deficit to zero.[6] A more coherent policy approach relied on the expansion of labor-intensive sectors such as farming, construction, and services. Likewise, recomposition in demand helped reduce unemployment to near traditional levels. Nevertheless, high rates of unemployment among young people and regional disenfranchised groups (who do not benefit from overall economic growth) still persisted.

Since 1984, Chile's economy has grown at an unusually rapid pace, not typical of Latin American standards. Moreover, growth has been constant, with current average rates reaching about 8.5 percent, annual inflation of around 13 percent, and a notable recovery in investments, which has exceeded 20 percent of GDP. In the labor market, wages have also maintained sustained growth, with a rate currently at 6 percent, and with unemployment steady at around 4.5 percent. Finally, the greater diversification of assets in capital markets has been supported by an open trade policy.

The high degree of consistency in macroeconomic policies is critical in understanding Chile's rapid economic recovery. As was pointed out, a series of institutional transformations were introduced toward the end of the 1970s which increased the flexibility of market operations. Among the most important was the establishment in 1979 of a legal labor structure after a long hiatus during which the country lacked a specific legal framework. Particularly worth noting are the following provisions: entitling workers to five months severance pay; permitting dismissals for economic reasons; replacing striking workers 60 days after the start of the strike; and allowing more than one union to operate within each company. The introduction of more flexible operation norms brought about formal improvements recognized by both sides, and facilitated wage determination and labor mobility.

Also noteworthy were the significant changes that took place in those years in social services that focused on the neediest groups. This was achieved by de-

---

[5] The real rate of exchange index increased by 49 percent between 1984 and 1988.

[6] This, however, had a negative social impact which, apparently, was addressed by providing greater assistance to the extremely needy.

centralizing decision making. One reform worth noting was the creation of privately-managed pension funds which helped overcome the financial crisis and improve the efficiency of state institutions. This reform helped to strengthen capital markets and to promote improvements in the flow of financial information and decision-making. Also, the adoption of a more efficient pension system meant a reduction in contributions earmarked for its funding, which had a positive impact on employment.[7]

In summary, despite a sustained pace in reforming Chile's economy, two distinct periods emerge in which the economy underwent alternate declines and recoveries. In the first period, during the mid-1970s, an important structural change took place involving sectoral realignment of resources and a possible decline in workers' skills which, because it occurred simultaneously with macroeconomic adjustment, led to persistently high rates of unemployment. The second period, in the early 1980s, was not a structural adjustment. Events in that period were responsive to the effects of the macroeconomic cycle which, while guided by more coherent policies and an improved institutional framework designed to help companies make internal adjustments, allowed for a relatively quicker recovery.

Human Resources During the Adjustment Period

In the context of structural adjustment, human resource traits are crucial. The labor market's flexibility and capacity to absorb manpower is determined by the ability of human resources to adapt to emerging demands. Although flexibility is also important for determining labor's capacity to overcome recessions during macroeconomic cycles, the nature of the flexibility requirements and the consequences on human resources are different.

The most traditional concept derived from the human capital model suggests that in the event of a macroeconomic crisis, companies will preferentially dismiss individuals endowed with less specialized human capital, that is, women and young people. During a structural adjustment in addition to the economic downturn, the demand for acquired skills in certain professions also declines. During such a process, the loss of specific human capital is proportionately greater for these skilled individuals, that is, for middle-aged individuals and men. These groups suffer the greatest relative loss. In this scenario, employment of young people and women does not decline in comparison with other groups. An assessment of those most adversely affected, which is one of the objectives of this chapter, is of great interest because, in addition to identifying the groups most

---

7 Paredes (1994) provides a theoretical analysis on the importance of greater efficiency in social services and in reducing the cost of work.

affected by the crisis, it helps in designing a more suitable policy aimed at alleviating the effects of adjustment.

Flexibility and Wages

As previously mentioned, structural adjustment of the Chilean economy can be characterized as a recomposition of employment and production in the tradable and nontradable goods sectors. Even when this characterization is not clearly discernible in the aggregate sectoral production data (Appendix Table 3.1), drastic changes in relative prices enhanced the effects of institutional reforms and presumably resulted in freeing up more human resources in the nontradable goods sector.[8] It is also plausible that the relative increases in work demand in the tradable sector induced subsequent increases in the relative wages in this sector, a phenomenon which is consistent with the previous notion. Such effect is neither transitory nor relatively marginal. Therefore, as Table 3.2 shows, wages in the nontradable sector declined in the 1970s by 16 percent for unskilled workers and by 30 percent for skilled workers as compared to those in the tradable goods sector.

The dramatic changes in relative wages among the tradable and nontradable goods sectors, particularly true for skilled workers, are, in themselves, a reflection of sectoral labor dynamics. Since both sectors underwent adjustments, the decline in salaries in the tradable goods sector, as compared to that of the nontradable goods sector, represents a conservative indication of the level of sectoral inflexibility.[9] Thus, the trend in salaries suggests a high degree of inflexibility, which would be especially relevant for skilled workers in the nontradable goods sector.

Table 3.2 indicates the coexistence of several factors, such as type and level of human resource training, that would deter the transition of workers from shrinking sectors to expanding sectors. A hypothesis that helps to explain this situation is that, since many of the displaced skilled workers in the nontradable goods sector were public officials (highly-educated, low-productivity, nonspecialized individuals), they generally had little to offer the private sector. This would partly explain the slow and difficult adjustment and the extremely high and persistent unemployment that prevailed for nearly the entire period.

The skills mismatch can be explained by both supply and demand factors.

---

[8] The regional recomposition of employment in the 1980s is closely tied to the emergence of the tradable sectors. However, the lack of national aggregate data before 1980 does not allow related verification in the change of the composition of employment.

[9] For example, the structural change brought about a slump, as compared to the whole manufacturing industry, in the import substitution sector of that industry, relative to the whole sector. Likewise, the phasing out of many public services stimulated a strong expansion of financial and commercial services.

Table 3.2. Real Wage Index in Chile, 1970-90
(1980=100)

Year	Unemployment rate[1]	Legal minimum[2]	Average[3]	Unskilled[4]	Skilled[5]	Tradable/ Nontradable[6]	INE index[7]
1970	5.7	81.0	112.4	124.1	144.0	119.9	109.7
1972	3.1	101.7	104.3	138.4	157.7	109.3	119.0
1974	9.2	90.6	56.2	94.5	78.4	132.4	70.2
1976	15.9	100.1	71.5	77.0	77.7	118.8	78.9
1978	14.2	97.4	91.0	82.4	97.6	116.0	85.0
1980	11.8	100.0	100.0	100.0	100.0	100.0	100.0
1982	20.4	122.2	133.2	126.6	133.3	118.6	108.6
1984	19.1	82.1	89.4	77.8	89.8	122.3	97.1
1986	13.9	78.8	72.6	64.4	66.6	108.1	94.9
1988	12.2	74.2	72.1	66.8	62.3	108.9	100.9
1989	10.1	82.6	81.5	80.0	71.1	109.9	102.8
1990	9.3	88.0	76.0	80.0	79.0	107.6	104.7

Sources:
[1,3,4,5] Economics Department, University of Chile.
[6] Yáñez (1988).
[2,7] INE (National Statistical Institute).

On the demand side, adjustment was slow because of the low incentive companies have to quickly adjust staffing levels and rely on new skills, especially if the latter entails specialized retraining. Also, proceeding slowly helps to avoid costly errors. On the supply side, a portion of the displaced workers in the shrinking sectors might have been unwilling to accept lower wages. Lower salaries reflect deterioration or lack of skills that were once in demand. In this regard, Paredes and Riveros (1990) provide evidence of a strong structural component in the overall unemployment trend, which explains the significant increase in unemployment levels as compared to those in the 1960s.

Socio-demographic Characterization

It is particularly important to study the socio-demographic characteristics of the groups affected by the adjustment. These characteristics can help in the formulation of policy initiatives to assist these groups and prevent adjustment deterioration of their skills beyond what can be strictly attributable to adjustment effects. Characterization by age, schooling, and sex is particularly useful, since each of these groups is endowed with specific human capital, thus making it possible to formulate policies that foster the formation of such capital.

For example, young people are thought to have a low level of company-specific human capital. By definition, these individuals have little work experience and, from this point of view, are less qualified even when formally trained. Women, too, have limited job-related experience because of their intermittent participation in the labor force.

Such a characterization has been widely documented and allows empirical verification of the hypothesis that the macroeconomic crisis of the 1980s had significantly different results than those expected from a structural adjustment. Specifically, the claim is made that, had there been a structural adjustment, the individuals most strongly affected would have been those endowed with relatively higher human capital, since an adjustment harms existing skills. Thus, during the crisis, policies should encourage retraining of human resources rather than just provide assistance to the impacted skills.

Supply Factors

The incidence of high unemployment rates for young people and women during periods of crisis is often used to support the argument that these groups are particularly vulnerable to labor demand reductions. However, analyzing unemployment rates is not a specific aim of this study. Rather, we are concerned with what occurs during the adjustment process. Furthermore, one problem with directly analyzing unemployment rates is that they are strictly dependent on the labor market and, especially, on fluctuations in participation rates of those entering the market for the first time. This does not allow, then, determination of what happens to those who are laid off, which means that a change in the unemployment level could mistakenly be attributed to a recomposition in demand. Table 3.3 presents trends in participation rates by sex and age groups, thus allowing for direct analysis of supply factors. A general overview suggests a sustained but gradual decline in the participation of men, and a less gradual rise in the participation of women. However, when different age groups are considered, one can observe a large fluctuation in participation rates for younger individuals, particularly for men. The anti-cyclical trend in the participation of individuals between the ages of 14 and 19 and, to a lesser but still significant extent, of individuals between the ages of 20 and 25, suggests that when one member of the family becomes unemployed, other members enter the work force mainly to offset the decline in family income. Therefore, in periods of economic crisis, such as the mid-1970s and early 1980s, groups of young people entered the work force after presumably dropping out of school.

The data in Table 3.3 supports the notion that the marked growth in unemployment for certain groups during periods of crisis can be, at least partially, attributed to supply factors. The information also allows one to consider, and eventually discard, the hypothesis that young people and women were most affected by structural adjustment layoffs.

Table 3.3. Chile: Labor Participation Rate by Age and Gender, 1970-90
(June of each year)

Year	Men	Women	Total	14-19 Men	14-19 Women	20-25 Men	20-25 Women	26-65 Men	26-65 Women
1970	54.8	77.1	36.2	28.4	16.8	82.9	49.7	93.3	38.4
1972	53.1	73.4	35.7	18.4	16.6	76.7	49.4	91.1	37.8
1974	52.8	76.1	32.4	29.7	15.9	81.3	42.7	92.9	35.4
1976	53.6	74.1	35.9	25.5	16.2	78.2	51.3	91.2	38.1
1978	53.0	73.3	35.7	22.7	15.7	78.1	45.8	90.1	38.9
1980	52.1	72.6	34.3	17.1	12.0	77.9	46.8	90.3	36.6
1982	53.1	73.5	35.6	18.7	13.4	77.0	49.5	88.5	37.7
1984	54.7	73.5	38.2	20.6	12.7	77.9	49.4	87.3	40.7
1986	54.1	73.3	37.6	17.5	12.1	76.8	47.2	88.6	41.5
1988	55.8	73.7	40.0	19.3	13.4	72.3	49.2	90.4	43.4
1990	57.4	76.6	40.6	17.7	10.3	75.2	49.7	91.7	45.0

Source: Economics Department, University of Chile.

Demand Factors

Variations in the participation rate affect the unemployment rate equally. There-fore, a comparison of trends in layoff rates for different groups will tell whether, and to what extent, the cyclical unemployment trend responds to the recomposition of demand. However, layoff rates are also affected by variations in the participation of new entries. Table 3.4 shows the trend of an adjusted layoff rate defined as the ratio between individuals laid off and the sum of those employed plus those laid off according to different age and sex groups (that is, both the numerator and the denominator exclude individuals looking for their first jobs).

As can be seen in Table 3.4, men constitute one group affected by the ad-justment. It can be observed that, even though layoff and unemployment rates were systematically higher for young people than for adults, during the 1970s adjustment period individuals endowed with greater human capital (between 34 and 45 years of age) were particularly hard hit with layoffs. Using 1972 as a base year, the layoff rate for the youngest group increased 3.9 and 5.9 times in 1974 and 1976, respectively, while the rate for the older group during the same years increased 3.6 and 5.2 times. Although they represent significant increases, these rates are moderate when compared to those for the group endowed with greater human capital. Layoff rates for this group increased 3.6 and 7.9 times in those years. The profile of changes in unemployment is particularly interesting when data for the recession of the early 1980s are taken into consideration. In 1982 and 1984, when the layoff rates rose rapidly again, layoffs for young people

Table 3.4. Layoffs and Unemployment by Age and Gender in Greater Santiago, 1970-90
(Percentages: June of each year)

Year	Layoffs[1]				Age[2]		Unemployment				Age	
	Total	Men	Women	(1)	(2)	(3)	Total	Men	Women	(1)	(2)	(3)
1970	5.6	7.2	3.8	8.6	4.9	7.0	7.2	8.3	5.4	16.9	10.6	5.1
1972	2.3	2.6	1.7	3.4	1.6	1.8	3.6	3.7	3.4	14.3	6.1	2.0
1974	8.0	8.6	6.8	13.2	5.7	6.4	10.6	10.2	11.2	28.0	15.9	6.8
1976	14.1	15.0	12.3	20.0	12.6	9.5	18.0	17.6	18.8	43.8	23.9	13.7
1978	9.8	11.2	7.3	12.2	8.1	11.9	12.8	13.4	11.9	28.5	18.1	9.7
1980	9.1	10.7	6.1	13.4	8.2	7.5	11.7	12.2	10.8	26.5	18.5	8.6
1982	21.9	24.2	14.1	28.0	18.0	16.2	23.2	23.5	18.2	37.5	34.1	18.7
1984	15.5	16.7	13.4	19.7	14.0	15.2	18.4	18.3	18.6	35.7	26.9	14.8
1986	12.8	14.7	9.7	17.5	10.0	11.7	15.4	16.8	13.1	38.3	22.0	12.2
1988	9.4	9.4	9.4	15.3	5.6	6.6	11.1	10.9	11.6	33.5	17.5	8.1
1990	9.6	9.5	9.9	16.1	5.4	7.4	10.2	10.3	10.1	24.9	15.5	7.0

Source: Economics Department, University of Chile, Greater Santiago Survey.
[1] Laid off/(Employed+Laid off);
[2] Cohorts (1) 14-25 years; (2) 36-45 years; (3) over 55 years old.

and the intermediate groups were approximately 2.1 and 1.5 times higher than they were in 1980, while layoffs for the older group increased basically by the same proportion.

This and the fact that trends in unemployment rates for the young are more pro-cyclical suggests that supply rather than demand factors have particularly drastic effects on unemployment for women and the young. The data also suggest that the nature of the shocks were different for the two periods, with the 1970s shock being more structural. This shock had a particularly serious impact on groups who had previously acquired a high degree of human capital. Indeed, the fact that young people and women were relatively unaffected by the adjustment—despite their low levels of human capital that predated the adjustment period—suggests that the adjustment rendered a large part of existing skills and human capital obsolete. Thus, job-related skills acquired prior to the adjustment did not help older workers preserve their jobs during the adjustment period. Rather, the need for their skills declined considerably or disappeared altogether.

To supplement the findings of the preceding analysis, it is important to study the evolution of wages based on socio-demographic groups in the periods in question. While wages for men and women followed similar trends during the adjustment of the 1970s, their impact on men was stronger. Thus, taking the 1970 year as a base of 100, real wages for men and women dropped four years later to 34.3 and 40.7, respectively (Appendix Table 3.2).

Moreover, as a confirmation that the nature of the 1982-84 economic adjustment was different, men's wages dropped by 24 percent while women's wages dropped by 29 percent. Wage data for men, based on age and schooling, confirm our previous assessment (Appendix Table 3.3). In effect, wages for workers with fewer than eight years of schooling experienced a proportionately lower decline between 1970 and 1974 (actually, until 1976). Similarly, an analysis of wage trends between 1982 and 1984 reveals that wages of less educated workers dropped by 32 percent, while those of the higher educated workers declined substantially. Finally, the data confirm previous analysis that young people were relatively less harmed by the 1970s adjustment than by the 1980s recession.

Data on trends in the duration of unemployment is particularly useful since it can provide a measure of the severity of unemployment for specific groups and of their ability to adapt. Table 3.5 shows that the largest group of unemployed during the 1970s adjustment period was also the group out of work the longest. Thus, between 1972 and 1976, the number of unemployed who had been out of work for up to three months increased by 175 percent, while the number of those who had been out of work for more than a year increased by 850 percent. However, during the 1980s crisis, there is no clear difference in the duration of unemployment profile, suggesting that the proportion of individuals out of work for long periods remained high after the crisis.

Therefore, extended unemployment rates were high during the two decades

Table 3.5. Chile: Unemployed Individuals by Educational Level and Duration of Unemployment, 1970-90
(Thousands of individuals)

	Less than five years of basic education			Six years and middle school education			University			Total		
	(1)	(2)	(3)	(1)	(2)	(3)	(1)	(2)	(3)	(1)	(2)	(3)
1970	9.70	6.34	4.55	16.44	14.38	7.13	0.00	0.00	0.20	26.1	20.7	11.9
1972	3.12	1.25	1.04	7.69	7.27	2.70	0.42	0.21	0.00	11.2	8.7	3.7
1974	10.75	7.75	2.75	21.51	27.77	7.50	1.25	3.25	0.25	27.8	38.8	10.5
1976	11.72	22.95	7.08	28.57	63.01	26.62	0.24	0.97	1.47	30.8	86.9	35.2
1978	10.42	10.66	2.18	31.50	40.70	20.83	0.48	2.65	0.72	34.0	54.0	23.7
1980	6.45	6.14	4.98	33.97	41.60	22.55	0.88	1.76	1.17	41.3	49.5	28.7
1982	16.74	21.62	8.83	78.86	116.63	31.36	2.74	5.78	1.82	85.6	30.4	42.0
1984	10.10	9.12	8.14	47.21	78.45	64.46	2.29	4.59	5.86	49.5	92.2	78.5
1986	10.30	11.34	6.19	58.42	64.62	37.79	2.75	4.46	6.53	61.2	80.4	50.5
1988	5.14	2.57	3.67	61.94	53.88	26.38	2.57	3.30	2.20	69.7	59.8	32.3
1990	11.30	3.40	1.40	76.10	27.60	28.50	3.60	2.20	0.10	91.0	33.2	30.0

Source: Unemployment Survey, University of Chile.
Notes:
(1) Unemployed up to three months.
(2) Three months to one year.
(3) More than a year.

of the adjustment period. A breakdown by education shows that those most vulnerable to unemployment during the adjustment belonged to the group who had completed six years of basic and middle school education (12 years). Actually, during the most critical years of the adjustment period, there were as many individuals unemployed for more than one year as there were individuals unemployed for less than three months.

The substantial escalation in the number of individuals with relatively high periods of unemployment argues against the notion that unemployment in Chile had a voluntary component resulting from job refusals linked to higher salary expectations. This argument is strengthened when one considers unemployment trends wherein the proportion of unemployed for voluntary reasons increases considerably only during a general economic upswing (Table 3.6). For example, out of the total number of unemployed in 1982, 72.6 percent had been dismissed, while only 13.2 percent had resigned. In 1990, these percentages were 66.7 and 26.3 percent, respectively.

On the other hand, the percentage of unemployed willing to accept job offers only in occupations they held previously has been rising. While in 1982 this percentage was 27.8 percent, in 1988 it rose to 34 percent. An interpretation related to the one previously suggested is that, following the strong depreciation in specialized human capital during the 1970s adjustment period, workers have been reconstituting their human capital and today are unwilling to accept lower salaries for jobs that underutilize their human capital. Likewise, when assessing the propensity of the unemployed to emigrate, one notes that the highest percentage of emigration took place in June of 1982, precisely when the country was in the middle of the crisis, then it ebbed over time.[10]

Employment

While statistical information on the traits of the unemployed is important, an assessment of the skills employers require most is particularly relevant, because it helps in the formulation of policy recommendations on training. Such analysis can be carried out by focusing on the characteristics of the employed. One of the most significant trends observed in Table 3.7, which shows statistical data for selected groups of the work force, is the significant increase in the average education of the employed and unemployed. The change in educational level of the working age population implies that the structural change must have needed individuals with higher levels of education. Furthermore, if one considers that the

---

[10] Unfortunately, no information of this kind is available for the 1970s. A comparison would have provided support to the notion that, in the 1970s, specialized human capital should have declined significantly more than in the 1980s.

Table 3.6. Chile: Characterization of Reasons for Unemployment, 1980-90
(Percentages)

	1980	1981	1982	1983	1984	1985	1986	1987	1988	1990
Unemployment	100.0	100.0	100.0	100.0	100.0	100.0	100.0	100.0	100.0	100.0
Laid off	79.2	75.3	85.8	84.3	80.5	75.6	82.6	82.2	81.5	93.0
Reasons for Unemployment										
Fired	63.1	54.8	72.6	73.3	67.4	57.0	63.2	57.9	48.0	66.7
Quit	16.1	20.5	13.2	11.0	13.1	18.6	19.4	24.4	33.5	26.3
Only prior job	35.1	35.0	27.8	31.4	26.9	27.8	27.9	29.8	34.0	n.a.
First time search	20.8	24.7	14.2	15.7	19.5	24.4	17.3	17.8	17.8	10.1
Low family income	10.8	8.9	4.8	7.6	7.9	10.5	6.0	10.3	7.5	1.8
Others	10.0	15.8	9.4	8.1	11.6	13.9	11.3	7.5	10.3	8.3
Migrant worker	59.6	62.1	72.1	66.8	64.4	67.2	68.4	60.3	61.3	61.4

Source: Unemployment Survey; University of Chile.

tradable goods sector has been spearheading the country's economic development in recent years, and that it was precisely within this sector that the average level of education has grown proportionately more, the notion is reaffirmed that the structural changes in Chile's economy, in particular the requirements for greater international competitiveness, have required a better educated population. Therefore, in 1990 the average education of workers in the tradable goods sector, the most dynamic sector during the 1980s, was the same as that for workers in the nontradable goods sector. In 1980, workers in the nontradable goods sector had 0.9 more years of education than those in the tradable goods sector.

The trend in the educational make-up of employed workers shows definitive evidence of a recomposition of the work force rather than an increase in the educational level of workers previously employed in each industry. This is consistent with the observation that wages in the tradable goods sector grew at a faster pace than those in the nontradable goods sector, which explains the relatively greater growth of the former sector.

Human Resource Programs

The mobility of human resources between sectors during a period of structural adjustment can be facilitated by institutions able to reconvert these resources in a short time. It must be recognized, however, that a portion of the people who lose skills during the period of adjustment have intrinsic difficulties in adapting and eventually require retraining assistance. This section analyzes Chile's major assistance programs, as well as retraining programs that provide partial help in reconverting human resources.

Training Programs

Public concern over training culminated in the early 1950s with the signing of a technical cooperation agreement between the Corporation for the Development of Production (CORFO) and the U.S. government. A direct outcome of this agreement was the creation of the Technical Cooperation Service (SERCOTEC), whose Office of Professional Training trained 2 percent of the work force between 1960 and 1966. Increased coverage of these programs led the government in October 1966 to create the National Training Institute (INACAP), an autonomous institution that centralized training activities. From its early days, INACAP focused its training programs on the lower levels of the occupation pyramid through courses that concentrated on agriculture, mining, and the manufacturing industry. INACAP's main objectives were to provide accelerated training to unskilled personnel, training to mid-level personnel, and basic training. The institute also began to offer technical training courses in mechanics and industrial electronics.

Table 3.7. Chile: Average Years of Education by Occupational Group and by Productive Sector, 1970-90
(Years)

Year	Education						Sector		Age	
	Total labor force	Laid-off	Employed	Self-employed	Wage Earners	Others	Tradable	Nontradable	Laidoff	Employed
1970	7.9	5.9	8.2	7.6	11.1	5.7	7.8	8.4	34.0	35.9
1972	8.4	7.5	8.7	7.6	11.5	5.8	8.2	8.9	33.8	36.2
1974	7.9	7.0	8.2	7.1	11.1	5.8	7.9	8.3	31.9	35.6
1976	8.3	6.7	8.7	7.6	11.7	6.1	8.4	8.9	33.0	36.2
1978	8.7	7.8	9.2	8.2	12.2	6.6	8.7	9.3	35.6	35.8
1980	8.9	7.9	9.4	8.5	12.3	7.0	8.8	9.7	33.3	35.7
1982	9.0	8.3	9.6	8.4	12.4	7.2	9.2	9.8	33.3	35.6
1984	9.9	8.8	9.9	9.2	12.6	7.5	9.7	9.3	34.2	35.5
1986	9.5	9.1	10.2	9.0	12.8	8.1	10.1	10.3	34.1	36.1
1988	9.6	9.6	10.1	9.1	12.8	8.1	10.1	10.0	32.4	36.9
1990	10.2	9.7	10.8	9.5	14.0	8.6	10.6	10.9	32.9	36.9

Source: Department of Economics, University of Chile, Survey of Homes in Greater Santiago.

For this, INACAP signed agreements with different national universities (Echeverría, 1989).

During this first period, the state centralized control of training activities through the different programs that INACAP itself provided. Enactment of the Training and Employment Law in 1976 brought about a radical change in the assignment of occupational training responsibilities. In response to criticism regarding the extreme rigidity of the system in force in 1976, the state abandoned its role as direct implementor of training programs and became mainly an agency for funding and regulating training services through the National Training and Employment Service (SENCE). In 1989, companies at all management levels became legally responsible for the training of their employees. Thus, occupational training activities became the main responsibility of the companies. The state, acting in the general public interest, subsidized training activities that were carried out in accordance with the law and its statutes. In an effort to satisfy social fairness and efficiency requirements, SENCE implemented additional programs to train those individuals, particularly the unemployed, who did not have access to company-sponsored training programs. The state decentralized its training programs by refocusing training on specific requirements of potential beneficiaries. In order to ensure that training would actually bring about greater efficiency, beneficiaries were encouraged to state their training preferences. In this context, cost-recovery conditions were imposed on INACAP which, since 1973, had lost its international financial supporters (except Germany) and its preferential status with the state.

In summary, since the 1950s Chile's training programs are recognized to have had positive social impacts, thus justifying the government's intervention. The changes that have been observed over time mostly relate to emphasis and policy strategies. During a first stage, the state intervened directly by centralizing training programs. Then, in the 1970s, as a result of criticism concerning the efficiency and effectiveness of public institutions in providing training, direct state participation was replaced by increased private involvement. However, this change in emphasis resulted only in the creation of a political framework and of guidelines which, though important in the global economic context, failed to channel additional public resources to training, or to engender more activist state policies.

National Training and Employment Service (SENCE)

Several training entities were active in the mid-1970s. Among these were the Institute of Labor and Social Development, the National Employment Service, and the Department of Labor's Education and Union Extension Fund. The number of agencies presented coordination problems among the different organizations and a lack of clarity and consistency in the policies adopted. To alleviate these problems, SENCE was created by the Training and Employment Law pursuant to Decree 1446 of 1976. SENCE responds to the Ministry of Labor which, since enactment of the law, is solely responsible for training institutions.

The specific duties which SENCE currently carries out primarily involve supervision of training programs developed by private companies and the promotion of vocational training through subsidy programs. SENCE also provides occupational counseling to workers, supervises and funds the operation of municipal offices and private job placement offices, and sets technical standards. Since May 1988, SENCE has also been running an apprenticeship program.

Technical Implementing Agencies (OTEs)

OTEs are legal entities recognized or authorized by SENCE. Their main function is to provide training courses. For example, because of its training activities, the privatized INACAP is recognized by SENCE as an OTE. Also recognized as OTEs are several universities, professional institutes, technical training centers, and technical-professional schools. These institutions, which are largely private, finance courses through tuition fees.

Intermediate Technical Agencies (OTIRs)

OTIRs are private nonprofit corporations recognized by SENCE. They are established as sectoral or regional associations of companies whose purpose is to support their members through the promotion, organization, and supervision of occupational training activities. OTIRs are prohibited from directly providing courses. Such activities must be carried out by the OTEs contracted through public bidding. Companies can join an OTIR by paying a membership fee. Fees are considered as direct training costs and are deducted from a state subsidy granted in the form of a tax credit.

OTIRs must earmark at least 80 percent of the income they receive from companies to organize training courses for employees of member companies (except for their first year of operation, when they have the option to allocate only 50 percent to partly offset the cost of getting the OTIR started). The remaining 20 percent can be used for administrative costs. The balance of the money not used for training activities must be allocated the following year for scholarships for employees of member companies (Kodama, 1991).

By July 1993, seven OTIRs had been established. The most important are the following: Training Corporation for Industrial Development (manufacturing industry); Training Development Institution (construction, mining, fishing, forestry, industry, and services); Training, Education, and Cultural Corporation; Occupational Training and Labor Development Corporation (metallurgic industry); and the Land Transportation Development Corporation.

Description and Analysis of Training Programs

The Regulations for Training Agencies outline several means for providing training. These include direct in-house company training, training by companies through OTEs, and training through company affiliation with OTIRs.

As was pointed out earlier, current strategy which aims to decentralize the training process focuses on subsidies. The following four programs, which share a common objective to subsidize demands, have been developed mainly for this purpose.

Company Programs

The company programs are the most important training programs of all. They enable companies to deduct directly from their yearly taxes expenses incurred for SENCE-approved training activities. The company can deduct a maximum amount of one percent of the total value of its payroll, or up to three times the minimum monthly wage (approximately $300), if this amount is greater than one percent.[11] This provision seeks to involve small and medium-sized businesses in training activities. In this latter case, the lower limit of the deduction is one percent. If a company's training costs amount to less than the allowed maximum amount, the company is entitled to deduct all training costs.

The subsidy acts like a tax credit that is independent of the company's end-of-year earnings or losses, and it applies to companies that pay taxes in cash or on an estimated basis. To be eligible for the discount, however, courses need to be pre-approved by SENCE and must be conducted either by the companies themselves, or by a recognized agency (OTE). Companies can also organize their own courses and contract training services either outside or within the firm (in-house courses). SENCE controls and supervises the use of state subsidies and authorizes each course. Courses are then either contracted out to OTEs or conducted in-house.

Two additional regulations apply to the tax exemption. The first sets a maximum per hour cost for each trainee. In 1992, this cost was approximately $5. Courses whose trainee-per-hour-cost is greater than this amount are subsidized only up to the maximum rate. The second regulation stipulates that employees whose salary exceeds 10 times the minimum wage level (approximately $1,000 per month), are subsidized for only half the course costs. These measures are intended to promote the training of lower income workers to improve their skills and control training costs.

---

[11] Decree 1446. Law 18709, Art. 1, No. 15.

Scholarship Program

The scholarship program targets individuals who have no access to company training programs, that is, mainly those who have been laid off or are entering or trying to enter the work force. The scholarship program is funded with allocations enacted by the National Appropriation Law. The program depends on municipalities to select grantees among individuals registered in municipal placement offices. Training is conducted by an OTE selected through public bidding.

Apprentice Program

This program was created in 1988. It consists of a temporary on-the-job apprenticeship contract awarded to individuals under 21 years of age. The contract is not subject to minimum wage requirements and the apprentices work under the supervision of an instructor. This program is subsidized through the tax rebate program by which companies are allowed to deduct up to 60 percent of an apprentice's salary as a training expense. A monthly maximum limit has been established which amounts to 60 percent of each apprentice's minimum monthly salary (approximately $60). Contract coverage is for a maximum of two years, with only the first year being eligible for subsidies. Apprentices who receive a salary higher than two times the minimum monthly wage level are not eligible for benefits. Finally, the number of apprentices cannot exceed 10 percent of the number of the company's full-time employees.

Youth Training Program

Although this program has only recently been introduced, and although it lies outside the context of structural adjustment, it is worth describing because it has been designed, at least implicitly, to solve problems identified with the adjustment period. Therefore, a preliminary analysis of the program's results will help to understand some of the underlying policies that stimulated its adoption. This program is geared to young people between the ages of 15 and 24 who come from low-income backgrounds, are unemployed, underemployed or idle, are not enrolled in the regular school system, but who wish to work. The program provides resources for training activities using market mechanisms. In this context, the state fulfills a demand role for the training courses by promoting public competitions countrywide. A large number of state-licensed training agencies act as suppliers, competing for public funds earmarked for the program. The program is based on the following elements: (a) the state is solely responsible for the design, implementation, supervision, and funding of training, with operational responsibilities being left to the private sector; (b) private and public training institutions compete for contracts, thus ensuring acceptable standards of quality at reasonable prices; and (c) training agencies are responsible for deciding, without state interference, where and in what domains training should be offered, thus being responsive to identified needs within the productive system and enabling the formulation of relevant training activities. Training institutions, prior to submitting their bids to the government, must prove the existence of potential opportunities such as employment vacancies, apprentice contracts, or self-employment opportunities.

Performance of Training Programs

There has been a significant increase in the number of persons trained and the amount of money invested in the principal programs supervised by SENCE (Table 3.8). Although data are not available to estimate what percentage of the work force has received training, since a trainee may enroll in several courses, the outside limit is 20 percent. This percentage, however, seems quite high when compared with indirect information derived from employment surveys. This would suggest multiple benefits bestowed on single individuals, since the number of trainees enrolled simultaneously in several training courses is relatively high. Notwithstanding the steady increase in the number of trainees and the resources invested, training programs, on the whole, appear to be highly cyclical. Thus, it can be observed that the crisis in the early 1980s had an adverse impact on program enrollment. This is especially evident in the case of company-run programs, but is an unexpected event in the case of the scholarship program which is supposedly geared to the unemployed. Furthermore, during this period, while costs were dropping, training seems to have been concentrated in more sophisticated areas, since the cost per student increased.

Company Programs

Company-run programs involve the largest number of trainees and absorbs the greatest amount of resources. The uppermost percentage of the total work force trained annually by companies reached 5.2 percent in 1991. This percent increases to 6.6 percent if computed on the basis of trained workers and the employed work force.[12]

Three problem areas have been identified in the programs. First, it is evident that program operations are cyclical. This is mainly a consequence of the way funding is structured, whereby more funds are made available when activity lev-

---

[12] While this ratio places Chile in the forefront of Latin American countries, which train, on average, between 2 and 4.5 percent of their actively employed populations, it is far inferior to that in developed nations such as Japan, Germany, and the United States, which train between 20 and 30 percent of their work force annually.

Table 3.8. Chile: Individuals Trained and Investment in Training Programs, SENCE, 1977–90
(Thousands of US$)

Years	Total		Companies		Scholarships		Apprentices	
	No. of participants	Total expenditures[1]	No. of participants	Total expenditures[2]	No. of participants	Total expenditures[2]	Beneficiaries	Expenditures
1977	22,640	1,819	32,525	2,806	n.a.	n.a.	55,165	4,625
1978	59,546	5,097	48,897	4,409	n.a.	n.a.	108,443	9,506
1979	68,795	8,584	51,853	6,241	n.a.	n.a.	120,648	14,825
1980	97,223	10,992	51,853	5,930	n.a.	n.a.	149,076	16,922
1981	93,236	14,734	21,133	4,547	n.a.	n.a.	114,369	19,281
1982	88,171	11,597	20,885	3,348	n.a.	n.a.	109,056	14,945
1983	105,452	12,841	19,639	1,696	n.a.	n.a.	125,091	14,537
1984	122,890	14,384	21,682	1,652	n.a.	n.a.	144,572	16,036
1985	136,783	13,054	21,984	1,345	n.a.	n.a.	158,767	14,408
1986	138,125	11,108	14,807	1,199	n.a.	n.a.	152,932	12,307
1987	162,849	13,825	13,751	1,175	n.a.	n.a.	176,600	15,000
1988	174,724	15,135	9,317	792	518	97	184,559	16,024
1989	186,857	16,922	11,074	915	447	89	198,378	17,926
1990	199,604	19,196	4,863	400	441	205	204,908	19,801

Source: SENCE.
[1] Corresponds to the total amount of the tax exemption.
[2] Corresponds to national budgetary funds.

els increase. While this can be a plus from the fiscal balance point of view, it does not help in mobilizing human resources during periods of adjustment.

Second, there is clear evidence of a link between coverage and type of courses offered by company-run programs. Indeed, the coverage and quality of the courses, which are affected by budget restrictions, mainly depend on the value established by the trainee-per-hour-cost. The smaller the per hour cost, the higher the propensity for low-budget courses which are generally less topic- and infrastructure-intensive. Therefore, it is not surprising that most of the courses offered by this type of program are of the classroom variety ("chalk and blackboard") as compared to those that involve hands-on practice with machinery and materials (lathes, welding, etc.).[13]

While the mere fact that most courses are being offered in the above areas does not necessarily present a problem, it has been interpreted as a sign of inefficiency. This is because these subject matters are generally geared to the upper echelons of the corporate pyramid which, presumably, have a lesser need for state subsidized training. The notion that subsidized training is being provided, even during economic boom periods, to high-income company executives is supported by data on beneficiaries. In fact, subsidies granted to companies have mainly benefited the more skilled employees. Thus, only 3.8 percent of employees who were eligible to receive 100 percent of the subsidy because of monthly incomes below $1,000 (88 percent of the work force) were covered by the program. Moreover, 12.4 percent of the employees who were eligible to receive 50 percent of the subsidy (12 percent of the work force) were covered. On the other hand, the structure of curricula of company-run courses differ considerably from those provided by the youth program, in that the former provide a better match between course content and company requirements.[14]

A third design problem of company-run training programs relates to the time lag between outlay and reimbursement of training-related expenditures. Companies have to wait for log-in and approval of tax payments until the following year after expenses have been incurred. This can mean an interval of up to 16 months between outlays and reimbursements. The delays limit small companies and those with cash-flow problems from gaining access to the tax exemption program. This explains why the company-run programs have been mainly used by large firms. In fact, SENCE estimates that only 12,000 (or 4.5 percent) out of 270,000 potential enterprises, not including very small businesses, actually provide training for their employees. According to data from the Internal Revenue Service, only about

---

13 In the period January-October 1990, 59.6 percent of the trainees were enrolled in administration, computer, and language courses. (See Bosch, 1991.)

14 The reasons companies provide training that does not directly increase productivity is extensively documented in the literature. Ehrenberg and Smith (1988), for example, provide a broad analysis of fringe benefits which, because they are provided free of cost, are particularly attractive to executives.

5.4 percent of the annual amount allocated for training-related tax exemptions has historically been used. Moreover, 1990 data indicate that small and medium-sized companies used only 30 percent of the tax exemptions they were potentially entitled to that year, while large companies used 59 percent. The problems identified indicate that, despite the progress achieved in recent years, companies are not making full use of available exemptions.

Scholarship and Apprentice Program

Problems with the scholarship program relate to inconsistencies between the type of courses offered and labor market requirements. This seems characteristic of countries where training is centralized (Zerda, 1993). Thus, Galilea (1989) argues that since 1981 scholarships have been granted mostly through public bidding and are subject to prescribed program quality criteria, conforming to labor market requirements, and mainly to cost imperatives. This should have resulted in a decline in coverage of the scholarship program. If the preceding interpretation is correct, it would suggest that the scholarship program has not been successful in providing work opportunities to grantees.

As for the apprenticeship program, there is concern that it has been used by some businesses as a way to hire cheap labor and has not been an effective vehicle for training and introducing young people into the labor market. In any event, program coverage has been low, as only 2,324 apprentices were members of the program between 1988 and 1991. Furthermore, the target of this program, young, economically-deprived people, has been enlisted by the youth program described below.

Youth Program

The youth program was created in the aftermath of the structural adjustment. Nevertheless, an analysis of the program offers interesting insights because of the availability of valuable information which allows certain instruments used in the program to be evaluated, instruments that were designed to enhance the fit between needs and the assistance provided. Analysis of this program allows evaluation of several important elements which should generally be taken into account when designing retraining and training programs.

The data used in this analysis relates to trainees enrolled in courses of the First Call For Line of Work Training and Experience within Companies, as of July 1991. This represents 21 percent of the total number of the current enrollees.[15] Course specializations are in the following areas: trade, industrial, techni-

---

[15] The Census of the First Call surveyed 70.5 percent of the 8,553 trainees enrolled in the program.

cal, farming, and maritime. Out of a total of 441 courses in the survey, distribution was as follows: 32 percent were in the manufacturing area; 30.6 percent related to technical specializations; 20.2 percent to farming; 12.2 percent to trade; and the remaining 7 percent to other activities. This is very significant, particularly if one considers specializations and the orientation of training courses provided under company auspices. Thus, the distribution of young employees, according to the type of business activity their employer engages in, is similar to that for the country as a whole. The population of young workers active in the manufacturing industry accounted for approximately 25 percent of the young workers enrolled in this program, and for 17 percent of the national work force. The same is true in the construction sector, where 13.2 percent of young people work, accounting for 11.6 percent of young people enrolled in the program, and for 7.2 percent of the national work force. This trend is less marked in the service sector, which accounts for 26.6 percent of employment. Here, young workers active in the sector amounted to 20.6 percent and accounted for 18.6 percent of young trainees in the program.

The distribution of trainees in the company-run programs is much higher in industries in which large companies predominate (electricity, gas and water, communications and financial services) and notably lower in industries where small ones predominate (construction and trade) (Table 3.9).

To observe the degree to which programs focus on the lower-income segment of the population, the information is presented in two forms. First, based on direct observations by the census takers and on a pertinent data base, beneficiaries were divided into socioeconomic groups. Second, based on individual declarations of family income made by the beneficiaries themselves, beneficiaries were grouped into income quintiles. The quintiles correspond to those of the recent survey on socioeconomic characterization (CASEN) completed in December 1990, which were updated based on the consumer price index (CPI). Based on the classification by socioeconomic groups used by the survey takers, 96.1 percent of the young enrollees are found in groups C3, D, and E, with 53 percent concentrated in group D. It is important to point out that the characteristics of group C3 correspond to the characteristics of the middle- and middle-low income population.[16] Survey data on per capita family income show that 63.8 percent of the beneficiaries are among the poorest 40 percent of the population, and that 83 percent belong to the 60 percent of lower-income population.

The structure of the socio-demographic data leads to the conclusion that beneficiaries are clearly within the program's target group. Actual focusing generally corresponds to the goals targeted by the program. Likewise, the structure

[16] The definition of group C3 is as follows: middle-low income; barrio, large neighborhoods of houses and apartment buildings; old houses in normal state of conservation; sectors far from the city; housing: remote houses or apartments, attached, with areas between 45 to 60 meters square.

Table 3.9. Chile: Distribution of Employed Individuals by Area of Economic Activity
(Percentages)

	Country	Corporate program	Total
Agriculture, hunting and fishing	17.1	2.5	29.6
Mines and quarries	2.0	16.3	51.3
Manufacturing industry	17.0	24.6	45.2
Electricity, gas, and water	0.5	6.0	78.6
Construction	7.2	3.7	33.7
Commerce	17.7	13.0	28.7
Transportation and communication	7.0	12.2	64.5
Financial services	4.9	21.6	41.7
Community and personal services	26.6	—	—
Total	100.0	100.0	42.7[a]

Source: Ministry of Labor.
[a] Average

of this program, which entails a focused drive on the target population of young people, is based on individual recognition of the benefits granted to them upon entering the program.

Of the total number of enrollees, 51 percent were employed within 90 days after the end of the program courses. If the universe of all beneficiaries who completed training is considered, the employment level is 53.7 percent (Table 3.10). Furthermore, the idle rate for young people with practical experience is 14 percent and for those enrolled in the program is 18.6 percent. The data, which has been derived from a control group of young people previously unemployed who did not participate in the program, confirms that participation in the program generates greater opportunities for social integration. Within the control group, employment was 12 percentage points lower (42 percent), and the idle rate was nine points higher (23 percent) than among the young people who participated in the training program.

The preceding suggests that the program stimulated young people to seek some form of integration, whether employment-related or educational. Thus, the part of the census that addressed education shows that, of the total number of program enrollees, 2.9 percent of the unemployed and 6.2 percent of those who were idle were studying. As a result, out of all program enrollees, a total of 60 percent were carrying out socially integrated activities. Moreover, the data on time spent in search of jobs, among young people who participated in the training and those in the control group, show a considerable difference: 6 to 19 weeks, respectively. Therefore the data confirms that participants in the program were better equipped to deal with conditions in the labor market.

As to the relevancy of the training provided, of the total number of young

Table 3.10. Chile: Occupational Status of Youth Training Program Beneficiaries
(Control Group)

	Total enrolled		Completed		Control group
	(%)	Beneficiaries	(%)	Beneficiaries	(%)
Employed	50.6	3,052	53.7	1,870	42.3
Unemployed	30.8	1,857	32.3	1,127	34.3
Inactive	18.6	1,122	14.0	487	23.4
Total	100.0	6.031	100.0	3,484	100.0

Source: Ministry of Labor.

people who received training and found employment, 55.4 percent declared that their work was related to the courses they took. From this same group, 31.6 percent worked in the same company where they received training. Finally, it should be pointed out that the young people who were trained by the program and who were gainfully employed were evenly distributed among small, medium, and large companies: 38.1, 26.8 and 31.5 percent, respectively. Young people in the control group were more concentrated in small companies (49.6 percent) and in medium-size companies (30.1 percent). In comparison, young people employed in large companies amounted to a mere 19.9 percent (Table 3.11).

The preceding is important because it establishes a relationship between formality and size of the firm, and between companies and quality of employment. In this respect, it is quite interesting to note that, if one takes as an indicator of formality the entering into a work contract and gaining eligibility to social security benefits, significant differences exist between young people who received training and the control group. Of the young people in the program, 68.2 percent claimed to have signed work contracts, and 68.1 percent claimed to be eligible for social security benefits. In the control group, these figures were 55.8 and 58.7, respectively.

Social Assistance Policy

During the first stage of the economic restructuring of the 1970s and during the economic crisis of the 1980s, the government concentrated its efforts on social assistance for the unemployed. This meant that priority was assigned to social assistance and protection programs rather than to programs that could facilitate labor mobility and improve the available human capital. To deal with unemployment during the periods of structural adjustment, Chile relied on Emergency Employment Plans (PEEs).

Beginning in 1974, as layoffs and unemployment rates increased and reached their maximum level in 1983, the PEEs were used as a mechanism for reducing

Table 3.11. Chile: Youth Training Program—Employed Individuals by Company Size *(Control Group)*

	Total enrolled	Completed	Control group
Total	3,052.0	1,900.0	226.0
Percentage	100.0	100.0	100.0
No. of workers			
0-9	39.4	38.1	49.6
10-49	26.0	26.8	30.1
50 or more	30.7	31.5	19.5
No data (cases)	3.9	3.6	0.8

Source: Ministry of Labor.

unemployment and avoiding excessive deterioration of family incomes due to unemployment. Therefore, in 1975 the Minimum Employment Program (PEM) was created. The purpose of the program was to alleviate the high social costs resulting from the adjustment process and from the restructuring of Chile's economy in late 1973.

In order to focus subsidies on the most needy, the participants in the PEM were subject to the following conditions: (a) they had to be over 18 and under 65 years of age; (b) they were not allowed to receive any other contribution in the form of salary, pension, or subsidy; (c) they had to be physically and psychologically capable of working; (d) they had to be unemployed; and, (e) they could not be members of the program for owners of small farming combines, as these might be motivated to leave their work in order to receive program benefits.

Due to the rapid rise in program participation and low levels of economic activity, participants carried out tasks of very little aggregate value and, often, did not carry out any task at all. The official work schedule was seven hours per day, five days per week, or the equivalent of 35 hours per week, with very few of these hours actually involving effective work. As a result, a high percentage of individuals who were unemployed enrolled in the PEM.

In 1982, following the marked increase in unemployment caused by the financial crisis, new emergency employment programs were created. First, the Occupational Program for Heads of Household (POJH) was created. As its name indicates, this program added to the list of membership requirements the condition of being a head of a household and of not being a participant in any other state-subsidized program. It was hoped that these conditions would help to improve program focusing. In 1983, the PEE program achieved its maximum coverage and provided assistance to a total of 517,000 participants who represented 12.5 percent of the work force and 16.6 percent of the total number of those employed. That same year, the rate of unemployment which considered PEE

Table 3.12. Chile: Trend of the Number of Emergency Employment Plan Enrollees, 1975-87

(Monthly average each year)

	Programs					
Years	PEM	POJH	PIMO	Forest	Others	Totals
1975	72,695	—	—	—	—	72,695
1976	157,835	81,200	6,812	4,865	2,067	157,835
1977	187,646	—	—	—	—	187,646
1978	145,792	—	—	—	—	145,792
1979	133,891	—	—	—	—	133,891
1980	190,423	—	—	—	—	190,423
1981	175,607	—	—	—	—	175,607
1982	226,607	81,200	—	—	—	307,999
1983	341,578	161,228	6,812	4,865	2,067	516,554
1984	167,559	168,697	13,602	6,331	13,275	369,464
1985	134,468	184,680	4,797	12,002	32,727	363,877
1986	88,888	122,365	759	5,375	34,907	252,294
1987	40,653	75,775	8,760	2,008	28,382	155,578

Source: Central Bank of Chile.

participants as employed reached 22.5 percent. If PEE participants had been classified as unemployed, the unemployment rate would have been 33.5 percent, the highest rate in Chile's history. In 1984, about a dozen more employment programs were created, all of which had as their main goal to reduce unemployment and avoid deterioration of incomes.[17] However, participation in these programs was significantly lower than that for the PEM and the POJH (Table 3.12). The gradual economic recovery fostered a contraction in the programs, all of which ceased to function by the end of 1987.

The characteristics of PEE participants indicate that 22.4 percent did not belong to the work force. This percentage is striking in view of the fact that all programs required participants to be unemployed workers. As to the educational level of PEE participants, 5.9 percent were illiterate, a figure which is much higher than the 3.3 percent national average for illiteracy (Appendix Table 3.4). Furthermore, 54.8 percent took or completed basic education studies, 27.3 percent took or completed high school studies, and 3 percent attended university courses.[18]

Also interesting is the fact that almost half of the participants who had previously been employed had voluntarily quit their last job. This suggests that the

[17] Among the most important were the Program for Intensive Use of Manpower and the Forestry Program.

[18] See Department of Economics, University of Chile (1989).

state was inadvertently promoting state employment, since unemployed people preferred to participate in public programs rather than find employment in the private sector. Considering that the PEE salary was only 0.4 percent of the retirement pension, one must conclude that PEEs offered significant nonmonetary advantages which made these programs attractive despite their low salaries. These advantages included, for example, lower supervision and transportation costs as well as more flexible schedules. This confirms the opinion that the demand and efficiency of these programs were low and that these programs, rather than active, were more consistent with a passive type of policy whose purpose was to ensure a minimum level of income.

Notwithstanding the problems reflected in the prolonged participation of beneficiaries (30.9 months), it is important to note the redistributive role of the programs (Appendix Table 3.5). In fact, the income received by participants allowed them, on the average, to move from the poorest segment of the population (first decile and part of the second decile) to the next higher segment. These characteristics lead one to believe that the greatest spending on employment planning or services was concentrated on passive rather than active income programs which could bring about permanent improvement.

In summary, we can conclude that the PEEs fulfilled a dual role: they subsidized the unemployed and alleviated poverty among individuals directly or indirectly affected by unemployment. However, they were never part of an active policy framework aimed at endowing workers displaced by the structural change with greater human capital that would allow them to reenter the work force.

Other Programs Implemented During Structural Adjustments in Chile

In addition to training programs, several other programs were implemented which were designed to reduce unemployment spans for those who had lost their jobs, and to diminish the severity of the effects of unemployment. Among these were the unemployment compensation program, assistance programs, and retraining programs.

Unemployment Compensation

The unemployment compensation program acquired special importance as a result of legal changes introduced in 1974 and the increase in the rate of unemployment during that time. The subsidy consists of a payment equivalent to approximately one third the minimum salary and is granted to workers in the public and private sectors.[19] The subsidy is temporary and is granted for 90

---

[19] The law stipulates that the unemployment subsidy cannot exceed 80.19 percent of minimum income.

days, and can be extended up to 360 days. Furthermore, the subsidy is gradually reduced and is forfeited if the unemployed individual refuses, without reasonable cause, a job offered by SENCE. A reasonable cause for refusing a job is a salary offer amounting to less than 50 percent of the last salary received.[20]

There is no clear trend in the evolution of the subsidy since 1973. No relation with the trend in unemployment rates is observed, only a constant decline in subsidy spending beginning in 1983. The decline in subsidy spending resulted primarily from political measures and can be partly explained by the decline in the layoff rate since 1984. Because the government believed that the subsidy discouraged job searches, the amount of the subsidy was substantially cut. The consequences were clear: while in the early 1980s almost 25 percent of laid off individuals received benefits, this percentage began to decline in 1984 and, by 1989, had dropped to 10 percent.

Unemployment Offices

In 1977, SENCE initiated a free employment assistance program that carried out decentralized operations through Municipal Placement Offices (OMCs). The law stipulates that OMCs should operate in all municipalities, except for certain municipalities exempted by the Ministry of the Interior. Currently there are 124 OMCs in as many communities, out of a total of 335 municipalities. In addition, a system of Private Employment Offices (OPCs) started operations beginning in 1982. These agencies are supervised by SENCE. Approximately 150 OPCs exist, 60 percent of which are in the metropolitan area.

The number of jobs generated through these programs has been increasing, possibly because of greater involvement since the mid-1980s by private placement offices (Appendix Table 3.6). A significant rise in enrollment was recorded during 1982-83, which coincides with the high unemployment generated by the economic recession which began that year. An increase in the number of total job vacancies was also observed.

As can be seen in Appendix Table 3.6, the placement rate for enrollees suggests that the programs have become more efficient. While during the first years of the program, only 20 percent of enrollees were placed in a job, towards the end of the 1980s and in the early 1990s, this rate increased to nearly 50 percent. Even so, it is important to point out that only about 50 percent of those who enrolled in these programs were subsequently hired. Moreover, the vacancy/placement ratio was very stable during the period, hovering around 1.6 percent. This means that approximately 63 percent of the positions offered

---

[20] Two other requirements for receiving this subsidy are that the individual may not be involved in any other paid activity and must have been dismissed for reasons beyond his control.

Table 3.13. Chile: Trend of Unemployment Compensation, 1973-89
(Thousands of 1992 pesos)

Year	Total expense[1]	Unemployed individuals benefitted (%)	Expenditures per beneficiary (pesos)
1973	175,631	1	224.5
1974	336,885	1	133.7
1975	17,394,534	19	231.3
1976	18,769,854	22	173.1
1977	17,105,508	21	223.6
1978	22,439,969	23	270.2
1979	24,101,681	24	267.5
1980	19,082,650	21	256.9
1981	22,811,436	23	304.5
1982	34,675,055	20	265.1
1983	33,038,374	20	231.8
1984	18,163,796	16	185.7
1985	16,571,633	18	170.3
1986	10,630,426	18	125.9
1987	6,553,201	15	99.2
1988	4,755,220	12	93.1
1989	3,031,575	10	77.2

Source: Ministry of Labor.
[1] Between 1973 and 1979 estimated on the basis of Social Security Service beneficiaries.

through these programs were filled, which reflects a mismatch in job skills caused by the structural change. Finally, it should be pointed out that the total placement/unemployment ratio in the country has increased, reflecting the importance of placement programs as mechanisms for job assistance.

Labor Retraining Programs

Beginning in 1992, in order to facilitate labor entry in different economic sectors, SENCE implemented labor retraining programs primarily aimed at reeducating specific segments of the work force. These programs were created because certain groups were rooted in specific geographic areas. The programs include the retraining of coal miners, women heads of household, longshoremen, and handymen. The programs are geared towards specific and localized segments of the work force, and involve few workers. Also, the volume of resources allocated to the programs is relatively low, even though they receive considerably more resources than, for example, the unemployment compensation program (Appendix Table 3.7).

Conclusions and Policy Lessons

Structural adjustment processes, such as those implemented in Chile since the mid-1970s, produced significant changes in the structure of the productive sector. Unemployment caused by a mismatch in skills was quite high during these processes. The Chilean experience shows that the persistent unemployment of the late 1970s, at a time when the GDP was growing, was largely due to skills imbalances. Employment in Chile was also adversely affected by policies which provided misleading signals to the private sector and which did not allow the sector to develop by investing in sectors where it enjoyed relative advantages. This study provides abundant proof that the training system and the handling of human resources did not facilitate intersectoral labor mobility because policies aimed at correcting the skills misalignments were not implemented.

Thus, during the 1970s, programs supporting labor mobility, particularly programs for the development of human resources, were not appropriately enacted. Only a first step was implemented, which consisted of transferring certain training activities to the private sector and reserving for the state the role of subsidizing and supervising the training system. This scheme is compatible with the needs of a dynamic adjustment process which is market-driven, and constitutes a core element in the development of a human resources training system. Undoubtedly, the state placed great emphasis on assistance policies, particularly through emergency employment programs, but did not allocate larger resources that would have allowed a better and more efficient labor training operation. Also, subsidies granted to companies to carry out training programs failed to reach those most affected by the adjustment process, such as the unemployed. Furthermore, the subsidy system did not promote a division of training tasks between the public and private sectors, whereby the public sector would specialize in general training, aimed essentially at improving aptitudes for industrial training, and the private sector would emphasize specialized training related to production activities. In fact, financing and subsidizing training through companies, as it was mostly done, implied allocating the responsibility for specialized training mainly to existing companies. These companies were ill-suited for general training or training pertinent to emerging firms.

The consequence is the poor result of the training system. An economy undergoing adjustment requires implementation of a system which can provide, in timely fashion, the human resources required by the private sector. In Chile, however, the relatively few initiatives taken in training labor were compounded by the lack of a macroeconomic policy to stimulate production, so that the poor condition of the productive sector made the lack of human resources less noticeable.

The Chilean case also points out another typical problem that arises during adjustment processes and which affects the design and efficiency of training systems. Unemployment brings about undesirable social consequences, and makes it necessary to enact a social assistance program to reduce the social cost of the adjustment. However, training qualified manpower does not constitute per se a social assistance program, but rather an active type of program aimed at increasing labor mobility. Similarly, social assistance programs, such as emergency employment plans, do not help to increase training. On the other hand, despite the general acceptance of the separate nature of the two types of programs, reactive or social assistance, and active or labor mobility assistance, it is clear that in real adjustment processes the two types of programs should complement each other. A greater integration and coordination between the two types of assistance programs would allow an increase in the overall efficiency of employment services. For example, those applying for unemployment compensation should have direct access to sources of work offered by employment assistance offices and to other active employment programs. Also, a high degree of integration would imply important savings in the total operating costs of employment services. On the other hand, greater integration between the two types of programs could generate excessive centralization of duties and loss of flexibility. This consideration is particularly important, considering the different nature of the programs. Active assistance programs should be dynamic and should quickly adapt themselves to changes in the economy, while passive income programs are highly regulated and devote a large part of their efforts to supervision and controlling fraud. The need for complementarity is clearer in the case of unemployed young people because of such unwanted consequences as lower formal schooling, delinquency, and structural poverty. Coordination, however, requires the creation of government structures in order to make the combined assistance to the unemployed more effective and expeditious.

Subsidy mechanisms were not created for the purpose of increasing labor mobility and reentry. The results of this study show that subsidies for company-run training programs benefit higher paid and skilled workers. At the same time, these subsidies do not benefit medium and small companies, and do not target priority training areas. The state needs to assume a more active role in focusing training subsidies, while providing the resources needed by the private sector through general training to employees.

Finally, when training young people, it is fitting to point out some interesting ideas concerning adjustment policies. The role of the private sector as a training agent is once again to be commended. Unlike company-run programs, the mechanism utilized to focus help on the neediest groups is innovative. Also, the apparent success achieved in meeting private sector requirements constitutes an important advance in the training provided by government institutions. The most noteworthy result relates to the procedures that allow specialized agencies to provide training courses. This guarantees that some of these trainees will acquire on-the-job practice in private sector firms.

Recommendations

A highly crucial issue during an adjustment period is the design of an adequate system for the development of human resources. A basic need to be addressed is the design of a flexible system responsive to the changing needs of individual companies in terms of their human resource requirements. The latter objective presents a number of difficulties because of the uncertainties the economy faces during an adjustment process, particularly knowing which sectors are likely to expand. The nature of the response provided by a training system will depend on its links to the private sector and on government incentives that foster the creation of training institutes.

The need for greater flexibility in the labor market makes unemployment an effective focusing agent. It should be remembered that the promotion of labor mobility within a company, rather than mobility that results in open unemployment, is very important. Therefore, it is necessary to create a second focusing criterion within the companies themselves, as well as related implementation structures. With regard to general training, the role of the OTIRs should be highlighted. These organizations "internalize" the external effects that make general training unattractive to companies. An incentive scheme, such as the one described here, could greatly alleviate the problem.

Another conclusion that can be drawn from the Chilean experience is that assistance and training systems should be flexible, both in adapting to changes and in providing a wide range of programs for different target groups. For example, several of the unemployment subsidies, such as the emergency employment programs, were created as open alternatives targeted to specific groups of the labor force. On the other hand, other programs supporting higher incomes acted more like job maintenance programs rather than subsidy programs for the unemployed. This allows for better focus and more efficient administration. Likewise, training programs should and can be structured to meet the demands of the target populations and projected goals. This requires proactive diagnoses and administrative decentralization in favor of regions, and public services to guarantee the effectiveness of subsidy programs. Implementation of the programs should be temporary, and they should be modified according to imperatives dictated by experience and the adjustment process itself. Dynamic and modern economies undergo constant adjustment processes. This requires implementation of a training system that fosters labor mobility and employment, rather than a rigid administrative structure that does not easily adapt to changes in demand.

Flexible institutional and legal mechanisms should be created to allow external and internal mobility within companies and to promote labor costs that reflect productivity. In the context of a market economy, the role played by labor unions and collective bargaining structures are fundamentally important in the definition and creation of such a legal framework.

Also imperative is the implementation of policies intended to shorten the duration and reduce the costs of the adjustment period. The lack of institutional mechanisms to facilitate the retraining of the work force are in juxtaposition with the skill mismatches that are usually generated during adjustment processes. Market forces alone cannot be sufficiently responsive to emerging needs in an environment dominated by uncertainty and externalities. Design of an appropriate institutional framework is especially important for the development of human resources during and after the adjustment stages. The role of the private sector in training should be recognized and encouraged. However, it is important to look for improvements, if training is to be effective in expediting resource mobility and retraining during the adjustment period. The performance of the OTIRs as training tools illustrates a new approach that deserves further study. Priority should be assigned to the training provided by these institutions, which groups private companies from the same line of business, since it alleviates one of the most harmful externalities that makes state intervention necessary—the lack of general training.

The company-run program is not very effective in providing general training nor does it promote the reentry of the unemployed into the work force. Therefore, direct worker subsidy schemes which avoid intermediaries are recommended (e.g., vouchers).

In this context, it should be pointed out once again that the latter financing scheme is crucial for focusing training and retraining programs. The Chilean company-run training program, because of the short-term financing requirements it generates, is cyclical. Financing schemes should, however, be formulated so that their coverage is anticyclical.

Bibliography

Abaigar, F. 1986. Promoción del empleo juvenil. *Revista de la Juventud* (no. 31).

Alarcón, P., V. Pola, and P. Wainer. 1990. Los jóvenes y el mercado del trabajo. Análisis del período 1958-1989 en el Gran Santiago. Master's thesis, Department of Economics, University of Chile, Santiago.

Arriagada, A.M. 1990. Labor Market Outcomes of Non Formal Training for Male and Female Workers in Peru. *Economic Evaluation Review* 18 (35).

Ashenfelter, O., and D. Card. 1985. Using the Longitudinal Structure of Earnings to Estimate the Training Effect. *Statistical Economic Review* (November).

Barandiarán, E. 1987. The Adjustment Process in Latin America's Highly Indebted Countries. World Bank, Washington, D.C. Mimeo.

Bosch, M. 1991. Proyecto fondo nacional de capacitación. Department of Industrial Engineering, University of Chile, Santiago. Mimeo.

Bowman, M. J. 1990. Overview Essay: View from the Past and the Future. *Economic Evaluation Review* 13 (4).

Casas, J. 1986. Medidas para combatir el paso juvenil: Descripción y reflexión sobre resultados. *Revista de la Juventud* (no. 31).

Cerda, M., and M. Marcel. 1990. Capacitación laboral y educación para el trabajo. Apuntes sobre la Agenda del Gobierno Democrático. Santiago. Mimeo.

CIEPLAN. 1989. Capacitación y empleo de jóvenes. Revisión y análisis de experiencias. CIEPLAN, Santiago. Mimeo.

Confederación de la Producción y el Comercio. 1987. Capacitación y acceso al mundo laboral de la juventud chilena de bajos recursos: Un desafío para el sector productivo nacional. Santiago. Mimeo.

Corbo, V. 1985. Reforms and Macroeconomic Adjustment in Chile During 1974-84. *World Development* 13 (8).

Corbo, V., and P. Meller. 1984. Trade and Employment in Chile in the 60s. *American Economic Review* 69 (2).

Cortázar, R., and J. Marshall. 1979. Working Papers. Research Series No. 34. Department of Economics, University of Chile, Santiago.

Corvalán, O. 1985. Formación profesional de la juventud en América Latina: Crisis y oportunidad. Santo Domingo, Dominican Republic. Mimeo.

Department of Economics, University of Chile. 1989. *Programas de empleo de emergencia*. Santiago: Editorial FACEA.

Echeverría, C. 1989. El estado y la capacitación en Chile. In *Apuntes CIEPLAN* (no. 85), ed. Mario Marcel. CIEPLAN, Santiago.

Edwards, S., and A. Edwards. 1987. *Monetarism and Liberalization: the Chilean Experiment.* Cambridge, Mass.: Ballinger Publishing Co.

Ehrenberg, R., and R. Smith. 1988. *Modern Labor Economics: Theory and Public Policy*, 3rd edition. Glenview, Ill.: Scott, Foresman and Co.

Freeman, D. 1985. Políticas de empleo para la juventud en los países desarrollados. International Labor Organization, Geneva. Mimeo.

Galilea, S. 1989. Experiencias del aparato del estado en capacitación ocupacional y sus perspectivas en la transición democrática. In Apunte*s CIEPLAN* (no. 85), ed. Mario Marcel. CIEPLAN, Santiago.

Hachette, D., and R. Lüders. 1987. Aspects of the Privatization Process: The Case of Chile 1974-85. World Bank, Washington, D.C. Mimeo.

Harberger, A.C. 1985. Observations on the Chilean Economy, 1973-83. *Economic Development and Cultural Change* 33 (April).

Heckman, J., and J. Hotz. 1989. Choosing Among Alternatives to Experimental Methods for Estimating the Impact of Social Programs: The Case of Manpower Training. *American Statistical Association Journal* (December).

Hidalgo, M. 1993. Los organismos técnicos intermedios reconocidos (OTIR) en el sistema de capacitación ocupacional. Master's thesis, Department of Economics, University of Chile. Santiago.

Kanawaty, G. 1985. Formación para un mundo en plena evolución: Algunas reflexiones de carácter general. *Revista Internacional del Trabajo* 104 (3).

Keithm, G., and J. Knight. 1989. El desarrollo humano: Razones para reafirmar su importancia. *Revista de la Planificación del Desarrollo* 19.

Knight, J. 1989. Cuestiones de política educacional en un período de estabilización y ajuste estructural. *Revista de la Planificación del Desarrollo* 19.

Kodama, K. 1991. Diagnóstico de la oferta de capacitación laboral en Chile. Master's thesis, Civil Industrial Engineering Department, University of Chile, Santiago.

Larraín, F. 1988. Public Sector Behavior in a Highly Indebted Country: The Contrasting Chilean Experience 1970-85. LAC Region, World Bank, Washington, D.C. Mimeo.

Levy, B., A. Stone and R. Paredes. 1991. Public Institutions and Private Transactions: A Comparative Study of the Legal and Regulatory Environment for Business Transactions in Brazil and Chile. CECPS, World Bank, Washington, D.C. Mimeo.

Marcel, M. 1989. Capacitación y empleo de jóvenes, revisión y análisis de experiencias. *Apuntes CIEPLAN* 85. Santiago.

Pardo, L., and I. Irarrázaval. 1990. Factores determinantes en los niveles de educación formal de los jóvenes: Alcances y significados en el mercado del trabajo. *Estudios de Economía* 17 (2).

Paredes, R. 1994. Job Security Regulation in Less Developing Countries. In *Impediments to Competitive Labor Markets,* eds. V. Adams, E. King, and L. Riveros. Washington, D.C.: World Bank. Forthcoming.

Paredes, R., and L. Riveros. 1990. *Political Transition and Labor Market Reforms.* Background Paper, Chile Country Economic Memorandum. World Bank, Washington, D.C.

Riveros, L. 1990. Empleo y salarios en un contexto de ajuste macroeconómico. *Estudios de Economía* 17 (no. 2, November).

_____. 1986. Labor Market Mal-Adjustment in Chile: Economic Reforms and Friction Among Submarkets. *Análisis Económico* 1 (November).

Sapelli, C. 1990. Ajuste estructural y mercado del trabajo. Una explicación de la persistencia del desempleo en Chile: 1975-80. *Estudios de Economía* (December).

Servicio de Cooperación Técnica (SERCOTEC). 1990. Diagnóstico sobre capacitación laboral en sectores comprendidos entre los CIIU 31 al 39. Santiago. Mimeo.

Torres, C. 1982. Evolución de la política arancelaria: Período 1973-1981. *Reporte 16.* Banco Central, Santiago.

World Bank. 1991. *Vocational and Technical Education and Training.* World Bank Policy Paper, Washington, D.C.

Yáñez, J. 1988. Estudio sobre los programas especiales de empleo. *Indice General de Remuneraciones del Gran Santiago 2.* Santiago.

Zerda, A. 1993. *Capacitación e intermediación de recursos humanos en el proceso de ajuste económico en Colombia.* Working Paper No. 139. Inter-American Development Bank, Washington, D.C.

Appendix Table 3.1. Chile: Trend of Sectoral GDP, 1969-90
(Millions of 1977 pesos)

	Tradable[1] goods	%	Industry	%	Nontradable goods	%	Total	%
1969	42,287	—	68,555	—	166,351	—	277,393	—
1973	38,179	-9.7	74,906	9.3	174,665	5.0	287,750	3.7
1974	47,546	24.5	72,994	-2.6	170,014	-2.3	290,554	1.0
1975	46,088	-3.1	54,405	-25.5	152,550	-10.3	253,143	-12.9
1977	48,117	4.4	57,678	6.0	156,150	2.4	261,945	3.5
1980	56,108	16.6	78,322	35.8	229,006	46.7	363,446	38.7
1982	60,447	7.7	63,500	-18.9	205,576	-10.2	329,523	-9.3
1984	62,692	3.7	71,858	13.2	213,376	3.8	347,926	5.6
1986	68,630	9.5	78,507	9.3	229,490	7.6	376,627	8.2
1988	73,251	6.7	89,997	14.6	264,282	15.1	427,530	13.5
1990	79,079	8.0	99,043	10.1	302,201	14.3	480,323	12.3

Source: Figures based on Central Bank of Chile newsletters.
[1] Tradables does not include industry.

Appendix Table 3.2. Chile: Real Wages, 1970-90
(Base 1970=100 and 1982=100)

	Totals	Men	Women
1970	100.0	100.0	100.0
1972	72.0	70.2	76.2
1974	36.8	34.3	40.7
1976	46.7	44.3	55.3
1978	67.2	65.9	74.1
1980	88.1	84.7	97.6
1982	100.0	100.0	100.0
1984	74.8	75.9	70.4
1986	58.2	57.9	59.0
1988	73.4	70.9	79.3
1990	92.2	93.6	90.4

Source: National Institute of Statistics (INE).

Appendix Table 3.3. Chile: Real Wage by Educational Level and Age, 1970-90
(Men 1970 and 1982=100)

	Educational level			Age			
	8 or less	8-12	12 or more	12-18	14-24	35-44	55 and more
1970	100.0	100.0	100.0	100.0	100.0	100.0	100.0
1972	74.2	67.0	62.2	59.5	96.0	73.1	53.5
1974	39.0	34.0	28.2	34.6	49.5	36.1	21.5
1976	45.7	39.6	34.4	45.3	89.0	44.1	37.7
1978	65.6	45.7	46.2	64.0	78.6	71.9	76.0
1980	78.1	72.1	70.7	72.4	95.2	99.0	75.9
1982	100.0	100.0	100.0	100.0	100.0	100.0	100.0
1984	67.8	72.7	67.0	90.8	62.5	88.1	59.4
1986	61.7	60.3	50.0	56.5	54.2	66.1	51.1
1988	77.1	62.0	56.4	83.5	64.5	74.1	72.4
1990	76.7	76.5	68.1	90.3	73.6	101.6	95.5

Source: Department of Economics, University of Chile.

Appendix Table 3.4. Chile: Educational Level of Emergency Employment Plan Enrollees
(Percentages)

Programs	Illiterates	Basic education	Middle education	Special education	Univ. education	Men	Women
PEM	5.8	50.4	31.7	11.0	1.1	27.4	72.6
POJH	5.1	56.5	27.2	8.9	2.2	71.9	28.1
PIMO	1.9	79.2	17.0	—	1.0	98.1	1.9
Forest	5.3	55.1	27.4	9.0	3.2	71.2	28.8
Average	5.9	54.9	27.3	8.9	3.0	49.5	50.5

Source: Ministry of Planning.

Appendix Table 3.5. Chile: Average Length of Participation in Emergency Employment Plans
(Months)

Programs	Length of participation in program	Length of participation in other programs[1]	Total length of participation
PEM	40.8	2.3	43.1
POJH	25.1	4.0	29.1
PIMO	1.2	6.0	7.2
Forest	17.9	4.4	22.3
Average	27.3	3.6	30.9

Source: Ministry of Planning.
[1] Shows the length of participation in other employment programs both before and after participation in the program in question.

Appendix Table 3.6. Chile: Jobs Filled by Employment Offices, 1977-91

	Total jobs filled	Jobs filled		Applicants		Vacancies	
		OPC	OMC	OPC	OMC	OPC	OMC
1977	8,216	—	8,216	—	61,456	—	13,760
1978	15,211	—	15,211	—	71,035	—	24,474
1979	17,066	—	17,066	—	83,749	—	26,797
1980	20,473	—	20,473	—	96,234	—	31,528
1981	28,686	—	28,6861	—	13,424	—	38,971
1982	27,480	1,389	26,091	9,329	194,466	3,539	31,531
1983	32,487	6,751	25,736	16,694	166,288	12,458	31,873
1984	37,424	9,639	27,731	20,353	113,089	18,858	34,078
1985	42,752	12,836	29,916	27,052	105,022	29,184	36,408
1986	55,309	15,608	39,701	35,837	113,566	37,999	49,959
1987	65,954	15,980	49,974	36,256	99,836	40,417	62,863
1988	76,112	16,557	59,555	33,718	104,528	39,485	80,351
1989	68,764	17,994	50,770	38,381	83,021	41,934	68,078
1990	53,168	17,387	35,781	41,334	80,221	38,946	49,715
1991	51,099	16,543	34,556	39,072	94,392	35,116	49,711

Source: SENCE.
Note: OMCs are municipal employment offices; OPCs are private employment offices.

Appendix Table 3.7. Chile: Worker Retraining Programs, SENCE, 1992
(Thousands of 1992 pesos)

	Amount	Total number of beneficiaries	Expense per beneficiary (pesos)
Worker retraining			
Coal miners	192,609.4	541	356.0
Housewives	145,891.9	610	239.1
Prospective port workers	33,659.7	655	51.4
Total	372,161.0	1.806	206.0

Source: SENCE.

CHAPTER FOUR

COLOMBIA

Alvaro Zerda[1]

This chapter analyzes the human resource conditions in Colombia during the current structural adjustment, as well as the country's institutions charged with resource training and intermediation. It identifies a series of policy initiatives that could supplement and strengthen government-sponsored activities, and formulates a comprehensive response to the challenges posed by the adjustment process so as to lessen their impact on the population's most vulnerable groups.

The chapter analyzes the evolution of Colombia's training and skills development system over a 20-year period, and its labor market and human resources over a 10-year period.[2] During this time span, the country underwent three economic cycles that were influenced by both foreign and domestic events and policies. Meanwhile, Colombia became a predominantly urban and democratic society, despite social and political problems due to two very serious sources of unrest, guerrillas and drug trafficking.

The country's economic structure was only slightly affected by these internal and external episodes. However, its industrial sector was not able to foster the expected economic growth during the 1970s. Therefore, beginning in 1990 the government adopted a structural adjustment program aimed at enhancing growth and social welfare.

The study shows that current socio-labor government policies and programs must be expanded to ensure their success during the transition and to alleviate adverse impacts on labor. This entails formulating clear short-, medium-, and long-term policy initiatives that would allow implementation of a comprehen-

[1] The research team for this chapter included Oscar Arcos, María I. Agudelo, Julio Silva, Manuel da Silva, Oscar Benavides, Ximena Lombana and Gabriel Misas. The author is grateful for the valuable comments and suggestions of Jere Behrman, Rainer Dombois, and Victor Manuel Gómez. He is also grateful for the remarks of participants at the Seminar for the Centers for Applied Research Network which took place in Montevideo in March, 1993, and participants at the Seminar on Human Resources in the Adjustment Process which took place in Bogota that same month.
[2] Ideally, both analyses should have covered equal time periods, but the data were incomplete.

sive and integrated system capable of managing human resources and facilitating labor mobility.

The chapter is divided into six sections. Following an introduction, the second section analyzes the evolution of Colombia's economy and the economic policies enacted by different governments. Its purpose is to establish the nature of economic changes over the past 20 years and to determine whether a structural adjustment was associated with them. The third section examines the condition of human resources during periods of recession in order to identify the groups most affected by adjustment changes. The fourth section assesses the role played by institutions responsible for human resource training and intermediation, and proposes an expedient and appropriate solution to problems in that area. The fifth section reviews government policies dealing with adjustment costs and identifies the system's quantitative and qualitative needs. The final section summarizes the study's main conclusions.

Nature of the Adjustment Process

In the last 20 years Colombia has undergone three clearly identifiable cycles marked by economic upswings and recessions. While these changes were mostly driven by foreign events, they were also shaped by domestic administrative considerations and by the economic policies of successive governments (Table 4.1).

In the first half of the 1970s, the economy was emerging from a period marked by rapid creation of wealth—the result of foreign investment inflows during the 1950s and of an expanding domestic market bolstered by the import substitution and export diversification policies then in effect.[3]

In the second half of the 1970s, GDP began to rise rapidly at a rate of 6.3 percent (Figure 4.1). It reached its highest level in two decades in 1978 owing to two booms in foreign trade: the coffee boom resulting from the Brazilian frost, and the marijuana boom resulting from increased consumption in the United States. The effects of these booms, however, evaporated before policies could be enacted to harness economic development benefits, and the country began to exhibit clear signs of "Dutch disease" (overvaluation of the exchange rate, two-digit inflation rates, low levels of investment, domestic and foreign trade deficits). These symptoms reduced economic growth close to zero during the 1982 crisis.

The crisis had a major impact on the financial and industrial sectors, resulting in massive bank failures and a 2 percent industry contraction. The crisis is

---

[3] During the 1950s and 1960s, GDP grew at an annual average rate of 4.8 and 5.9 percent, respectively.

Table 4.1. Colombia: Macroeconomic Trends by Periods and Phases, 1970-90
(Average percentage rates)

Variable	Period I Rise (70-72)	Period I Decline (73-75)	Period II Rise (76-78)	Period II Decline (79-82)	Period III Rise (83-86)	Period III Decline (87-90)
GDP growth	6.91	3.93	6.31	2.44	4.08	3.86
Investment/GDP	17.08	15.80	15.22	17.03	17.43	17.63
Domestic investment/GDP	16.64	15.50	14.87	16.33	15.46	12.95
Foreign investment/GDP	0.44	0.29	0.34	0.69	1.96	4.68
National savings/GDP	15.27	17.96	20.47	17.33	18.14	21.34
Exports/GDP	12.81	15.16	16.80	13.03	14.69	18.34
Imports/GDP	14.33	14.21	13.62	15.05	12.43	14.02
Foreign debt growth	14.17	8.00	17.30	17.70	11.26	0.98
Interest debt growth	16.00	21.14	10.19	40.39	8.14	9.05

Sources: Figures based on data from the Colombian National Office of Statistics (DANE), National Accounts, and the Banco de la República.

now slowly ebbing—though at a slower pace than the previous recovery—and a third cycle is beginning. Economic growth is once again being driven by two external factors: a short-lived boom in international coffee prices in 1986 and a second boom in cocaine trafficking spanning the 1980s.[4] Meanwhile, the peso continues to depreciate, the terms of trade are recovering, and inflation is rising (Table 4.2).

As in the past, however, the upswing in foreign trade did not engender sustained growth. Rather, it slowed economic activity, and led to a series of alternate ups and downs until 1991, when GDP growth was 2.3 percent. Export levels, however, were not affected by the recession (Table 4.1) because of a recovery in petroleum and coal exports and, partly, because of the dynamic growth in "nontraditional" exports (other than coffee and petroleum) such as flowers, manufacturers, and graphic arts. The exchange rate continued to depreciate while inflation rates reached their highest levels (32.6 percent) in Colombia's history in 1990 (Table 4.2). Taxes and spending in the public sector were also high (Table 4.3).

The year 1992 was critical for Colombia's economy since industry had to ration as much as 25 percent of its energy during the most acute phase of the crisis. Meanwhile, the war against guerrillas and drug traffickers intensified,

---

[4] There is no consensus on the quantitative impact of drugs on Colombia's economy. Some researchers minimize the impact and others estimate it at 20 percent of GDP. Kalmanovitz (1992) estimates that mafia income contributes between 6 and 8 percent to the country's GDP, and that 10 percent of the illicit income is deposited or invested abroad as flight capital.

Figure 4.1. Colombia: GDP Growth, 1971-92
(Percentages)

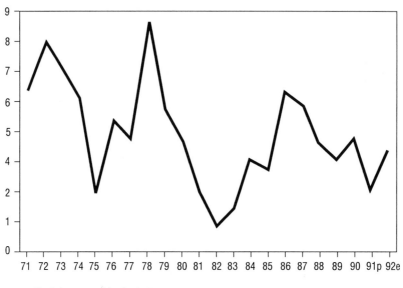

e: estimated   p: provisional or temporary

diverting considerable state resources from social and infrastructure invest-ments.[5] International coffee prices during the year dropped to their lowest level in 15 years (to 50 cents per pound), as did the price of cocaine.[6] The open trade policy adopted in 1990 strengthened after a brief interval in 1991 when imports rose 30 percent and exports, including the so-called "lesser" exports, stagnated or declined (Table 4.4). This decline was partly attributable to the revaluation of the peso (Banco de la República, 1993).

Preliminary estimates place overall GDP growth in 1992 around 3.5 per-cent. Industry grew at a rate of 5 percent, while farming and livestock grew only 1.2 percent in 1991, thus showing signs of stagnation. Economic expansion was led by the construction sector which, with a growth rate of about 10 percent, accounted for a significant portion of employment and offset unemployment in other sectors.

---

[5] It is estimated that in 1992 the government diverted 30 million pesos from the budget to military expenditures (Sarmiento and Zerda, 1993).

[6] This could explain the increase in poppy cultivation (Kalmanovitz, 1992).

Table 4.2. Colombia: Price Trends by Periods and Phases, 1970-90
(Indices and average percentage rates)

Variable	Period I Rise (70-72)	Period I Decline (73-75)	Period II Rise (76-78)	Period II Decline (79-82)	Period III Rise (83-86)	Period III Decline (87-90)
Real exchange rate	94.33	92.22	83.11	75.78	89.76	113.48
Inflation	11.55	22.82	21.01	26.29	19.57	27.71
Interest rate	15.00	23.16	27.86	36.12	34.17	34.54
Terms of trade	84.86	91.57	141.07	105.53	105.10	94.35

Sources: Figures based on data from the Banco de la República, DANE, and the International Monetary Fund.

Table 4.3. Colombia: Consolidated Public Sector Indicators by Periods and Phases, 1970-90
(Millions of 1980 pesos and percentages)

Variable	Period I Rise (70-72)	Period I Decline (73-75)	Period II Rise (76-78)	Period II Decline (79-82)	Period III Rise (83-86)	Period III Decline (87-90)
Public savings	121.522	168.140	311.093	314.093	345.167	484.051
Public investment	176.498	188.517	237.960	466.423	623.536	532.715
Public spending	493.946	571.458	600.052	1.190.256	1.543.131	1.740.250
Fiscal deficit (surplus)[1]	-54.976	-20.377	73.133	-152.330	-278.369	-48.664
Deficit/GDP (%)	-1.86	-0.58	1.81	-2.40	-3.98	-0.03

[1] Savings less investment.
Sources: Figures based on data from DANE, National Accounts, and General Accounting Office.

Official projections for the coming years are optimistic based on the performance of the mining and construction sectors, and on the assumptions that the economy will be driven by public and private investments and exports will make a significant recovery (Presidency of the Republic, DNP, 1993) (Table 4.4). However, the accuracy of these projections has been questioned based on several domestic and foreign factors. The latter include the international economic recession, protectionist pressures in several industrial countries, and the low prices of primary commodities. The domestic factors include a drop in consumption due to stagnation in real salaries and the peso revaluation policy enacted to control inflation (Sarmiento and Zerda, 1993).

In summary, economic fluctuations in Colombia during the 1970s and 1980s did not have a significant impact on the country's overall economic performance. As can be seen in Table 4.5, the GDP drop in agriculture was offset by growth in

Table 4.4. Colombia: Selected Economic Indicators during the Structural Adjustment Phase, 1990-93
(Percentage rates and indices)

Indicator	1990	1991	1992 (1)	1993 (2)
GDP growth	4.1	2.3	3.6	4.5
Per capita GDP growth	1.9	0.0	0.8	—
Growth in industry	6.6	-0.9	5.1	3.3
Growth in agriculture and livestock	0.1	0.0	1.2	2.8
Growth in exports	0.2	0.1	-3.0	5.0
Growth in imports	0.1	-0.1	28.7	16.0
Inflation	32.6	26.8	25.1	22.0
Real exchange rate	126.6	113.9	102.1	—
Interest rate	38.2	36.2	27.2	—
Terms of trade	85.2	80.6	76.2	—
Fiscal balance (%)	0.1	0.9	0.1	-1.4
Unemployment rate (7 cities)	10.2	9.8	9.9	—
Variation in real wages	-4.8	-0.6	-1.6	—
Poverty level (basic needs)	16.0	15.5	n.a.	—
Poverty level (poverty line)	40.8	40.7	44.8	—

Sources: Banco de la República newsletter, DANE, National Planning Office (DNP), ECLAC, and author's calculations.
Column (1) Preliminary.
Column (2) DNP.

coal and oil production, mostly during the 1980s (the reason for which several local analysts claim a "primarization" of the economy). The highest production level ever achieved by the mining industry was 21 percent of GDP. Per capita income did not improve, however, and even declined in some years. Furthermore, although poverty indicators declined during the early 1980s, they rose again in the second half of the decade and in the early 1990s (Table 4.4).

Economic Policy in the 1970-90 Period

The economic policy backdrop for events during this period can also be divided into three easily identifiable phases. While these did not exactly coincide with the previously mentioned periods, their impact on them was clearly observed. The phases can be defined as ones of liberalization (1974-82), protectionism (1983-88), and openness (1989-90).

The government of President Alfonso López (1974-78) enacted two reforms whose goals were to liberalize the financial system and lighten tax burdens on companies. The first reform resulted in rapidly rising interest rates, which in 1974 grew by more than one-third and, subsequently, exceeded 30 percent. This

Table 4.5. Colombia: Sectoral Structure of GDP by Periods and Phases, 1970-90
(Percentages)

Variable	Period I		Period II		Period III	
	Rise (70-72)	Decline (73-75)	Rise (76-78)	Decline (79-82)	Rise (83-86)	Decline (87-90)
Agriculture	24.2	24.1	23.9	19.4	17.5	16.6
Construction	4.0	3.9	3.9	4.9	6.3	5.6
Industry	20.8	23.1	23.7	21.9	22.0	20.7
Trade	12.5	13.3	13.1	13.5	13.8	11.2
Mining	2.2	1.9	1.6	2.3	3.9	7.6
Transportation and communication	8.7	7.9	8.3	8.5	8.1	8.6
Private services	5.3	4.9	5.0	5.5	5.3	7.9
Public services	8.7	8.0	7.8	9.6	10.7	10.2
Financial services	14.0	13.4	13.2	14.2	12.4	11.0
Credit-related bank services	-2.6	-2.6	-2.5	-2.8	-2.6	-3.0
Tax claims on GDP	2.1	2.0	2.1	2.7	2.7	3.3

Sources: Figures based on data from DANE and National Accounts.

caused investments to stagnate at less than 17 percent of GDP (Table 4.1). In order to reduce inflationary pressures associated with the economic boom and related foreign currency inflows, the government slowed down the gradual devaluation of the peso adopted in 1968. By 1982, the peso had been revalued upward by 30 percent. The enactment of an import liberalization policy did not immediately impact on the economy.

The government of Turbay Ayala (1978-82) continued the liberalization policy implemented by the previous administration. The coffee boom had ended and the current account balance showed a running deficit. This situation was compounded by the administration's import policy focusing on major investments. These investments were mainly financed through foreign debt and heightened inflationary pressures. High volumes of contraband imports led to a decrease in domestic industrial production, constrained investment returns, and formed the basis on which Colombia was diagnosed as having the "Dutch disease" (Berry and Thoumi, 1986).

Colombia's next president, Belisario Betancur (1982-86), enacted a stabilization program designed to control the foreign and domestic deficits inherited from his predecessor. The result was a significant reduction in public spending, particularly social spending. In 1985 President Betancur carried out a 52 percent nominal devaluation of the peso (30 percent real) and, at the same time, restored import controls, raised nominal tariffs, and significantly increased effective tariff rates to protect domestic producers. These recessionary measures and a major domestic credit squeeze were accompanied in 1986 by a short-lived coffee boom which increased that year's GDP by about 6 percent.

This peculiarity of Colombia's economy—periodic trade booms that foster temporary increases in GDP—has greatly influenced the country's economic policy stance which, until recently, had considered structural adjustment programs unnecessary. Instead, the stabilization measures fought inflation by controlling credit (through monetary restriction) and by constraining public spending.

The administration of President Virgilio Barco (1986-90) continued these stabilization policies based on restricted public spending and, in 1987, had all but eliminated the fiscal deficit. Past economic liberalization policies were again reinstituted, price controls were lifted, and tariffs and administrative import barriers were reduced.

At the end of his term, President Barco embarked on a policy for modernizing the country's industry by opening the country to inflows of foreign goods and capital (Presidency of the Republic, DNP, 1990). This policy held that Colombia's sluggish industrial growth was due to its delay in adopting modern technologies, the result of both excessive industrial protectionism and a narrow domestic market with limited potential for expansion. Greater competition would force business to modernize, thus spurring a rise in the economy's overall production. The policies of César Gaviria's government aimed to strengthen market liberalization, and accelerate and support the process with legislative measures in areas such as labor, finance, taxes, and exchange rates. These measures are embodied within a complete structural adjustment program.

In 1993 practically all imports were liberalized. A decree issued in 1992 mandated a gradual lowering of average tariff rates by 11 percent between 1991 and 1994. Labor regulations, as amended in 1990 by Law 50, became more flexible, enabling mobility of productive resources and thus making it easier for workers to move from one job to another. The hope is that these measures will encourage companies to modernize their production processes.

In the area of finance, the reform package in Law 45 of 1990 caters to industry's new needs and, at the same time, seeks to induce the adoption of modern technologies and processes. This goal may be achieved either by infusions of foreign capital (the reason why barriers to foreign investment were significantly reduced) or through initiatives by domestic producers forced to improve production efficiency because of increased competition.

A complete currency float was instituted in foreign exchange. Congress granted the government broad permanent powers to deal in these matters. The trading of government foreign exchange holdings was freed, as was the holding and sale of gold. The government was also empowered to choose and regulate its intermediaries in the exchange market. In foreign investment, the law granted an amnesty for flight capital invested abroad prior to September 1990.

Finally, the state's withdrawal from direct involvement in economic activities became more explicit through the liquidation or privatization of several large public companies, particularly in the area of communications, ports, and financial services. At the same time, public administration agencies were restructured and the number of government employees reduced. Between 1991 and 1992 an estimated 40,000 government employees were retired. In late 1992 the government introduced a set of measures that liquidated or restructured 87 public entities, eliminating about 25,000 jobs. The goal for 1994 is to eliminate 130,000 jobs, or 13 percent of total public employment (Sarmiento, 1992).

The Colombian economy is just beginning to feel the effects of the late 1992 changes. The impact of the employment measures was barely felt in early 1993. The open rate of unemployment at the end of 1992 reached 9.9 percent, a rate in line with historic averages despite the growth in the economically active population. However, it should be pointed out that the economy's ability to generate employment has weakened in the past few years, affecting job quality and increasing the importance of training programs and their management.

Evolution and Characterization of Human Resources

The decline in Colombia's rate of population growth during the last 20 years, from 3.1 to 2.1 percent, has not decreased the size of the work force due to an increase in both male and female participation rates. This trend began to turn around toward the end of the 1980s and is expected to become stronger in future decades as a result of the so-called "demographic transition" (Ocampo and Ramírez, 1987).

Characteristics of the Labor Market

Colombia's labor market has evolved into two distinct sectors: the salaried and the informal sectors. The salaried sector is regulated by labor laws defining minimum wages, social security policies, and work conditions. The two distinctive traits of the informal sector are exemption from labor regulations and self-employment. In reality, there is no clear separation between the two sectors because workers frequently cross from one sector to the other (López, 1990a). Labor market trends between 1970 and 1990 were characterized by fluctuations in economic activity and by changes in real salaries. Between 1982 and 1984 employment rates were stable and real salaries grew noticeably (Tables 4.6 and 4.7). Although employment rates during 1984-88 increased *pari passu* with rates of economic growth, real salaries were severely affected.

The educational level of employees also improved along with the growth in the employment rate. During 1982-92, the number of workers with a specific

Table 4.6. Colombia: Evolution of Labor Market Variables, 1982-92
(Percentages and years)

	1982	1983	1984	1985	1986	1987	1988	1989	1990	1991	1992
WAP growth	—	—	2.6	—	—	2.6	—	—	2.5	—	2.5
EAP growth	—	—	2.7	—	—	5.8	—	—	4.6	—	3.0
Percentage of employed	90.5	88.5	86.8	86.1	87.0	88.8	89.8	91.0	89.7	89.8	90.1
Men	57.4	52.5	53.8	53.6	53.7	54.1	54.6	55.1	54.2	52.7	53.5
Women	33.1	36.0	33.0	32.5	33.3	34.7	35.2	35.9	35.5	37.1	36.6
Average age of employed	34.0	—	34.0	—	—	34.0	—	—	34.0	—	34.0
Men	35.0	—	35.0	—	—	35.0	—	—	35.0	—	35.0
Women	32.0	—	32.0	—	—	32.0	—	—	33.0	—	33.0
Percentage of unemployed	9.5	11.5	13.2	13.9	13.0	11.2	10.2	9.0	10.3	10.2	9.9
Men	5.0	5.7	6.6	6.5	6.1	5.1	4.3	4.1	4.9	4.5	4.2
Women	4.5	5.8	6.6	7.4	6.9	6.1	5.9	4.9	5.4	5.7	5.7
Average age of unemployed	25.0	—	26.0	—	—	27.0	—	—	28.0	—	27.0
Men	26.0	—	27.0	—	—	28.0	—	—	28.0	—	28.0
Women	24.0	—	25.0	—	—	26.0	—	—	27.0	—	27.0
Percentage of idle individuals											
Men	—	—	—	—	—	28.1	28.2	28.3	29.3	28.9	27.2
Women	—	—	—	—	—	71.9	71.8	71.7	70.7	71.1	72.8
Percentage of temporal employment	13.3	14.7	14.9	21.6	17.0	14.7	13.3	12.2	16.1	15.9	19.1
Percentage of under employed individuals	11.5	14.3	15.7	20.7	16.2	15.9	19.3	11.5	13.9	16.9	16.4
Men	7.5	9.2	10.3	13.6	10.3	10.3	12.1	7.3	8.4	7.7	10.0
Women	4.0	5.1	5.4	7.1	5.9	5.6	7.2	4.2	5.5	9.2	6.4
Average years of education	7.4	—	7.6	—	—	8.5	—	—	8.5	—	8.7
Men	7.4	—	7.6	—	—	8.4	—	—	8.4	—	8.7
Women	7.3	—	7.5	—	—	8.5	—	—	8.6	—	8.8

Source: Figures based on data from DANE, Household Survey.
WAP: Working-age population.
EAP: Economically active population.

level of secondary or university education increased from 42.8 to 46.6 percent and from 14 to 17.6 percent, respectively. This trend corresponds to an increase in the average years of education which, because of expansion in education, rose from 7.4 years to 8.7 years and boosted individual incomes.[7] Moreover, during 1970-90 unemployment levels fluctuated between 8.1 percent and 13.9 percent. Open unemployment reached its highest level in 1985 as a consequence of the crisis in the early 1980s. The crisis resulted in an economic slowdown and the implementation of restrictive measures for that year. It is notable that since 1983 women account for more than 50 percent of total unemployment.

The strong devaluation of the peso in 1985 stimulated a rapid growth in exports, particularly nontraditional exports. Together with the coffee "mini-boom" which stimulated domestic production, the devaluation made possible a recovery in urban employment in late 1986. At the same time, the composition of urban employment was changing because of the continued decline in government employment (Table 4.8). Services, construction, and the informal sector accounted for the highest employment levels, to the extent that 48 percent of jobs in 1990 were found in enterprises with fewer than 10 workers, and 73 percent were registered in trade and service activities (National Office of Statistics, 1992).

The data show that during the 1980s Colombia displayed a marked tendency towards informal employment (nonpaid family workers, domestics and independent workers, the self-employed), which accounted for 33.2 percent of employment in 1982 and 32.1 percent in 1992, and a decline in the growth rate of real labor incomes. The decline in the number of blue collar workers or government employees attests to the effects of the state modernization policy, one of whose components is downsizing.

Pricing in the informal sector was flexible since the sector was not subject to the regulations of the modern sector. While this helped to reduce open unemployment, it also produced considerable fluctuations in per capita incomes in the informal sector. A 5 percent increase in the unemployment rate, such as occurred between 1979 and 1986, represents a decline of about 10.7 percent in average incomes for the informal sector. This results when more people enter this sector when employment in the formal sector declines (Reyes, 1990).

Age

During 1982-92, the average ages of employed men and women were 35 and 32 years, respectively. In contrast, the average age of those unemployed was 27 (Table 4.6). This has been a general characteristic in Colombia during the past 20

---

[7] Studies carried out in recent years on the rate of return for education agree on an average of 10 percent for the last decade (Psacharopoulos, 1988; Londoño, 1990).

Table 4.7. Colombia: Annual Growth Rates of Employment and Average Labor Income by Periods and Categories, 1982-92
(Percentages)

Employment	1982-84	1987-89	1990-92	1982-92
Employers	29.2	18.7	51.6	30.5
Men	30.9	18.1	50.5	28.3
Women	20.7	21.2	67.5	41.6
Manual worker/Government worker	1.0	7.0	4.2	2.2
Men	2.1	3.7	1.9	0.8
Women	6.2	2.1	7.3	4.5
Manual worker/Private sector worker	0.4	4.5	11.5	6.1
Men	-0.4	4.0	10.7	4.9
Women	2.0	5.3	12.9	8.6
Self-employed	6.7	0.3	6.9	4.4
Men	5.8	0.0	3.4	2.7
Women	8.9	0.9	13.1	8.2
Non-paid family workers	30.9	-1.2	63.4	14.5
Men	29.3	-7.6	109.3	12.8
Women	32.0	2.3	46.5	15.6
Domestic worker	7.7	-1.1	5.3	2.0
Men	-6.7	-1.1	-8.5	-1.0
Women	8.3	-1.1	5.9	2.1
Average real income by occupation				
Employers	8.0	n.a.	n.a.	n.a.
Manual worker/Government worker	32.8	4.5	1.2	-0.8
Manual worker/Private sector worker	30.0	2.5	-1.4	-1.5
Self-employed	13.0	n.a.	n.a.	n.a.
Domestic worker	37.6	3.7	-0.4	-0.8

Source: Figures based on data from DANE, Household Survey.

years and reflects a problem in the qualifications of first-time job seekers and the inability of the production sector to absorb new workers. Studies show that job turnovers occur every 14.4 months on average because companies prefer to replace their older employees with younger ones who represent cheaper labor (López, 1990b). This practice will undoubtedly gradually disappear as the demographic transition takes hold.

Table 4.8. Colombia: Employment Structure by Occupations, Selected Years, 1982-92 (Percentages)

Category	1982	1984	1986	1988	1990	1992
Nonpaid family worker	1.6	2.4	1.7	1.5	1.3	2.4
Private worker or manual worker	52.4	49.1	51.9	52.0	52.6	52.3
Government worker or manual worker	11.7	11.1	10.6	10.5	10.7	8.9
Domestic worker	6.5	7.0	6.3	6.2	6.0	4.8
Self-employed	25.1	26.5	26.0	24.5	23.7	24.9
Employer	2.7	3.9	3.5	4.0	5.5	6.7

Source: Figures based on data from DANE, Household Survey.

Female Employment

The participation of women in the work force has increased considerably, from 33.1 percent of total employment in 1982 to 36.6 percent in 1992. This trend was accompanied by an increase in the education indices for women, to the extent that women now outnumber men in school enrollments at all educational levels. In other words, female participation in the work force increased by 70.8 percent between 1982 and 1992, while male participation increased by 50.8 percent. The integration of women in the labor market, particularly women over 25, explains the growth in employment. However, women continue to prefer working in the services (40 percent) and trade (25 percent) sectors, while between 55 and 60 percent of all active women work in the informal sector. The higher participation of women in the work force also reflects an increase in their family responsibilities, since 16 percent of employed heads of household in 1992 were women as compared to 13 percent in 1982.

The discrepancy in male and female wages has also decreased dramatically, although women still earn less than men (Bonilla and Rodríguez, 1992).

The Unstable Nature of Employment

Temporary employment has grown in Colombia (Table 4.6). Most temporary workers are independent and nonpaid family workers (21.8 percent and 17.3 percent, respectively, in 1982). These levels increased considerably in 1992 for practically all categories, but particularly for nonpaid family workers (30.9 percent), blue collar or private white collar employees (20.7 percent), and domestic workers (15.1 percent). Although exhibiting much lower levels in other occupations, temporary employment has been on the rise over the past two years, perhaps reflecting the effects of the 1990 labor reform which made fixed-term contracts more flexible.

Fixed-term hiring has been used along with temporary employment to counter the impact of economic cycles. During the recession in 1985 temporary jobs accounted for 21 percent of total employment, exceeding the 1980s average by 7 percent. Mostly affected were blue and white collar workers, domestics, and nonpaid family workers.

The volume and quality of employment seems to decline in periods of recession. Thus, 1985 registered the highest percentage of employees dissatisfied with their work schedule (20.7 percent). Although this percentage subsequently declined thereafter, it has been increasing in recent years.

Groups Affected by Economic Fluctuations

It is well-known that the origins of a recession, as well as its manifestations and consequences, are different from those in an adjustment period. During an adjustment process, the hope (and goal) is to restructure output favoring sectors capable of producing goods efficiently. This entails a total rethinking of sectoral needs and human resource training, a situation which does not necessarily occur in a recession. Because the country did not experience a structural adjustment, and considering the main conclusion of the second part of this study, it is useful to examine the labor market developments during the past economic cycles. This would allow us to evaluate the economy's reaction during economic crises and, in particular, to examine the response of training and labor assistance programs during these situations.

As a result of the economic recession of the early 1980s, the rate of open unemployment exceeded the highest levels in the country's history. The post-1985 recovery brought about a steady decline in the rate of unemployment to an average of 10 percent by the end of the decade. In general, unemployment affected mostly women and young people. The increased participation of women in the labor market caused the women's share of total unemployment to increase from 47.6 percent in 1982 to 57.8 percent in 1992. As a consequence, the men's share of total unemployment decreased by 10 percent, from 52.4 to 42.2 percent. This resulted in higher female unemployment levels during the 1982-92 period (135 percent), as compared to the increase in male unemployment (51 percent). Between 1991 and 1992, the trend in the growth of female unemployment is similar to that for the period in question (3.8 percent).

An analysis of unemployment figures by age and sex groups (Table 4.9) confirms the presence of two situations. One situation, which is structural in nature, shows young men up to 25 years of age and young women up to 31 years of age with the highest rates of unemployment. The other situation, which relates to observed changes in the unemployment rate, shows evidence that women between the ages of 26 and 38 and men over the age of 39 experienced the greatest increase in unemployment during the critical stages (1985 and 1991). These results are, to a certain degree, consistent with a practice previously mentioned, whereby Colombian businesses replace older workers in periods of crisis and bring high numbers of young people (many of whom are women) into the labor market.[8]

An examination of unemployment by educational levels (Table 4.10) also shows evidence of a structural tendency. Higher rates of unemployment for the period were recorded for workers with intermediate levels of education, particularly women. However, focusing on the critical years, it is evident that the greatest increase in unemployment was for groups with the lowest level of education (no schooling) and those with the highest levels (completed secondary and even university). Thus, if one wishes to define a "profile" of those affected by the economic adjustment, it would consist of women between 26 and 38 years old, and men over 38 whose education placed them at either the highest or the lowest ends of the scale.

An additional employment problem is the time needed for finding a job. Lack of job market information and inefficiency of labor intermediation programs have resulted in young people requiring more time to find employment. Indeed, young people invest a significant amount of time looking for jobs that offer acceptable salaries. The average time individuals claimed to be unemployed increased from 36.8 weeks in 1982 to 45.4 weeks in 1987, and to 41.3 weeks in 1992. The average time that workers were out of work before finding gainful employment was eight months in 1992. The structural characteristics of Colombia's economy offer the only explanation for such lengthy job search periods.

Labor Market Trends

Employment growth in the country during the last few years can be explained by an increased supply of labor, mainly resulting from the massive integration of women into the labor market. This integration has primarily occurred in the trade and services sectors, in low productivity enterprises, and in sectors of independent or self-employed workers linked to the informal sector. Of the 511,790 new jobs created between September 1991 and June 1992, approximately 70 percent pertained to the commercial sector, restaurants and hotels, and other services, reflecting the diminished growth in primary manufacturing activities.

---

[8] It should be noted that this trend may decline in the future as a result of the already mentioned "demographic transition" or because of higher work-related expertise being acquired by employees as a result of increased competition in production quality.

Table 4.9. Colombia: Unemployment Rate by Age Groups and Sex, Selected Years, 1982-91
(Percentages)

Age Group	1982			1985			1988			1991		
	Total	Men	Women	Total	Men	Women	Total	Men	Women	Total	Men	Women
12-18	21.48	19.87	23.54	26.45	26.68	26.18	22.03	20.87	23.44	24.51	22.27	27.01
19-25	16.71	14.84	19.18	22.98	18.75	27.88	17.98	14.28	22.31	16.78	13.86	19.84
26-31	8.15	7.19	9.57	13.19	9.14	18.55	9.95	6.53	14.24	9.61	6.92	12.81
32-38	4.67	3.46	6.74	8.55	5.51	3.10	6.41	4.49	9.12	6.90	4.65	9.67
39 or more	3.14	2.96	3.57	6.49	5.89	7.84	3.85	3.57	4.42	4.40	4.05	5.08

Sources: DANE, National Accounts.

Table 4.10. Colombia: Unemployment Rate by Level of Education and by Sex, Selected Years, 1982-91
(Percentages)

Group	1982			1985			1988			1991		
	Total	Men	Women	Total	Men	Women	Total	Men	Women	Total	Men	Women
Uneducated	6.43	7.72	4.85	9.53	10.63	8.08	6.34	6.35	6.34	7.68	9.11	6.22
Elementary (incomplete)	8.40	7.49	9.81	11.81	10.51	13.78	8.88	8.14	9.93	9.36	8.44	10.59
Elementary (complete)	8.17	7.20	9.98	11.08	9.08	14.56	8.54	6.80	11.37	8.26	6.93	10.28
High school (incomplete)	13.10	10.23	18.09	18.61	13.49	26.60	13.63	9.48	20.18	12.89	9.21	18.47
High school (complete)	9.48	8.26	11.17	14.72	11.06	19.12	10.89	7.78	14.62	10.77	8.13	13.82
University (incomplete)	10.42	8.28	13.43	16.77	13.36	20.78	11.03	9.40	12.99	10.58	8.15	12.97
University (complete)	3.53	3.14	4.41	7.14	5.26	10.72	5.43	3.90	7.95	5.02	3.52	7.27

Source: DANE, Household Survey.

The economic outlook for the next several years seems to indicate a worsening of the employment situation, particularly in urban areas where higher rates of underemployment are expected. It also seems to indicate more temporary jobs and a higher level of informality in the economy. According to the employment trends of the past few months, women and the young are those most affected by unemployment. Moreover, the government decrees issued in December 1992 for the sale or restructuring of public enterprises pursuant to the state reform program will result in more than 25,000 government layoffs.

According to the Labor Ministry's survey of industrial establishments, employment levels and growth during recent years have been conditioned by fluctuations in demand and by changes in production structures. Those most affected were unskilled workers and general administrative and sales personnel (Zerda, 1992b). From a private sector perspective, issues that will impact employment levels in the coming years will be economic liberalization policies and high wage and interest rates. Employers also predict greater difficulty in recruiting highly qualified personnel, such as professionals or individuals with technical expertise, supervisors, and machine operators. However, most employers trust that they will be able to cope with these difficulties through increased training or improved production operations. This notion makes it important to review the status and outlook for human resource training, a topic that will be dealt with in the following sections.

Training and Employment Assistance Programs

The growth and modernization projections of a structural adjustment program are based on technological improvements and human resource training. The development plan must emphasize investment in human capital to be able to train, in the medium term, a flexible, competitive, and productive labor force. This, in turn, will improve the quality of life. In this respect, priority objectives of education policies should be to increase coverage at the early levels of education (particularly secondary education where the hope is to increase coverage from 46 to 70 percent in 1995), improve the quality of education, and strengthen the complementarity between the formal education system and the National Training Service (SENA). Achieving this means: (a) converting technical and diversified high school diplomas into academic diplomas with professional courses in major areas of training; (b) extending and adapting SENA's programs for the young; and (c) sponsoring technical development programs between universities and SENA.

Table 4.11. Colombia: Spending on Education and Training, Selected Years, 1972-90
(Rates of growth and percentages)

	1972	1975	1980	1985	1990
Literacy rate[1]	n.a.	n.a.	n.a.	96.1	95.8
Growth in education spending	9.9	4.2	9.5	5.5	0.7
Growth in social spending	11.9	2.1	11.3	3.4	6.8
Growth in spending on training	n.a.	n.a.	n.a.	1.8	2.0
Education spending/GDP (%)	2.2	2.1	2.4	3.0	2.3
Social spending/GDP (%)	4.0	3.9	4.8	4.9	5.2
Education spending/social spending (%)	51.6	54.6	51.6	56.2	43.5
Training spending/GDP (%)	n.a.	n.a.	0.3	0.2	0.3
Training spending/social spending	n.a.	n.a.	6.2	4.8	5.9

[1] As a percentage of the population over the age of 12.
Sources: Figures based on data from the General Accounting Office, financial reports, and DANE, National Accounts.

Spending on Education

Judging by the literacy rate for the population over 12 years of age (Table 4.11), it can be stated that state spending on education has been quite effective. However, major differences are noted at different levels of education. As in most Latin American countries, Colombia has in the last two decades achieved close to 100 percent (gross rate) coverage in primary education (Table 4.12). This figure does not hold for secondary education, however, where coverage, despite high levels of growth observed for 1970-90, does not exceed 46 percent of the population between the ages of 12 and 18. The situation is similar for higher education, where coverage by the end of the 1980s reached only 14 percent of the population between the ages of 19 and 24.

High repetition and dropout rates are the norm in both primary and secondary education. Both levels are plagued by significant problems in quality resulting from rote teaching methods, inadequate teacher training, lack of educational materials, unstructured curricula, and deteriorating buildings. In mid-1992, the Educational Framework Law, aimed at overcoming these difficulties, was submitted to Congress. Also under consideration is the possibility of establishing several lines of credit for financing the investments of the Open Education Plan formulated by President Gaviria's government.

Since the 1970s, social spending has accounted for a growing share of GDP. However, after the significant drop recorded in 1985 as a result of stabilization policies, social spending has not recovered its prior levels (Table 4.11). This situation may persist because of military spending priorities and the recent gov-

Table 4.12. Colombia: Gross Rates of Coverage in Formal Education, Selected Years, 1970-90

	1970	1972	1980	1985	1990
Elementary	6.0	83.0	102.0	103.0	90.0
Secondary	31.0	22.0	35.0	44.0	46.0
Higher	7.0	5.0	9.0	10.0	14.0

Source: Ministry of Education.

ernment policy measures focusing on social spending. The latter program aims at resolving poverty issues through initiatives such as the National Rehabilitation Program (PNR) and the Integrated Rural Development Program (DRI). These programs are designed to cope with needs in those areas where state control is lacking and there are serious problems of unrest.

Although the rate of GDP spending on education increased until 1985, when it declined significantly, the opposite is true for social spending on training which, despite economic fluctuations during the last 20 years, has accounted for a steady GDP share thanks to special financing support from SENA. The support has allowed this spending to optimize budgetary levels even during periods of economic crisis.

Career Training in Colombia

Human resource training in Colombia is provided by four types of institutions, which are detailed below.

Mid-level Technical Schools

This type of training in formal secondary education is slowly being phased out. Enrollments in the classical program have grown from 74 to 78 percent during the last two decades, while enrollments in other types of technical teaching have been decreasing. Particularly affected has been the industrial program which includes the Institutes of Diversified Middle Education (INEM). Enrollment in this program declined from 4.3 percent in 1970 to 3.4 percent in 1990.

Technical and Technological Institutes

This type of educational program is accredited by the Colombian Institute for the Development of Higher Education (ICFES). Training lasts two years at the technical level and three years at the technological level. The impact of this program has been particularly important in the small business sector.

Companies

Public and private companies provide training programs based on their own specific needs. In the public sector, several schools specialize in training, complementarity, and skill specializations. These include the Finance Ministry's Tax and Customs Schools, and the Communications Ministry's Technical Institute of Telecommunications (ITEC). In the private sector, a recent Labor Ministry survey showed that 26 percent of the country's companies provide formal, on-the-job training programs (Zerda, 1992b) and several sectors (industrial design, leather, textiles, plastics and rubber) are opening their own research and technical training centers.

National Training Service (SENA)

Created in 1957, this service has established teaching programs for young people and training systems for employed adults to meet the needs of the formal economy. However, in the mid-1970s, SENA also began to support informal economic activities and participate in the development of social policies at the national level. SENA has promoted the development of small businesses and self-starting programs. It has also supported DRI programs which aim to bring modern production methods to the farming community, and those of the PNR which aim to establish government presence in the country's depressed areas and areas susceptible to armed conflict. All of these activities, carried out with limited resources, distracted SENA's planning and development efforts from its principal mission and weakened its strategic function, which is to provide the training and technical education required by industry.

Career Training Through SENA

As coverage at the elementary and secondary levels of education expanded and the population's educational indices improved, SENA gradually changed admission requirements for its programs. It selected apprentices with high levels of education and instituted technical and technological curricula for high school graduates. Economic evaluations attest that the rates of social and private return on investment related to SENA's programs have been high and that they exceed the cost of social opportunity of capital by 14 to 36 percent (Jiménez, Kugler, and Horn, 1986).

Courses

SENA classifies its manpower training courses into five categories: (a) training, (b) development, (c) complementarity, (d) skill development, and (e) specialization.

In view of the extended training needed by young people entering the labor market, apprenticeship training has been losing ground, both in absolute as well as relative terms, to complementary training for workers already active in the labor market (Table 4.13). Compliance with the training law (SENA, 1987)—to train one apprentice for every 20 factory workers—would mean that 120,000 apprentices would have been in training in 1993, instead of the mere 17,000 now enrolled.

However, SENA's apprenticeship training courses annually absorb on average 25 percent of the total number of instructor hours. This indicates a proliferation of diverse courses and a lack of depth in numerous programs.[9]

Complementarity (training in skilled trades) absorbs about 50 percent of the total number of instructor hours and accounts for average enrollment growth rates of 1.4 percent annually. As this education is meant to complement training in specific trades, it involves the acquisition of specializations that apply directly to the company's operations.

Training Programs

SENA offers six types of career training programs: (a) training in centers; (b) training in companies; (c) the Program for Public Career Training of the Rural Population (PPPR); (d) the Program for Public Career Training of the Urban Population (PPPU); (e) correspondence training; and (f) technological dissemination (Table 4.14).

The disparity in technical development among Colombia's economic tiers and the lack of resource availability outside the public sector led to government-sponsored social programs, provided through SENA. The programs were designed to overcome unemployment and poverty and to provide social assistance to the urban informal sector, the farming sector, and to special target groups (women, young people). This goal is reflected in the dynamic nature of the rural and urban Programs for Public Career Training (PPP). These programs accounted on average for 43.1 percent of total SENA enrollment during 1970-90, while the training carried out in centers accounted for 39.8 percent. The latter program has been declining in importance despite the fact that it constitutes the main training vehicle for industrial production activities (Table 4.15).

This is even more obvious if one observes the level of enrollment in technological development centers, advanced career training centers, and in company-sponsored training programs. In reality, courses for technicians at the post-secondary level (construction, topography, industrial maintenance) and courses for high-level technicians absorb between 50 and 55 percent of total instructor hours.

---

[9] Programs include areas such as a national rehabilitation plan, small-scale fishing, the handicapped, prison inmates, armed services, basic health, and retail.

Table 4.13. Colombia: Structure of SENA's Professional Training by Type, Selected Years, 1970-90

(Percentage of enrolled students)

Type	1970	1975	1980	1982	1985	1990	1991
Apprentice	0.9	8.7	3.5	4.6	4.3	1.8	1.8
Qualification	18.6	22.6	24.8	18.6	16.51	6.4	19.5
Complementarity	47.3	6.0	68.9	74.1	77.5	80.7	77.4
Promotion	0.8	1.9	1.2	1.0	0.8	0.4	0.5
Specialization	0.2	0.7	1.6	1.6	0.8	0.7	0.7
Other	32.1	0.1	0.0	0.1	0.0	0.0	0.1
Total	100.0	100.0	100.0	100.0	100.0	100.0	100.0

Source: Figures based on data from SENA, Statistics Department.

Table 4.14. Colombia: Structure of SENA's Professional Training by Location, Selected Years, 1970-90

(Percentage of enrolled students)

Types	1970	1975	1980	1982	1985	1990	1991
Centers	42.5	64.2	53.5	56.4	24.0	21.2	23.9
In-company training	6.0	4.3	5.2	4.7	25.4	10.0	11.2
Rural and urban PPP[1]	51.5	31.5	41.3	38.9	38.9	56.8	53.3
Technical instruction (offices)	0.0	0.0	0.0	0.0	11.6	11.9	1.6
Correspondence training	0.0	0.0	0.0	0.0	0.0	0.0	10.0
Total	100.0	100.0	100.0	100.0	100.0	100.0	100.0

Source: Figures based on data from SENA, Statistics Department.
[1] Programs for Public Career Training.

Training by Economic Sectors

The growth in enrollment in industrial career training courses during the 1970s was reversed in 1982 and 1983, mainly due to the crisis of those years (Table 4.15). As a result of the crisis, even by the late 1980s enrollment levels had not returned to levels achieved during the previous decade. Thus, during 1970-90 the rate of growth of trained students in the trade and services sectors averaged 3.3 percent annually, with an annual rate of decline in instructor hours of 1.3 percent. In contrast, the industrial (including construction) and the agricultural sectors registered negative annual average growth rates of -4.1 and -0.5 percent, respectively.

Nevertheless, the industrial sector continued to account for a high propor-

Table 4.15. Colombia: Structure of SENA's Professional Training by Economic Sectors, Selected Years, 1970-90
(Percentage of enrolled students)

Sector	1970	1975	1980	1982	1985	1990	1991
Agriculture and livestock	46.6	23.6	27.7	31.8	25.1	23.3	23.3
Industrial	21.7	32.6	34.9	28.6	32.9	20.5	21.3
Trade and services	37.7	43.8	37.4	39.6	42.1	56.2	55.4
Total	100.0	100.0	100.0	100.0	100.0	100.0	100.0

Source: Figures based on data from SENA, Statistics Department.

tion of training courses and an even greater number of instructor hours, which reflects the technical complexities of career training for new workers and specialized training for active workers in manufacturing. On the other hand, the trade and services sectors accounted for a fair number of complementarity courses with training periods lasting under 880 hours.

The marked decline in career training and increased training in the trade and services sectors beginning in the 1980s lend support to the previously discussed notion that these sectors enjoy greater growth and employment opportunities. Therefore, it could be said that SENA's training activities simply followed the evolution of the economy. It did not hamper or influence the trends.

Different studies have pointed out that shortcomings in Colombia's career training system are due to weak training programs and the use of obsolete techniques and technologies. The most serious training weaknesses are found at the technician level and at the higher level of engineer and administrator, the latter indicative of poor university training. For example, as yet the country has no training programs in engineering production processes needed to meet the requirements of the industrial restructuring (Misas, 1992). SENA's extremely rigid and centralized administrative structure, marked by highly bureaucratic planning (guided by day-to-day performance criteria), hampers any attempt to make prompt and timely changes in training programs and curricula required by modern production methods and technologies.

Financing Mechanisms

SENA's budget is endowed by a 2 percent payroll tax, which since 1982 has been assessed on all companies regardless of their capital or number of employees. In the early 1980s the trade and services sectors contributed 50.6 percent of SENA's budget, the industrial sector 41.8 percent, and the farming and livestock sector 7.6 percent. In 1991, the contribution of the trade and services sectors increased significantly (60 percent), while that of the industrial sector declined considerably (30.6 percent), and the farming and livestock sector remained relatively stable (9.4 percent). The contribution structure shows a close relationship with the training structure by economic sectors.

SENA's income grew during 1970-90 at an average annual rate of 3.1 percent, while its expenditures grew at an average annual rate of 3.5 percent. SENA has been increasing its social assistance outlays (operational expenses for training centers and their programs, including housing and pension funds, and interinstitutional arrangements) at an average annual rate of 2.8 percent. Likewise, it has been reducing its operational costs (2 percent between 1987 and 1991). Nevertheless, about 50 percent of SENA's employees (8,317) belong to the administrative staff in a one-to-one relationship with its teaching personnel. This type of staffing structure is extremely inappropriate, especially since half of the instructors hold temporary contracts.

SENA's actual outlays, which peaked in 1984 (1,601 million pesos at 1980 constant prices), have been steadily declining and largely explain the institution's technological shortcomings. The predicament stems from a 1985 government requirement that obliged SENA to allocate part of its budget to maintain and endow several levels of secondary education and to support other spending prescribed by the Ministry of Education. These "transfers" accounted for 40 percent of SENA's outlays in 1990.

SENA relies on several agreements signed with other countries to finance training in specific industrial fields such as machine tooling and woodworking. While the agreements have allowed SENA to acquire new equipment, the type of equipment is more appropriate for large-scale production than for the kind of courses SENA provides. Therefore, the equipment in these training centers is greatly underutilized and the program is somewhat inflexible.

Trends in Career Training

Changes in SENA's training methods and results of its new courses addressing industrial restructuring problems do not yet appear in the statistical data. Institutional goals proposed at the end of 1992 for the 1993-94 period include a new focus on human resource training through decentralization of SENA's regional training centers. Notwithstanding the institution's goals for the next two years, however, the government decided to reorganize SENA to better adapt it to private sector needs and facilitate the process of industrial restructuring. Accordingly, SENA will be restructured into a number of mixed corporations located at different training centers throughout the country. These corporations will cater to, and be administered jointly by, industrial or service labor unions, nongovernmental organizations, and centers of higher learning.

A well-known major shortcoming of the system is, however, the weak relationship between the particular training provided by SENA and actual company needs. The Ministry of Labor recently surveyed 700 industrial sector companies in order to evaluate labor market activities at the beginning of the adjustment process. The survey showed that only 7 percent of companies with in-house training programs use SENA's services for training skilled new workers, and 15 percent use SENA for retraining active workers (Zerda, 1992b). When asked about the main problem encountered in training workers, 5 percent felt that SENA's training was inadequate. The problem lies in the fact that, despite attempts to modernize, SENA's training is still rooted in traditional manufacturing methods that involve an increasingly specific division of shop labor, defined as "one job-one person-one task." However, nowadays more flexible training is required that will endow workers with multifaceted abilities and make it easier for them to adapt to specific company training (Zerda, 1992a).

Changes in the international marketplace and domestic reforms related to open trade, modernization, and industrial restructuring require a multifaceted work force flexible enough to respond to technological change. Career training should be reformed to meet this need. SENA has allocated much of its resources to social programs and to government-mandated initiatives, neglecting its main objective of training and providing technical skills to labor. The institution should adopt a new approach to training by revising existing programs—methodologies, availability of equipment and laboratories, and teacher evaluation methods—and by reviewing their relevance to the needs of the manufacturing and services sectors. SENA should make such an initiative an immediate priority.

Intermediation Employment Services

Another form of assistance available to the country's work force is provided by intermediation employment services. These services are not widely used, partly because of informal recruiting practices such as personal recommendations from friends or relatives of company executives (for high- or mid-level positions) or from the workers themselves (for operation-level jobs) (Zerda, 1992a). Colombia has two types of organizations providing intermediation services.

Official Services

In July, 1970, the Ministry of Labor created the National Employment Service (SENALDE). SENALDE has an office for enrollment, selection, and placement of candidates located in Bogota. Coverage was expanded in 1976 by establishing 12 offices in the main regional capitals. In 1989, SENALDE's duties were transferred to SENA.

During its 20 years of operation, the service received applications from over 1 million candidates. Of these, 20 percent were ultimately placed (Table 4.16).

Table 4.16. Colombia: Placement Assistance by the National Employment Office, Selected Years, 1970-89
(Thousands of persons)

	1970[1]	1975[1]	1980	1985	1989[2]	Total
Supply	4.8	21.3	79.4	99.1	52.9	—
Demand	2.1	11.1	30.6	19.8	15.3	421.5
Referred	2.4	15.7	52.1	37.0	28.8	715.2
Placed	0.4	2.5	18.8	13.8	10.1	229.2

Sources: Ministry of Labor and Social Security.
[1] Data from the Cundimarca region.
[2] Data up to July.

The poor results can be attributed mainly to the fact that companies made little use of the service (36 percent demand) and to problems in processing applications and placements. The latter problems came about because of a lack of complementary services—such as certification, validation, and retraining—that could match job candidates to employer demands.

Private Services

Hiring in Colombia since the 1970s has mainly been carried out by lucrative placement exchanges, and also since the 1980s by temporary employment services. Many of the latter are simply extensions of major companies wishing to circumvent existing regulations related to probation periods, fixed-term hiring, and employee benefits. The Ministry of Labor has been collecting data on temporary services only since 1984 and coverage is incomplete (60 percent). One conclusion drawn from the survey is that this type of temporary hiring has mostly centered on "non-agricultural" workers.

Government Policies and Incentive Mechanisms

In the context of its general economic modernization strategy, Colombia's current government has introduced changes into the general education system in order to foster growth in human capital. Accordingly, the government decided to strengthen general basic training within the formal education system by introducing flexibility in training and versatility in new areas of knowledge and technologies. Based on a rather quick assessment, it decreed that the "early specialization" provided by institutes of diversified middle education (INEM) was inadequate and that technological and technical education should thus become the exclusive responsibility of SENA (Presidency of the Republic, DNP, 1991).

Furthermore, the labor reform sought to eliminate several microeconomic factors that the government identified as obstacles to economic growth and productivity. Law 50 of 1990 abolished compulsory rehiring injunctions and pension sanctions enacted as a result of high labor turnovers. Because of this provision, employers were dismissing workers before they completed 10 years of service in order to circumvent the labor law then in effect, which obliged them to reinstate workers and pay them compensation for damages if dismissals were made without justifiable cause after 10 years of service.

The labor reform also eliminated retroactive benefits for laid-off employees, which had become the employers' key argument for explaining their inability to generate employment. It was considered an obstacle to capitalization plans because unemployment reserves could not be tapped. Under the new regulations, companies are obliged to deposit an annual unemployment amount into a worker's account under a special fund. These unemployment funds invest the resources in the financial market and deliver market returns to their users.

Other provisions of Law 50 deal with remuneration rights not considered part of the salary, such as bonuses and incentive payments. The law provides the option of negotiating a lump sum salary for those who earn the equivalent of more than 10 minimum salaries, so as to alleviate liquidation costs of high level executives. Likewise, it extends job probation periods from two to six months and allows for flexible work schedules, including a 36-hour work week, so that three daily shifts can be set up without overtime. Other provisions make it possible to defer for 10 years new investments by company units in areas approved by the Ministry of Development.

A final aspect of the labor reform relates to collective rights issues. It expedites the creation of labor unions by eliminating bureaucratic controls and sets democratic standards for exercising the right to organize. It also extends maternity leave to 12 weeks.

It should be noted that for the moment the social security system is still under congressional debate and has not been incorporated into the reform. In addition, the reform did not include existing labor legislation for the public sector, a body which is marred by the lack of a merit-based performance system.

To facilitate the process of economic transition, the government implemented the activities described below.

Delivery of Technological and Training Services

SENA's restructuring is part of the overall structural adjustment program. This initiative aims to bring SENA's technological services and human resource training in line with industry needs. It was decided that SENA's regional technology centers would work directly with and for private companies (in sectors such as machine tooling, leather and shoe production, and graphic arts), on company sites and through corporate entities (92 in total) charged with carrying out specific technological tasks (research and development, technical assistance, consultation, tests and trials). The hope is that the career training provided by SENA under contract to the centers would comply with modern production and technology standards. Such training would be supplemented by programs that upgrade and reconvert human resources and tailor the training of technicians to specific business and regional interests of corporate entities (registered under private law).

These corporations would be funded by SENA contributions sourced from the 2 percent payroll tax, by contributions from the private sector, and by contributions derived from the sale of goods and services. The corporations' technical and teaching staff would be provided by SENA. SENA's own staff of 8,317 would be reduced to some 300 employees responsible for administering, managing, providing guidance, and coordinating networks of entities (including corporations) which carry out career training, provide technological services, and administer employment information systems. In practice, the scheme reorganizes SENA and transfers its training activities to the private sector through a national training system. However, Law 50 of 1990 preserves SENA's responsibilities for training related to social policy activities. Under the decree, SENA is still responsible for transferring resources to the central government. Debate on these provisions has resulted in a congressional resolution that would invalidate SENA's restructuring. This resolution has been pending in Congress since the first quarter of 1993.

Strategy for Socio-Labor Adjustment

A broad strategy has been outlined for helping labor face the transition during the structural adjustment period. This "socio-labor adjustment strategy" involves measures aimed at alleviating losses for workers displaced from their jobs and in need of training or retraining to meet new market conditions. These measures involve employment intermediation activities, professional development and training services, and assistance to companies that have an urgent need to update workers' skills or transfer them to new assignments within or outside the work place. These programs are under SENA's coordination and are described below.

National Labor Intermediation System

Colombia's state employment services are the National Employment Service (SENALDE) and SENA's regional service in the provinces of Antioquía and Chocó. SENALDE's duties were transferred to SENA in 1989. SENA, in turn, plans to extend its coverage countrywide through private sector corporations. The proposed scheme aims to integrate two diverse systems: a national intermediation system involving different tiers of employment information and made up

of private employment agencies and SENA, with a national employment information and job training system involving all organizations that document data on
employment, the labor market, and career training. This approach clearly identifies labor's skill and training needs in order to refocus SENA's training services.

The goal of the intermediation service is to provide coverage to 25 percent
of the country's unemployed, or five times the number covered by SENALDE. It
intends to achieve this goal through application and enrollment services, job information and counseling, training on finding jobs, legal advice, and private placements. In dealing with employers, the intermediation service will seek to identify
job opportunities, pre-select personnel, and provide legal advice.

Complementary Employment Services

The purpose of this assistance is to achieve a balance between available supply
and demand, as well as to provide productive work opportunities to those who
are unable or uninterested in working for others. The services seek to reduce the
gap between labor supply and job opportunities while at the same time providing
self-employment alternatives for workers.

The unemployed are offered education, training for self-employment, certification, and validation. Employers are offered job position evaluations and assessments of company training plans. The assistance also includes training services provided on SENA or company premises as well as career training. Active
workers are also offered trade certification and validation, training (updating,
complementarity, and retraining), legal information, training on finding jobs, and
training for self-employment.

Integrated Labor Adaptation Service (SALI)

SALI is a program whose objective is to develop joint employee-employer planning and to achieve employee-employer consensus on the development and use
of human resources when changes in industrial infrastructure take place. The
program is a vehicle for facilitating the relocation of displaced workers. It is
structured along the lines of similar programs in Canada and in other countries
and applies to personnel dismissals and company dissolutions. Assistance is provided to private and public companies and to regional or labor union workers.
The program relies on financial support from the World Bank for coverage in the
manufacturing, agro-industrial, mining, and associated services sectors. Its main
function is to relocate workers displaced as a result of economic liberalization.
The program proposes to carry out the following functions: analysis of displaced
workers' skills; professional and labor orientation; implementation of job search
and short-term training programs; and development of feasibility studies for the
creation of new companies.

Employee-employer agreements are achieved in joint committees with equal representation run by a nonpartisan president elected by the committee. If necessary, the committee can rely on help from consultants. By December 1992 committees had been formed in the machine tool and flower export sectors. Their membership includes 1,989 workers, 242 requalified workers, and 110 entrepreneurs who created new companies.

SALI relies for start-up capital on $5 million from the World Bank included in a credit of $200 million granted to the government in support of the industrial restructuring process. Financial support to SALI committees is granted on the condition that beneficiary companies belong to eligible sectors and are in need of human resource training activities. Financing will only cover the committees' operating expenses.

Labor Adaptation Service for the Public Sector (SAL-SP)

The Labor Adaptation Service was created in 1992 to help displaced government workers reenter the labor market. The general focus of SAL-SP is to provide employment services, define trade profiles, and requalify and adapt labor and micro-company projects, in a scheme similar to that described for SALI. However, in this case the committees are financed with public funds for the entities that decide to go ahead with the program.

Policies for Young People and Women

To protect the weakest groups in the labor market, the government has established guidelines aimed at the social integration of young people and women (Presidency of the Republic, 1993a, 1993b). Human development initiatives have been proposed for both groups. Among them are activities related to education and its links to economic activity. These include a 70 percent increase in coverage at the high school level by 1995 with subsidies for young people; social service alternatives for high school graduates; and promotion of university social service activities that allow students to work on state- or community-sponsored projects.

Likewise, the formation of business groups, individual companies, and production workshops will be encouraged. Young people (12 to 24 years of age) who are self-employed and work in low productivity activities will become eligible to receive credit, savings, training, and entrepreneurial evaluation services. In the event of shaky business conditions, production replacements and access to training will be facilitated through the creation of revolving credit funds that have savings components for financing education. "Seeding" companies will also be created as integrated service structures in areas appropriate for seeding activities (including technology transfer). The goal is to coordinate the activities of unions, the private sector, nongovernmental organizations, and local governments.

Quantitative and Qualitative Needs of the System

The activities defined so far, while important, cannot fulfill all the needs of economic adjustment. These activities have been structured and implemented in isolated form rather than as part of a comprehensive system that integrates the different levels of human resource education, training, and intermediation, thus providing a long-term perspective for development.

In this regard technical and technological education clearly lack conceptualization. This is officially attributed to a kind of "final" education rather than to a permanent and comprehensive education that is responsive to the changing environment. In Colombia, this type of education has been considered as "secondary" since secondary education has been geared to the pursuit of a university career, an opportunity that only 14 percent of age-appropriate adolescents can achieve. The reform of the education system reinforces this trend by institutionalizing the role of high school diplomas to the detriment of technical and technological training options at intermediate levels.

In this context and within the guidelines defined by the government programs, several comments can be made. These are discussed below.

Redefining Long-term "Integrated Training"

The type of training that is provided needs to be matched to ever changing technological developments. The ability to master specialized training depends on the quality of trainees' general education: their capacity for conceptualization and abstraction as well as their willingness to continue schooling and to requalify and upgrade skills (Gómez, 1991). Therefore, every component of a training system should foster an eagerness for lifelong learning. It should also develop traits for acquiring new on-the-job knowledge and skills, whereby in-house "specialized human capital" training can be expedited.

Levels of Training

The training provided by companies aims, as expected, at developing specific job skills. In this regard, SENA's programs run the risk of prioritizing a more specialized training at the expense of a more general one, thus reintroducing rigidities in labor training and in labor's ability to mobilize and adapt. Therefore, SENA should assume an important role in education, providing general training and ensuring that corporations include it in their training programs. The institution should be freed of all financial burdens not pertaining to its main mission.

Fiscal incentives could be established for specialized training. These might include tax discounts to companies that provide financing to SENA, carry out training or requalification programs for their workers, or qualify new workers and offer them permanent job opportunities.

Intermediation System

There is a notion that employment intermediation implies only the implementation of an employment supply and demand information system. At best, such a system would be a kind of "information bulletin" and would hardly be adequate during a period of economic adjustment. It is therefore necessary to develop all aspects of intermediation with SENA's help. SENA should coordinate and carry out, through the corporations, activities related to the certification, validation, and retraining of worker trainees based on their abilities and company demands. It is also necessary to keep the system's channels of communication and dissemination permanently working so as to impact on traditional business practices and encourage their modernization.

Support for Displaced Workers

Besides the mechanisms and channels of information on employment opportunities that the National Intermediation System provides, it would be very important to supplement worker incomes with credit lines for the creation of single or multipartner entrepreneurial business projects. For this purpose, technical cooperation resources could temporarily be made available for special employment and requalification programs to groups affected by past economic fluctuations, such as women between the ages of 26 and 38 and men over 39, taking candidates' skills into account.

The impacts of the adjustment process have been uneven in different regions, some regions being more severely affected than others. Therefore, it would be necessary to establish, with the financial support of the regions, local and temporary programs for minor projects in order to facilitate the transition process for significant segments of the population, while the new government-sponsored employment activities take hold.

Promotion of Youth Employment

As has been seen, one of the most highly and permanently vulnerable groups are individuals between the ages of 14 and 25, particularly women, who have intermediate levels of education. Therefore, to take advantage of their productivity potential, it is necessary to design programs that increase employment opportunities for the young and that correspond to the skills required by expanding sectors. The integration of this group into the economy could be facilitated by the implementation of a scholarship or subsidy program that would cover basic needs during the training period and which private companies could subsidize. Furthermore, company compliance with the training law would also enable faster absorption of this group, particularly women, into the economy. The government would need to carry out a broad persuasive (incentives) and punitive (sanctions) campaign in order to broaden compliance with the law.

Assistance Activities

As mentioned earlier, a kind of minimum financial support could be established for displaced workers over the haul of the readjustment process (a type of "unemployment insurance"). A special credit line might also be established within the National Development Plan for Microbusiness for small business groups comprising displaced workers who show promising entrepreneurial ability.

Follow-up and Evaluation Mechanisms

Finally, there is the need to establish monitoring systems in the labor market, particularly for displaced workers, in order to carry out timely evaluations of the effectiveness of the activities implemented. This would allow timely corrections and adjustments that would increase the efficiency of the human resources management system.

Conclusions

The analyses in the preceding sections allow several conclusions to be drawn that serve as the basis for evaluating the government's activities in reducing adjustment costs and, therefore, identify guidelines for formulating an integrated human resources management system.

In the first place, it is clear that no real structural adjustment took place in Colombia. This is partly due to characteristics of the country's economy. Periodic trade booms allowed for periods of growth during the last two decades and, despite economic fluctuations, kept the country from experiencing crises of the magnitude experienced by other countries in the region. However, because of stagnation in industrial development and sluggish productivity indicators, the government implemented in the early 1990s a series of reforms that constitute a structural adjustment program.

A study of the performance of human resources in this context reveals several positive evolutionary effects such as a high rate of economic integration, particularly of women, and a gradual increase in education levels. Nevertheless, negative aspects have been the slow decline in real wages in the past decade, the loss of quality in jobs, and the persistent high unemployment of young people and women with intermediate levels of education. A detailed analysis of this situation in the recession periods reveals that in terms of the resulting changes, the greatest impacts were felt not by the structurally disadvantaged groups, but by women between the ages of 26 and 38 and by men over 39.

Institutions charged with training and intermediation of labor did not respond adequately to these circumstances. These institutions kept a low profile during the period, with minimal effective impact. SENA was overcome by new requirements stemming from recent and rapid technical changes. This predicament resulted from its institutional rigidity and from the fact that SENA was diverted from its main mission by government-imposed budgetary obligations and by duties foreign to its mission. Under these circumstances, training activities simply followed the economic trends without hampering and influencing anticyclically the general and specific training of human resources.

Finally, an analysis of the series of initiatives sponsored by the current administration leads to the conclusion that these initiatives lack a general framework within which they could be integrated, making labor training more flexible, and adaptable to change. Such training is currently being required, as are programs that facilitate human resource mobility in the labor market.

The initiatives designed to stimulate more direct private participation in training programs, while important and helpful in refocusing training, are not sufficient. SENA's job training responsibilities need to be defined, as do those of companies related to specialized training. In this regard, programs should be designed to establish a more direct link among the different entities that provide technological education, in order that appropriate knowledge and actions may be taken when changes in training are necessary.

With respect to government initiatives in response to the adjustment process, this study found a need to focus on issues related to employment of displaced workers and assistance to vulnerable groups through concrete programs. These programs envision significant private sector participation under the tutelage of the public sector.

Bibliography

Banco de la República. 1993. *Informe de la junta directiva al Congreso de la República*. Bogota: Banco de la Nación.

Berry, A., and F. Thoumi. 1986. Crecimiento y políticas económicas en Colombia, 1970-84. *Cuadernos de Economía* 7 (9):119-162.

Bonilla, E., and P. Rodríguez. 1992. *Fuera del cerco, mujeres, estructura y cambio social en Colombia*. Bogota: Canadian Office of International Development.

Gómez, V. M. 1991. La educación académica y la educación profesional. Dilemas de equidad, selectividad y calidad. Paper presented at the Latin American Seminar on Education and Work, CENEP-CID, Buenos Aires.

Jiménez E., B. Kugler, and R. Horn. 1986. Evaluación económica de un sistema nacional de formación profesional: el SENA. World Bank, Washington, D.C. Mimeo.

Kalmanovitz, S. 1992. Análisis macroeconómico del narcotráfico en la economía colombiana. Final report presented at the Centro de Investigación y Educación Popular (CINEP). Bogota.

_____. 1990. La economía del narcotráfico en Colombia. *Economía Colombiana*. Contraloría General de la República. Bogota.

Londoño, J. L. 1990. Income Distribution During the Structural Transformation. Colombia 1938-88. Doctoral thesis, Department of Economics, Harvard University, Cambridge, Mass.

López, H. 1990a. Areas problemas en materia de empleo e ingresos. In *Colombia, la Deuda Social en los 80* (2). Bogota: OIT-PREALC.

_____. 1990b. *Trabajadores urbanos independientes, ciclo de vida laboral y seguridad social en Colombia*. Medellín: Instituto de Seguros Sociales, CIE, Universidad de Antioquía.

Misas, G. 1992. La Reestructuración del SENA, un reto para enfrentar el siglo XXI. Bogota. Mimeo.

National Office of Statistics (DANE). 1992. *Censo económico nacional y multisectorial - 1990*. Bogota: DANE.

Ocampo, J.A., and M. Ramírez. 1987. El problema laboral colombiano. Contraloría General de la República, Departamento Nacional de Planeación, Servicio Nacional de Aprendizaje (SENA), Bogota. Mimeo.

Presidency of the Republic, National Planning Department (DNP). 1993. *Programa macroeconómico 1993*. Bogota: DNP. Consejería para la Juventud, la Mujer y la Familia. 1993a. Documento de política para la juventud. Documento No. 4. Bogota.

_____. Consejería para la Juventud, la Mujer y la Familia. 1993b, *Política integral para las mujeres colombianas*. Bogota.

_____. 1991. *La revolución pacífica. Modernización y Apertura de la Economía* 1. Bogota: DNP.

_____. 1990. El programa de modernización de la economía colombiana. *Políticas para el Cambio Económico y Social*. Bogota: DNP.

Psacharopoulos, G. 1988. Educación, habilidad e ingresos en Colombia, 1988. *Planeación y desarrollo* 23 (2).

Reyes, A. 1990. Impacto del salario mínimo legal sobre los salarios medios en Colombia. In *Colombia, la Deuda Social en los 80* (2). Bogota: OIT-PREALC.

Sarmiento, L. 1992. Los programas de ajuste estructural y el empleo en Colombia. Bogota. Mimeo.

Sarmiento, L., and A. Zerda. 1993. Ajuste estructural, desarrollo económico y social - Dos años de revolución pacífica. *Economía Colombiana* 241:16-42.

Servicio Nacional de Aprendizaje (SENA), 1987. El contrato de aprendizaje, normas. SENA, Bogota. Mimeo.

Zerda, A. 1993. *Capacitación e intermediación de recursos humanos en el proceso de ajuste económico en Colombia*. Working Paper No. 139. Inter-American Development Bank, Washington, D.C.

_____. 1992a. Apertura, nuevas tecnologías y empleo. Friedrich Ebert Stiftung de Colombia (FESCOL), Bogota. Mimeo.

_____. 1992b. Funcionamiento del mercado de trabajo industrial: análisis de una encuesta a establecimientos. Document No. 30. Project COL/90/007. Ministry of Labor and Social Security/United Nations Development Program/International Labor Organization, Bogota.

CHAPTER FIVE

URUGUAY

Marisa Bucheli[1]
Adriana Cassoni
Rafael Diez de Medina
Máximo Rossi

During the 1970s, Uruguay tried to enact several structural economic reforms. Some of these took hold gradually while others simply failed to materialize. A financial liberalization process was initiated in the mid-1970s and, by the end of the decade, measures leading to a gradual decline in tariff levels were introduced. Projected tariff cuts, however, were not reached and in 1982 the country began to enact a series of partial stabilization initiatives.

Between 1985 and 1989 the country underwent a period of political and economic transition. Since assuming power in 1990, the current government has undertaken several steps to liberalize trade, reduce the public sector, and control inflation. The steps, which have been relatively successful, were designed with a view to the country's integration in the Common Market of the Southern Cone (MERCOSUR) and required major macroeconomic and sectoral adjustments.

Although it cannot be said that the country underwent a systematic adjustment process, policies to this effect have been implemented and have impacted on sectoral, employment, and wage structure. The current outlook for integration into MERCOSUR augurs an inevitable structural adjustment for a country characterized by a small economy, a generally adequate skilled labor force, and an economically active population that has a high percentage of people over the age of 50.

A policy for training or reallocating human resources was not enacted during any of the phases mentioned above. However, there were several isolated public and private sector initiatives. Chief among these was the emergence of a

[1] Patricia Triunfo assisted in the preparation of this chapter. The second section is based on Adrián Fernández's report, which was prepared especially for this study. The authors are grateful for the collaboration of Carlos Mendívil and Teresita Ribas of the Ministry of Labor and Social Security and Luis Pigni of Uruguay's Labor University. The authors also wish to thank Rosario Domingo, Héctor Pastori, Ruben Tansini, Inés Terra, Raúl Trajtenberg and Marcel Vaillant for their suggestions.

large number of private training centers and in-house training programs. In 1993, the National Employment Office was created. One of its main objectives was to retrain manpower and design specific programs within the framework of a comprehensive employment policy. However, for these policies to be effective, an assessment of the current status of human resources is needed and target groups within the population need to be identified. Also, training and retraining programs need to be evaluated with regard to their effectiveness in matching private sector requirements.

Macroeconomic Aspects

Trends from 1974-92

Following World War II, Uruguay's economy developed in an atypical fashion. While other world economies—including those in Latin America—grew at rapid rates, Uruguay's per capita output declined at an annual rate of 0.4 percent during 1955-73. Between 1973-84, the country underwent an institutional breakdown, with the installation of a military regime and the suppression of labor unions.

During this time, measures favoring economic liberalization and deregulation were introduced and were accompanied by an unprecedented decline in real wages (Figure 5.1). GDP grew rapidly until 1981, with income distribution showing signs of regression as evidenced by high unemployment rates (Figure 5.2).

The preannounced exchange rate policy implemented in 1978 resulted in a serious trade imbalance which led to a major devaluation by the end of 1982. A strong recession followed and lasted until 1984, as the country tried to restructure relative prices and its external sector. When democracy was restored in 1985, the government enacted a wage adjustment program and focused its attention on fiscal adjustments and the external sector. Output increased significantly due to favorable external shocks. Finally, in 1990-92 emphasis shifted to fiscal adjustment, price stabilization, and state reform.

The changes introduced in the 1970s have helped Uruguay integrate into the international economy (Figure 5.3) and have resulted in a reshaping of the country's production sectors, particularly its industrial sector.

Financial Liberalization and Export Promotion: 1974-78

In 1974, Uruguay's economy faced a particularly difficult external situation. Oil prices quadrupled at the end of 1973 and primary export prices declined sharply. This led to a major deficit in the country's balance of payments current account.

The country dealt with this situation by expanding its export base primarily

Figure 5.1. Uruguay: Real Wage and Real Exchange Rate Performance, 1970-91
(Index 1985=100)

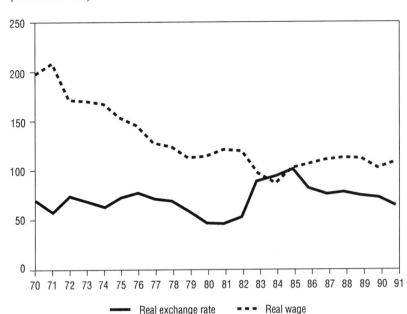

through indirect tax "rebates" and subsidized credit policies. The signing of trade agreements with Argentina and Brazil also helped to increase exports, as did the elimination of several nontariff measures affecting imports.

At the same time, the country liberalized foreign currency exchange flows, thus establishing in 1978 a free and unified exchange market. Foreign currency deposits (for residents and nonresidents alike) were allowed, and controls on credit and interest rates were eliminated. The liberalization of the exchange market and the numerous devaluations that followed resulted in a significant increase in real exchange rates that lasted until 1978.

The labor market was deregulated by outlawing labor unions. The economically active population grew and export earnings were enhanced by a drop in real wages. Also, unemployment rates reached double digits beginning in 1976.

These policies were effective in balancing trade. Exports grew, accounting for two-thirds of the increase in output, and became diversified.

Trade Liberalization and Stabilization: 1979-82

The key to the stabilization pricing policy during this period was the adoption of a preannounced exchange rate policy (tablita) which consisted of a series of nomi-

Figure 5.2. Uruguay: GDP and Unemployment Rate Performance, 1970-91
(Percentages)

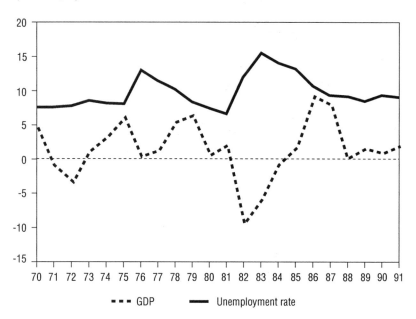

nal devaluations. The favorable external demand shock of 1979—caused mainly by increased competitiveness in Uruguay vis-à-vis Argentina—resulted in higher domestic prices rising annually by 83 percent against a nominal devaluation of 21 percent. This led to a significant drop in real exchange rates, and further deterioration in following years.

Beginning in 1980, effective trade liberalization measures were adopted through tariff reductions. Rates declined from 100 to 55 percent while tax bracket spreads were narrowed. These two initiatives, along with reduced export incentives, generated a high trade imbalance. Expanded global liquidity, instability in neighboring countries, and repatriation of flight capital generated a favorable capital account balance and a considerable increase in foreign exchange reserves which lasted until 1981.

In 1982, concerns that exchange rates would deteriorate became pervasive in the private sector. This contributed to considerable capital flight which, together with the trade imbalance, forced a devaluation in November of that year. Half of the output growth for this period resulted from higher consumer spending which contributed to a recovery in real wages. Part of this growth was, however, attributed to an unprecedented boom in construction. Growth in this sector came from Argentinean capital inflows and previous public investments.

Figure 5.3. Uruguay: External Indicators, 1970-91
(Ratios)

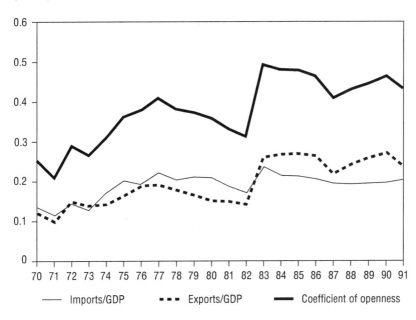

| | Imports/GDP | • • • Exports/GDP | Coefficient of openness |

The Restructuring of Relative Prices: 1983-84

With the demise of the pricing stabilization policy, emphasis again shifted to adjustment of the external sector. Despite the sharp increase in inflation, the real exchange rate began to recover in November 1982 with the elimination of the tablita.

In mid-1981, the economy suffered a serious recession. The GDP dropped 15 percent between 1981 and 1983 and industrial sector output dropped by 23 percent. A reduction in imports again helped to balance trade. In 1983, unemployment reached its highest level in 20 years, and real wages once again declined.

The private sector's high level of hard currency debt incurred prior to the 1982 devaluation created a serious problem for companies, and hindered their recovery. Furthermore, by "selling loans," private banks transferred part of their riskier outstanding credits to the state, causing an enormous quasi-fiscal deficit.

Economic Recovery: 1985-89

The onset of this period was characterized by a high foreign debt exposure—which rose to 133.2 percent of GDP—and by a large fiscal imbalance. When democracy was restored, labor unions resumed their efforts to raise real wages. These factors forced delays in long-range policies. However, external factors helped Uruguay's economy. These included a drop in international interest rates and oil prices, and positive external demand shocks resulting from the stabilization plans implemented in Argentina and Brazil, particularly as a result of the 1986 Cruzado Plan. This paved the way for a new phase of economic expansion, sustained by increases in both exports and domestic demand. The latter was supported by a significant growth in real wages which were indexed to inflation rates of previous years.

The private sector's problems of overindebtedness contributed to the bankruptcy of some major banks which owned mostly company stocks. These banks were temporarily taken over by the public sector.

In 1987, favorable economic trends ebbed and forced an accelerated devaluation. Domestic credit tightened and the indexing of private sector wages to past inflation rates slackened, with wage levels remaining flat in public sector nominal terms. The result was an economic slowdown. Public spending rose in this year—an election year—resulting in a fiscal deficit of 6 percent of GDP. Public debt, particularly that denominated in foreign exchange, rose. Thus inflation, which had been declining until 1987, also rose by 89 percent in late 1989.

The Fiscal Adjustment: 1990-92

One of the main goals of the government that took office in March 1990 was fiscal adjustment through deficit and public debt reduction. More effort was exerted in raising fiscal revenues, particularly social security contributions and consumer taxes, and also in reducing public spending. The latter included an explicit policy for reducing real wages in the public sector. Tariff barriers were reduced and additional tariff reductions were planned in preparation for accession to MERCOSUR.

Favorable external economic conditions, like those that prevailed in the past, made it possible for these objectives to be met without a recession.

The Labor Market

Uruguay's latest Population and Household Census (1985) recorded a population of approximately 3 million people. Slightly more than 50 percent of the population lives outside the state of Montevideo (interior) and only 11 percent lives in rural areas. A comparison of these figures with data from the 1975 census reveals an average annual population growth rate of slightly over 6 percent.

Emigration has affected the country's population growth rate. A factor since the 1960s, emigration intensified in the 1970s and reached record levels during 1973-76. It has been estimated that 180,000 people—whose average age is 27 and half of whom are women—have left the country. Studies carried out in the countries where the emigrants settled (mainly Argentina and Brazil) show that a significant percentage of emigrants were qualified workers who became quite successful abroad. It was difficult for Uruguay to replace the loss of this human capital. Though no data exist, some studies have pointed out a recent exodus of workers with tertiary education, which is a comparatively new phenomenon (Fontana *et al.*, 1988).

Despite the emigration of working-age people, the country's rate of activity has increased significantly—from 48 percent in the early 1970s to approximately 60 percent today. This has been due to the growing number of young people under 25 years of age and the massive incorporation of women into the labor force. Besides other contributing social factors, emigration and the increased participation of women and young people in the work force are linked to the evolution of real wages. From the 1970s until 1984, the downward trend in wages was noteworthy and nearly constant. The related drop in family income may explain why family members, who traditionally had not been participants in the labor market, entered it. A subsequent economic recovery did not reverse this trend.

The average unemployment rate for the 1970s (8 percent) was lower than that for the 1980s (11 percent). The unemployment rate peaked during the adjustment years of economic liberalization and export promotion (1976-78). During those years, the entrance of women into the labor force resulted in high rates of structural unemployment. Unemployment rates for workers over 45 more than doubled (Table 5.1). People with university and high school education were less affected than those who had technical training.

The crisis of 1982-84, which brought about an unprecedented rise in the unemployment rate, had a strong impact on men and less educated workers, including graduates of the Labor University of Uruguay (Universidad del Trabajo del Uruguay). Unemployment levels for young people and women are generally higher than average during a recovery.

The decline in unemployment during the recovery of the mid-1980s can be linked to the technological changes introduced in the 1970s. These changes were characterized by heightened use of capital (Rossi and Tansini, 1989) and were induced by industrial promotion laws which promoted such use. Since labor demand has a high price elasticity (Tansini and Zejan, 1990), the reduction in wages during the 1970s attenuated the consequences of the decline in unemployment.

As mentioned, average productivity and real wages in the manufacturing sector have evolved in a similar fashion during the last two decades and their relative spread has narrowed since 1985 (see Annex). This implies that the positive wage gap (higher wage than productivity) that existed in 1975 has been steadily narrowing under the impact of external shocks and adjustment policies. This is viewed as a sign of flexibility in industrial wage fixing, since there is

Table 5.1. Uruguay: Unemployment Rates by Educational Level, Sex and Age. Selected Years
(Percentages)

	1970-73	1976-78	1979	1983-84	1988-90
Overall rate	7.6	11.5	8.4	14.8	8.9
Educational level					
5 years or less	7.8	11.6	7.8	13.4	6.2
Elementary school completed	7.1	11.1	8.0	14.6	7.3
7 to 10 years	8.1	12.6	10.6	16.5	11.0
11 or 12 years	8.6	13.9	9.1	16.2	12.1
UTU	11.9	13.6	7.4	16.0	9.4
University	7.6	9.7	11.2	11.6	8.9
Sex					
Male	7.1	8.3	5.9	11.2	6.9
Female	8.6	16.8	14.2	19.1	11.8
Age					
14-19	25.6	34.4	25.0	44.1	34.6
20-24	15.4	17.0	12.6	23.7	19.1
25-34	6.4	10.1	6.6	12.0	8.1
35-44	4.2	7.6	5.4	8.9	4.9
45-54	3.8	6.1	4.6	9.0	3.4
55-64	2.4	7.3	4.7	10.4	3.2
65 and over	1.8	9.1	8.2	8.9	1.9

Source: Ongoing Household Survey (OHS) of the National Statistical Institute.

evidence that industrial wages adjust rather quickly to changes in relative prices and productivity.

The overall economy showed a relatively high degree of flexibility considering the response of nominal wages to rises in unemployment and inflation. The suggestion that a rigid structure of relative prices was responsible for the high unemployment of the 1980s is not supported by the indices used to measure labor flexibility. This argument holds even when allowing for any adverse impacts that the reemergence of labor unions in 1985 may have had in this regard. Moreover, 1980-90 estimates predicted by a Beveridge curve show that the vacancy/unemployment ratio worsened in the 1980s. In view of the preceding evidence, this trend cannot be fully explained by inadequate relative wage levels. Problems in labor mobility and declining efficiency in identifying job opportunities seem more likely to be causes. The first hypothesis is supported by the discrepancy that existed between company labor requirements and the level of skilled labor available, while the second is based on increased participation of young people for whom, as shall be seen later, the companies are unwilling to hire.

Assessment of Human Resources

Description of the Work Force

Of Uruguay's urban population, 76 percent are of working age (14 years and over) and 58 percent of these are active in the labor market. The distribution of the economically active population (EAP), by age, shows a significant group over the age of 50 (Table 5.2).

This group's large share of the labor market reflects the population's age distribution and labor losses due to the young average age of emigrated workers. The integration of young people (under 25) and of women groups in the labor market markedly increased these groups' specific rates of activity during the period under study. In 1991, the groups' rates of activity reached 65 and 44 percent, respectively (Table 5.3).

Along with the growth in activity for these groups, there has also been a steady increase in the level of human resource training. This is quite a remarkable outcome considering that the emigrants were highly qualified personnel. In 1991, only 1.3 percent of active urban workers had no training at all, and half of these had completed between six and nine years of education. It can be said, therefore, that the country disposes of an important pool of people with basic education who can endow the labor market with the flexibility it needs in restructuring the country's production sectors.

The country's level of education is uneven: the younger generation is better educated while a significant percentage of individuals over 50 (in relation to the average) have fewer than five years of formal education (Tables 5.4 and 5.5). Most skilled workers are attracted to the capital city, which has a strong tertiary sector. Furthermore, unemployment mostly affects first-time job seekers (Table 5.6). Only 10 percent of the unemployed in Montevideo and 19 percent of those from the urban interior have completed elementary school. This suggests that the majority of unemployed find it difficult to adapt to new work requirements, and do not as yet have the required expertise.

Noteworthy is the relative increase of private sector as opposed to government employees, both in Montevideo and the interior of the country. There were approximately 259,000 government employees in 1991, 79 percent of whom worked for central and regional government agencies. It is expected that the number of government employees will continue to decrease in response to current policies. On the one hand, budgetary considerations have led to a deterioration in real government wages, as compared to those in the private sector, with the in-

Table 5.2. Uruguay: Distribution of the EAP by Age, 1991
(Percentages)

Bracket	Montevideo	Rural cities
14-19	7.9	9.8
20-24	12.3	11.0
25-49	54.9	55.6
50 and more	24.9	23.6
Total	100.0	100.0

Source: Based on the Ongoing Household Survey (OHS) of the National Statistical Institute.

tent to encourage reduction in public sector employment through specific policies. On the other, monetary incentives have been introduced that encourage these
workers to retire voluntarily. These incentives are not automatic. Immediate supervisors must declare workers dispensable without, in so doing, setting a universal labor norm.

An analysis of the underutilization of the labor force is quite interesting. The
informal labor market can be defined as comprising individuals who are self-
employed and do not conduct business through offices, nonpaid family workers,
salaried employees, and employers in companies with fewer than five employees
with the exception, in all cases, of skilled personnel, technicians, administrators,
or managers. Using this definition, it can be concluded that in Montevideo, 18
percent of the EAP and one-fifth of all employees belong to the informal sector.
Most informal employees are individuals who are self-employed and conduct
business through their own offices (32 percent), private sector employees (29
percent), and self-employed individuals without offices (27 percent). Most of
these workers belong to the trade (34 percent) and industrial (22 percent) sectors.
Moreover, more than 60 percent of the informal workers that meet the above
definition are men.

By labor instability standards, defined in their strictest sense, 9 percent of
the EAP and 10 percent of employees in Montevideo have no job security.[2] Of
these workers, 43 percent belong to the services sector, 20 percent to industry,
and 17 percent to the trade sector. Almost 60 percent of these workers are women.

Of the above groups, three warrant special treatment in the assessment and
design of employment and human resource policies. The groups comprising
women and young people are currently those most affected by high levels of
unemployment. Similarly affected are individuals over the age of 50 who, be-

---

[2] Empirically, labor instability refers to private sector workers who have no health insurance, workers who are looking for another job because their current one offers no security, and nonpaid family
workers.

Table 5.3. Uruguay: Labor Activity Rates, 1991
(Percentages)

Bracket	Montevideo	Rural cities
All:	60.3	55.1
14-19	38.4	37.5
20-24	80.2	73.0
25-49	85.1	78.6
50 and more	37.7	32.8
Women:	48.2	39.4
14-19	27.6	24.0
20-24	73.3	57.5
25-49	74.0	61.5
50 and more	24.7	18.9
Men:	75.0	72.6
14-19	49.3	50.4
20-24	87.6	88.6
25-49	98.2	97.4
50 and more	55.6	50.1

Source: Based on the Ongoing Household Survey (OHS) of the National Statistical Institute.

cause of their age and relatively low educational level, are vulnerable to the impacts of a reconversion. Since the current policy for reducing public spending leads to an explicit reduction in public sector employment, government officials can also be included among the groups most affected by the adjustment.

Institutional Aspects

To better understand the recommendations pertaining to labor training— particularly those pertaining to target groups affected by the adjustment—it is helpful to describe the current functioning of the labor market.

Wage Determination

The return of a democratic government in 1985 resulted in renewed labor union activity. Beginning that year, public sector wage adjustments were calculated on a quarterly basis. In the private sector, negotiations between industrial associations and labor unions were encouraged (Wage Councils met every four months). Mediation by the Executive Office set a pattern for wage adjustment. During the first year, wages were indexed to past inflation; in the following years, past inflation was averaged with that predicted by the government for the following quar-

Table 5.4. Uruguay: Economically Active Population by Years of Education and Age Groups, Montevideo, 1st Half of 1991

(Percentages)

Years of education	Age groups								
	14 to 19 years			20 to 24 years			25 to 29 years		
	Men	Women	Total	Men	Women	Total	Men	Women	Total
Employed	100.0	100.0	100.0	100.0	100.0	100.0	100.0	100.0	100.0
0 to 5	5.2	2.6	4.4	3.0	0.3	1.8	3.2	2.4	2.8
6 to 9	72.6	67.0	70.8	45.2	42.5	44.0	47.3	33.1	41.2
10 to 12	21.8	26.1	23.2	38.2	37.0	37.6	27.0	32.8	29.5
13 and more	0.4	4.3	1.6	13.6	20.2	16.5	22.5	31.6	26.4
Laid-off	100.0	100.0	100.0	100.0	100.0	100.0	100.0	100.0	100.0
0 to 5	7.1	0.0	4.2	8.1	1.6	4.8	4.0	8.0	6.7
6 to 9	64.3	85.0	72.9	50.0	51.6	50.8	56.0	50.0	52.0
10 to 12	28.6	15.0	22.9	30.6	20.3	25.4	20.0	26.0	24.0
13 and more	0.0	0.0	0.0	11.3	26.6	19.0	20.0	16.0	17.3
First Time Job Seekers	100.0	100.0	100.0	100.0	100.0	100.0	n.a.	n.a.	n.a.
0 to 5	1.9	0.0	0.9	0.0	0.0	0.0	n.a.	n.a.	n.a.
6 to 9	55.8	45.8	50.5	27.8	28.6	28.3	n.a.	n.a.	n.a.
10 to 12	40.4	54.2	47.7	22.2	21.4	21.7	n.a.	n.a.	n.a.
13 and more	1.9	0.0	0.9	50.0	50.0	50.0	n.a.	n.a.	n.a.
EAP	100.0	100.0	100.0	100.0	100.0	100.0	100.0	100.0	100.0
0 to 5	5.0	1.4	3.7	3.6	0.5	2.1	3.2	3.1	3.1
6 to 9	68.9	64.5	67.2	45.2	43.0	44.2	47.2	35.1	41.8
10 to 12	25.6	31.8	27.9	36.6	33.3	35.1	26.3	31.5	28.7
13 and more	0.6	2.3	1.2	14.6	23.2	18.6	23.3	30.3	26.5

	30 to 49			50 or more			Total		
	Men	Women	Total	Men	Women	Total	Men	Women	Total
Employed	100.0	100.0	100.0	100.0	100.0	100.0	100.0	100.0	100.0
0 to 5	8.4	6.0	7.4	24.3	26.0	24.9	11.4	9.6	10.7
6 to 9	43.8	37.6	41.0	44.8	45.3	45.0	46.6	40.7	44.1
10 to 12	29.9	30.3	30.1	18.2	15.1	17.0	26.7	27.5	27.0
13 and more	17.8	26.1	21.5	12.7	13.6	13.1	15.3	22.1	18.2
Laid-off	100.0	100.0	100.0	100.0	100.0	100.0	100.0	100.0	100.0
0 to 5	10.3	14.1	13.0	20.0	38.7	27.6	10.1	10.9	10.6
6 to 9	59.0	47.5	50.7	51.1	45.2	48.7	55.9	53.9	54.8
10 to 12	20.5	30.3	27.5	22.2	16.1	19.7	25.6	23.6	24.5
13 and more	10.3	8.1	8.7	6.7	0.0	3.9	8.4	11.6	10.2
First Time Job Seekers	n.a.	n.a.	n.a.	n.a.	n.a.	n.a.	100.0	100.0	100.0
0 to 5	n.a.	n.a.	n.a.	n.a.	n.a.	n.a.	1.3	0.0	0.5
6 to 9	n.a.	n.a.	n.a.	n.a.	n.a.	n.a.	45.5	42.1	43.5
10 to 12	n.a.	n.a.	n.a.	n.a.	n.a.	n.a.	32.5	39.3	36.4
13 and more	n.a.	n.a.	n.a.	n.a.	n.a.	n.a.	20.8	18.7	19.6
EAP	100.0	100.0	100.0	100.0	100.0	100.0	100.0	100.0	100.0
0 to 5	8.5	6.6	7.6	24.1	26.5	25.0	11.2	9.4	10.4
6 to 9	44.2	38.5	41.6	45.1	45.3	45.2	47.1	41.9	44.8
10 to 12	29.7	30.2	30.0	18.4	15.2	17.1	26.7	27.6	27.1
13 and more	17.6	24.7	20.9	12.5	13.0	12.7	15.0	21.1	17.7

Source: Based on the Ongoing Household Survey (OHS) of the National Statistical Institute.

Table 5.5. Uruguay: Economically Active Population by Years of Education and Age Groups, Rural Cities, 1st Half of 1991

Years of education	14 to 19 years			20 to 24 years			25 to 29 years		
	Men	Women	Total	Men	Women	Total	Men	Women	Total
Employed	100.0	100.0	100.0	100.0	100.0	100.0	100.0	100.0	100.0
0 to 5	6.6	4.4	5.9	7.7	3.3	6.0	6.0	3.7	5.2
6 to 9	73.8	57.7	68.8	59.2	46.7	54.3	60.5	42.0	53.6
10 to 12	19.2	37.2	24.8	30.8	39.6	34.2	28.9	39.9	33.0
13 and more	0.3	0.7	0.5	2.4	10.4	5.5	4.6	14.4	8.2
Laid-off	100.0	100.0	100.0	100.0	100.0	100.0	100.0	100.0	100.0
0 to 5	5.3	6.9	5.7	9.1	0.0	5.1	10.0	5.6	7.1
6 to 9	75.0	75.9	75.2	65.9	67.6	66.7	70.0	63.9	66.1
10 to 12	19.7	17.2	19.0	22.7	23.5	23.1	10.0	30.6	23.2
13 and more	0.0	0.0	0.0	2.3	8.8	5.1	10.0	0.0	3.6
First Time Job Seekers	100.0	100.0	100.0	100.0	100.0	100.0	n.a.	n.a.	n.a.
0 to 5	3.4	1.8	2.6	0.0	0.0	0.0	n.a.	n.a.	n.a.
6 to 9	74.6	57.1	66.1	40.0	28.6	32.6	n.a.	n.a.	n.a.
10 to 12	20.3	41.1	30.4	33.3	50.0	44.2	n.a.	n.a.	n.a.
13 and more	1.7	0.0	0.9	26.7	21.4	23.3	n.a.	n.a.	n.a.
EAP	100.0	100.0	100.0	100.0	100.0	100.0	100.0	100.0	100.0
0 to 5	5.9	4.1	5.3	7.6	2.6	5.6	6.2	3.9	5.3
6 to 9	74.1	59.9	69.3	59.2	47.4	54.3	60.8	44.5	54.4
10 to 12	19.5	35.6	24.9	30.0	38.7	33.6	28.0	39.2	32.4
13 and more	0.5	0.5	0.5	3.2	11.3	6.5	5.0	12.4	7.9

	30 to 49			50 or more			Total		
	Men	Women	Total	Men	Women	Total	Men	Women	Total
Employed	100.0	100.0	100.0	100.0	100.0	100.0	100.0	100.0	100.0
0 to 5	18.4	12.0	15.8	45.8	42.9	44.9	22.5	16.4	20.2
6 to 9	54.1	46.9	51.2	42.4	39.9	41.6	53.7	45.5	50.7
10 to 12	22.5	25.2	23.5	8.9	10.4	9.4	20.1	25.8	22.2
13 and more	5.0	15.9	9.4	2.8	6.7	4.1	3.7	12.3	6.9
Laid-off	100.0	100.0	100.0	100.0	100.0	100.0	100.0	100.0	100.0
0 to 5	45.3	13.3	25.7	63.6	52.2	58.9	24.3	13.2	19.0
6 to 9	49.1	61.4	56.6	36.4	39.1	37.5	61.1	62.4	61.7
10 to 12	5.7	20.5	14.7	0.0	4.3	1.8	13.3	20.5	16.7
13 and more	0.0	4.8	2.9	0.0	4.3	1.8	1.3	3.9	2.6
First Time Job Seekers	n.a.	n.a.	n.a.	n.a.	n.a.	n.a.	100.0	100.0	100.0
0 to 5	n.a.	n.a.	n.a.	n.a.	n.a.	n.a.	2.6	5.7	4.4
6 to 9	n.a.	n.a.	n.a.	n.a.	n.a.	n.a.	65.8	47.2	54.9
10 to 12	n.a.	n.a.	n.a.	n.a.	n.a.	n.a.	23.7	40.6	33.5
13 & more	n.a.	n.a.	n.a.	n.a.	n.a.	n.a.	7.9	6.6	7.1
EAP	100.0	100.0	100.0	100.0	100.0	100.0	100.0	100.0	100.0
0 to 5	19.2	12.2	16.3	46.3	43.3	45.4	22.2	15.7	19.7
6 to 9	54.0	48.0	51.5	42.2	39.8	41.4	54.3	46.9	51.5
10 to 12	21.9	24.8	23.1	8.7	10.1	9.2	19.8	26.0	22.2
13 & more	4.8	15.0	9.1	2.7	6.8	4.0	3.7	11.4	6.6

Source: Based on the Ongoing Household Survey (OHS) of the National Statistical Institute.

Table 5.6. Uruguay: Unemployment Rate, 1991
(Percentages)

	Montevideo	Rural cities
Both sexes:	8.3	8.5
14-19	34.7	27.1
20-24	17.6	17.3
25-49	4.8	6.0
50 and more	2.8	2.6
Women:	10.2	11.5
14-19	43.7	33.5
20-24	22.1	24.2
25-49	6.7	8.9
50 and more	2.4	3.5
Men:	6.7	6.6
14-19	29.6	24.2
20-24	13.5	12.8
25-49	3.2	4.0
50 and more	3.1	2.1

Source: Based on the Ongoing Household Survey (OHS) of the National Statistical Institute.

ter, thereby reducing the index. Minimum wage requirements did not allow wage levels to be set below specified thresholds. These were established by the Executive Office until 1985 and, after that date, by the Wage Councils themselves.

In 1986, sectoral wage contracts in the private sector were encouraged to cover at least one year so as to avoid periodic labor disputes caused by quarterly adjustments. These agreements set different standards in different sectors. Since not all sectors entered into wage agreements, wages of some private sector workers remained closely linked to the guidelines established by the Executive Office. Of those sectors that did sign agreements, some adopted different wage readjustment periods, although in general the quarterly increase was maintained. In most agreements, wage increases were calculated on the basis of past and projected inflation rates and included clauses for periodic restructuring of real wages in the event inflation worsened.

Beginning in 1990, the new government's economic policy eliminated coordinated quarterly adjustments for those who had not signed agreements. Following a six-month period of open negotiations in which the conflict with labor unions worsened, it was agreed to grant the private sector an adjustment for an endogenous period based on past inflation. In the public sector, increases continue to be set by executive decrees within the framework of a stabilization policy which has reduced public spending and personnel levels.

The Tax Burden

The tax burden associated with labor costs is rather high. Social security taxes constitute 20.5 percent of the gross salary for employers and 16 percent for employees. Added to this are wage taxes of 1 percent for employers and, depending on wage levels, between 3.5 and 7.5 percent for employees. In 1993, the latter rates were reduced to 1 and 2 percent, respectively. Vacation and bonus payments increase labor costs by an additional 15 percent.

Hirings and Dismissals

While term contracts are being entered into in the private sector, clauses related to social security, severance pay, and workmen's compensation are similar to open-ended contracts. Not included are contracts that are less costly for companies and that encourage the employment of young people or training for those who are entering the labor market for the first time.

Unilateral reduction of work schedules by companies is not permitted except in well-founded cases as, for example, in the case of a restructuring in work operations. Overtime must be paid at twice regular wages during work days and at 2.5 times wages during holidays.

Dismissal regulations in the private sector do not require specific cause. However, unless "considerable bad performance" is proven, the employer is required to pay an indemnization which can amount to as much as six monthly salaries, including the payment of bonuses, vacation time, and other pay (such as tips, overtime, etc.).

Wage earners in the public sector are subject by law to special rules. Hiring must be carried out on the basis of admission tests, except in cases of highly qualified people and emergencies. However, over the two decades covered by the study, hiring was mostly through contracts without prior testing. Public officials (except those hired under term contracts) can only be dismissed by the Executive Office, if ineptitude, omission or commission of a crime is proven. Dismissal follows legal proceedings initiated by the Attorney General and is subject to approval by the Senate of the Republic. These requirements, with some exceptions for state-owned enterprise employees, have made it practically impossible to remove public officials from office. Fixed-term contracts can be revoked with an indemnization of two-thirds of the total salary for the term.

Special Cases

Women are protected during pregnancy: they are entitled to three months of pre- and post-partum leave and have the right to shorter work days during the nursing period. During the nine months of pregnancy and the month and a half following delivery, dismissal is subject to six months severance pay. With the exception of these particular situations, the same rules apply to men and women. Legal provisions address working conditions of underage workers as to schedules (work day less than eight hours), restricted participation in specific activities, and other issues.

Unemployment Insurance

While unemployment insurance has long been established in Uruguay, it was only in 1981 that it came into general use because of the significant increase in the rate of unemployment. Benefits consist of monthly cash subsidies for six months, which are discontinued if the worker reenters the job market before the stipulated term.[3] The subsidy amounts to 50 percent of the average nominal monthly wage received in the six months immediately prior to job cessation, and cannot be lower than half of the national minimum wage. Workers who are married or have handicapped dependents receive an additional 20 percent.

Private sector workers who are involuntarily unemployed for reasons not attributable to their work abilities are ineligible for this insurance. There are also subsidies which take into consideration partial work suspensions or reductions in work hours. To be eligible for this insurance, however, it is necessary to have worked at least 180 days or 150 shifts in the 12 months prior to requesting the benefit. Therefore, the insurance covers only workers with a minimal degree of job retention. Furthermore, these benefits do not apply to farm workers, domestic workers, and bank employees; retirees or early retirees; those who receive incomes from other activities; and those who are laid off or suspended for disciplinary reasons.

While the monthly benefit is the same, the duration of the subsidy depends on the causes underlying the unemployment condition. For layoffs, the duration of the benefit is dependent on the contractual provisions between the company and the worker. For dismissals, however, the benefit duration will depend on the ability, luck, or will of the worker to reincorporate into the labor force.

National Employment Office

In order to soften the impact on the labor market of the process of integration and productive restructuring, the government in 1993 created the National Employment Office under the jurisdiction of a National Board. This Board is composed of representatives of the Executive Office, workers, and businesses. Besides be-

---

[3] It has been suggested that the purpose of this subsidy is frequently distorted because companies use it to hold on to their personnel in periods of low production, thus avoiding wage costs during that interval or avoiding dismissal and rehiring costs.

ing responsible for national employment policies, the role of the National Employment Office includes the design of job placement plans for special groups of workers, the sectoral and regional reorganization of human resources, and the implementation of manpower retraining programs.

All workers covered by unemployment insurance will have access to these programs. They will receive during their training period an additional income equivalent to a percentage (to be determined) of the insurance benefit. If retrained individuals are rehired by their previous employers, these companies must reimburse the expenses incurred by the programs.

To fill vacancies, companies will have access to the list of available workers on the National Employment Office list. Companies will not be allowed to dismiss workers hired from the list (except for blatant poor performance) for a period of six months. As an incentive, these companies will be exempt from employer contributions during the first 90 days of the worker's employment. They will have to give 50 percent of the exonerated amount to the Labor Restructuring Fund which finances these programs. The fund will also be supported by an additional tax of 0.25 percent on wages to be paid by the company beginning in January 1993. This rate will increase to 0.50 percent beginning in 1994.

Status of Groups Targeted by the Labor Policy

As previously mentioned, young people and women constitute the main labor resource with a change in activity level. These groups qualify for assistance since they show high levels of open unemployment and underutilization, thereby warranting an evaluation of their status and an effort to reintegrate them into the labor force.

Moreover, individuals over the age of 50, who represent a significant proportion of the total active population and who have a relatively low level of education, constitute a potential problem insofar as they are employed in sectors impacted by the restructuring process.

Finally, to complete this analysis it is essential to identify those sectors that may be affected by future structural adjustment processes and the characteristics of the work force employed within these sectors. This makes it possible to improve the evaluation of training programs in companies that adopt new production processes, and of programs that would facilitate the mobility of workers when certain production processes are discontinued. Among the latter workers, it is worth mentioning public officials, since the shrinking of public employment will exert additional pressure on the private sector.

Youth

The Montevideo work force between the ages of 14 and 25 years increased considerably from the early 1970s until 1984 (40 percent), and has leveled off since that time (55 percent in 1991). While data are not available for the urban interior in the 1970s, the 1980s exhibit a slowdown in labor participation for young people between the ages of 20 and 24 years to a level lower than that of Montevideo, and an increase in the participation of young people under 19 years to a level comparable to that in the capital. This growth in the participation rates has been accompanied by high rates of unemployment, contributing more than 50 percent to overall unemployment.

Two groups of young people can be distinguished. The first group includes those who, because of their social environment, do not feel that they have the option to work or study. Therefore they enter the labor market in unfavorable conditions and with limited possibilities for a better education. The second group includes those whose level of education is higher than average and whose rate of unemployment can be associated with a high degree of selectivity. It should be noted that the practice of favoring seniority and on-the-job training over formal classroom instruction—in many cases explicitly, particularly in matters related to wages and promotions—has created job access problems for this second group.

The latter factor constitutes a problem for a country with high emigration patterns since it leads to feelings of frustration on the part of educated young people who, having made an investment in human capital for a prolonged time, are confronted with the fact that such studies do not help them gain employment. This does not mean, however, that education does not offer advantages, as will be seen later on in the chapter. It only indicates that in job searches, experience currently outweighs education. This is evidenced through the fact that rates for laid-off educated workers are similar to those of employed workers and are even lower for those who are seeking work for the first time.

As for those who are employed, most young people perform low-salaried tasks: men work in jobs related to the trade sector in Montevideo and to the farming and livestock sector in the country's urban interior, while women are concentrated in domestic service activities. Jobs that command higher wages are not bestowed on young people due to the previously mentioned seniority and hierarchy considerations. The probability of higher paid jobs increases with age, a trend noticeable when the young population is divided into two groups, those younger and older than 19 years of age.

Furthermore, job security declines among those between 14 and 24 years of age in all of the country's regions. This is particularly noticeable in adolescents between the ages of 14 and 19 who show a high rate of job instability (32.3 percent in Montevideo and 34.3 percent in the interior). The number of workers with unstable jobs and those facing underemployment is significant: 17 percent in Montevideo and 19.4 percent in the interior.[4]

Instability, underemployment, and the high level of informality of the jobs held by young people constitute a problem in that they fail to provide the desirable work experience compatible with stable jobs.

Women

The growth in female participation in Montevideo's labor market is one of the outstanding events of the 1970s. The rate of participation leveled off in the following decade. It reached 27.4 percent in 1968 and 44 percent in 1991. In an environment of declining real wages, this trend was interpreted as a contribution by women to raise household incomes. An additional cultural effect that explains the trend is the acceptance of new responsibilities by women. This is further evidenced by the marked increase in the level of education of women since the 1970s.

In the years following 1984, the growth in female participation extended to the country's urban interior, although the level of participation there remains lower than that in the capital. The trend suggests that Montevideo's level of participation will be hard to exceed and that in the interior the trend is to narrow the gap. With high rates of unemployment, women account for about 50 percent of the overall unemployment rate in Montevideo and 55 percent of that in the urban interior.

There is currently a higher participation of females with higher levels of education and higher household incomes (Diez de Medina and Rossi, 1991). This can be explained by the higher opportunity cost provided by work in lower-income households. Poorer households have greater numbers of members, which makes it necessary to care for minors; also, women in these households have lower levels of education and therefore their potential salary is less. Moreover, 35.3 percent of laid-off women in Montevideo and 24.4 percent of those in the country's interior have more than 10 years of education, indicating that education is not a factor impeding women's entry into the labor market. This target group, therefore, does not have particular problems adapting to labor restructuring programs.

Women are subject to a high level of segregation since they work mainly in lower-salaried occupations such as domestics, sales clerks, and textile workers. However, a high percentage of women employed in administrative jobs earn

---

[4] The concept of visible underemployment includes government or private sector workers who usually work fewer than 40 hours per week and who also are looking for work. It also includes self-employed or nonsalaried workers who are looking to change their present job and who are in search of higher incomes or full-time employment.

good salaries based on their relatively high levels of education. It is interesting to point out that in these jobs women are better educated than men and it is the tertiary education which allows them to overcome, to a large extent, segregation situations.

Another common type of employment for women involves part-time work (less than 30 hours per week): 32 percent of women in Montevideo and 35 percent of those in the interior are part-time employees, while the respective percentages for men are 13 percent and 8 percent. Women with higher levels of education have a greater propensity to engage in part-time employment. Children in the household have a negative influence on women's rate of participation. This is consistent with the fact that in Uruguay the law facilitates part-time activity for women who have recently had a child (half-time and pre- and post-delivery leave). School schedules (four hours daily) and Uruguay's inadequate day care and preschool services also make it difficult for women to hold full-time jobs.

People Over 50

One quarter of the employed population are over 50 years of age. Their work activity rate is 38 percent in Montevideo and 33 percent in the urban interior (1991). In recent years, however, a decline in the participation of men in Montevideo has been observed, suggesting two causes. First, pension increases since 1989 have motivated individuals of retirement age to leave productive activity. Second, this motivation may have been strengthened by a recovery in real household incomes.

Age and educational level present problems during a production restructuring process in which requirements for human resource training change. Of the individuals over 50 years of age who live in Montevideo and those who live in the urban interior, 25 percent and 45 percent, respectively, have not completed elementary education. Of the total number of individuals over 50, private sector wage earners are those in the most precarious position, since public officials can choose not to retire and self-employed workers, depending on the sector in which they are working, may be less affected. This subgroup represents 45 percent of the total employed in Montevideo and 38 percent in the urban interior.

Finally, the socio-occupational structure of individuals over 50 years of age also limits the number of persons affected. Self-employed workers are more apt to adapt to structural changes and those who receive higher incomes can opt for retirement. In Montevideo, 41 percent belong to one of these categories (university personnel, business owners, and employees) while in the interior the proportion is 23 percent.

Public Officials

The number of government employees has declined in recent years, from 272,000 in 1988 to 259,000 in 1991. This trend should continue as state reforms take hold. Therefore, it is important to assess the needs of this group as retraining and relocation in the private sector continues. The following analysis is limited to a comparison with workers in the private sector.

The difference in the level of education of the two sectors is quite significant, both in Montevideo and the rest of the country. The public sector generally has more qualified personnel, if qualification is measured by the years of formal education received. In Montevideo, 62 percent of public employees have more than 10 years of education compared with only 43 percent of private sector employees (1992); the same applies for the rest of the country (44 and 25 percent, respectively).

This difference is due to a concentration of women with relatively high levels of formal education in the public sector. In Montevideo, 50 percent of the men have more than 10 years of education and in the interior 40 percent, while the same figures for women are 77 and 73 percent, respectively. These figures suggest that gender-based discrimination is, in a sense, less pronounced in the public sector.

In addition to education, it is necessary to consider the average age of government employees in order to assess their potential for relocation through training programs. Within this group, 74 percent of the employees in Montevideo and 78.8 percent in the urban interior are under 49 years of age, which indicates that most government employees fall in an age bracket that should be amenable to structural conversion.

Training Programs

This section describes the country's human resource training system and assesses its coverage in recent years. In the analysis, general education and professional-technical training have been treated separately, since the latter can be adapted more quickly to the specific requirements of the production sector.

Institutional Description

Until 1973, compulsory education included six years of elementary education beginning at six years of age. Upon completion of the six years, students had two middle education options: professional-technical and general training. With the enactment of the General Education Law of 1973, compulsory education was extended to nine years, including the three years of both middle education options. In 1986, the curriculum of the three years of middle education was restructured by creating the Single Basic Cycle (CBU). This new program delays the selection of the professional-technical training option until the fourth year of middle education.

Once they complete the CBU, students can elect to enter a diversified high school curriculum or follow technical or professional training courses offered by the Labor University of Uruguay (UTU).[5] These three course options generally qualify the student to pursue higher-level studies.

Traditionally, higher education consisted of teacher and professional training, the latter being offered by a public institution. Beginning in 1984, several tertiary level degrees offered by other institutions, notably private sector schools, were recognized.

In addition to the above curricula, several institutes offer job-related training which sometimes requires prior formal education. These include private institutes and the semi-private Center for Professional Training (COCAP). COCAP is a semi-public, nonprofit institution funded by contributions from private sector exporters and tuition fees. The institution is managed by a board made up of representatives of the Executive Office and industrial and farm business associations. It was created in 1978 and began to offer courses in 1982. It was conceived in anticipation of the need to provide fast training for workers entering the export industry, in view of the projected growth of this sector.

Also worth mentioning is the public sector's Center for Training and Production (CECAP). This institute will not be discussed in detail here since its main objective is to attend to the needs of socially-troubled young people. It provides training to individuals between 14 and 24 years of age who are dropouts from the formal education system and who have behavioral and learning problems. Besides training, students receive scholarships and food assistance. CECAP has a placement unit for its graduates which assists them with entry into the labor market.

General Education

Between 1974 and 1991, the government allocated to social programs (education, social security, housing, urban and rural planning, and other community services) resources averaging annually the equivalent of 15 percent of GDP. Of this amount, 14 percent was allocated to education. Spending on education declined from 2.9 percent of GDP in 1974 to 1.4 percent in 1984. In 1985, however, spending on education started a recovery, reaching 1.9 percent of GDP in 1991 (Table 5.7).

---

[5] This does not preclude other options offered by the UTU, which are described later in the chapter.

Table 5.7   Uruguay: Education Expenditure Indicators, 1974-91
(Percentages)

Year	Education expenditure/GDP	Education expenditure/social expenditure	Education expenditure/ central government expenditure	Social expenditure/GDP
1974	2.9	17.7	24.6	16.5
1975	2.6	18.7	20.9	14.1
1976	2.6	16.8	22.3	15.6
1977	2.5	18.3	18.6	13.8
1978	2.1	15.8	14.7	13.5
1979	1.9	16.2	15.3	12.0
1980	2.0	14.1	16.9	13.9
1981	1.9	12.0	15.6	16.1
1982	2.3	11.7	16.1	19.9
1983	1.7	10.2	13.1	16.5
1984	1.4	10.2	10.9	13.7
1985	1.5	10.7	12.3	13.6
1986	1.7	11.7	14.0	14.3
1987	1.8	12.2	n.a.	14.9
1988	2.0	12.3	11.0	16.0
1989	1.9	12.0	10.6	15.9
1990	1.9	11.9	10.6	16.4
1991	1.9	20.3	10.1	9.5

Sources: National Accounting Office and Fundación de Estudios Sociales del Uruguay (FESUR).
Note: Social expenditures include education, social security, housing, urban and rural planning and other community services. Public expenditures per student include all educational leveles.

According to the last population and housing census (1985), only 4.3 percent of the population 15 years of age and older had not received formal education, evidencing an improvement in the system's coverage as compared to preceding decades (11.4 percent in 1963).

In 1985, all age groups showed a higher rate of illiteracy in rural areas (8 percent) than in urban areas (3.7 percent). While Montevideo's population undoubtedly enjoys better educational opportunities than those available in rural areas, the disparity has narrowed in the years between the two censuses.[6] In 1963, 2 out of every 10 inhabitants in the capital between the ages of 15 and 24 had not

[6] It is important to note that while compulsory elementary education has existed for more than a century in the country, in practice the six-year cycle has only recently (1967) been incorporated into rural areas.

completed elementary education, in comparison to 4 out of every 10 in urban centers of the interior and 7 out of every 10 rural youths. In 1985, the difference had narrowed to 1, 2, and 4, respectively.

Levels of Education

As the census data show, the elementary education program has slowly but steadily improved. Today, there is nearly total coverage throughout the country, with 95 percent of the students graduating. Growth in coverage has been mainly the result of free public education which, in the last two decades, accounted for more than 80 percent of student enrollment. Coverage of public education tracks the geographic distribution of the population, which is highly concentrated in urban zones, particularly in the capital.

All schools in rural areas are run by the public sector, while in urban areas public schools coexist with private ones. In Montevideo, private education accounts for 26.2 percent of student enrollment and 34.9 percent of schools, while in the urban interior these figures amount to 30.4 and 16.5 percent, respectively (1989).

For middle education (six years of secondary or professional-technical training), enrollment increased by 8.7 percent between 1970 and 1975, but declined in 1980 to 1970 levels. Thus, expansion of compulsory education to nine years has not had a positive impact. Beginning in 1980, enrollments at the middle education level began to grow rapidly. This increase is partly due to the increase in the number of elementary graduates, which rose from 42,000 in the 1970s to 52,000 in 1989. It may also be due to families starting to emphasize middle schooling for younger members of the household.

Beginning in the mid-1970s, the expansion of professional-technical training changed the make-up of secondary education, with enrollments in the former increasing approximately 31.2 percent between 1976 and 1984. In the following years, however, the situation reversed and the proportion of enrollees in secondary education increased in comparison to those in the UTU.

Finally, university enrollment increased significantly in the 1970s and 1980s. The teacher training program, on the other hand, was less successful, recording a reduction in the number of teaching graduates for both secondary and elementary schools. This was certainly due to the low salaries associated with these jobs.

Despite the creation of new institutions, more than 90 percent of university enrollments are concentrated in the public university. The public university is characterized by a student body increasingly interested in short curricula and in electives. University attendance by women and nonresidents of Montevideo has historically been high.

With respect to students from the urban interior, their participation has declined from 33 to 29.5 percent. These students tend to drop out of school more frequently than those from Montevideo. This may be related to the inability of the interior to generate better employment opportunities.

Economic Returns on Education

Wage differentials attributable to training are evidence that formal education is highly profitable and facilitates access to better paying jobs (Bucheli, 1992b). This suggests that there is an incentive for families to consider their children's education as an investment, which could explain the accelerated growth in middle school and tertiary enrollments experienced in the past 20 years.

However, recent studies (CEPAL, 1992) have qualified the expansion in education as a "leap forward," because graduates have more years of schooling at a time when fewer academic requirements exist. Since returns on education are equivalent for younger or older people, the market does not seem to place a premium on extended curricula. One explanation could be that education, regardless of its quality or demand in the market, serves more to provide employers with an indication of the applicant's degree of responsibility and discipline.

It is interesting to note that returns on education are higher for men than for women, except during the first years at the university. Higher levels of education allow women to secure better-paid jobs and, therefore, to partially break segregation barriers (Bucheli, 1992b).

As to the options provided by middle education, no apparent monthly wage differentials are observed. Graduates of UTU's professional-technical training program earn lower per hour wages, which are offset by a higher number of hours worked. This result is not surprising. Because of their specialized skills, UTU graduates find it easier to work part time on their own, even when employed by others, as compared to those with secondary education.

Professional-Technical Training

Four professional-technical types of institutions will be discussed: UTU, which had more than 36,000 students enrolled in technical courses in 1991 and which is part of the public education system; COCAP, with 1,900 students; private institutions, about 80 in number, which offer courses to more than 45,000 students in different work-related areas; and company-run training programs, which have found wide application in the last decade.

The Labor University of Uruguay (UTU)

UTU was created to provide general professional-technical training to qualify students for a trade rather than for work that is specific to a company.

In light of the establishment of the Single Basic Cycle (CBU) in 1986, UTU had to restructure curricula, since its courses were geared mainly to individuals who had completed elementary education and to early dropouts from secondary education. Thus, nine-year education programs were created. Courses for elementary school graduates were limited to students over the age of 15, so as to encourage completion of the CBU while providing a second chance to early dropouts of middle education.

Under the former system that provided technical training from the age of 12, students could achieve technical qualifications at age 14. The UTU was, therefore, a good alternative for training adolescents of low-income families who, as was mentioned earlier, are those who enter the work force at an early age (ANEP, 1992).[7] With the elimination of technical training, the option to master a trade at an early age disappeared, creating additional difficulties for young people belonging to low-income families.

UTU offers CBU courses for persons with little or no training, courses for rapid and specialized training, courses taught off campus by visiting instructors,[8] and courses on professional-technical education. The latter courses accounted for between 55 and 60 percent of enrollments in the last five years and covered different levels of training (Table 5.8). A positive aspect of the 1986 reform was that it facilitated the transfer of students from secondary education of the second cycle to professional-technical training, which allowed enrollment of students who attended higher average levels of middle education but who had not completed the course work.

The first level of technical education includes courses that are geared to early dropouts from the formal system (students who have completed elementary school and are older than 15 years of age) and to skilled training. Approximately 40 percent of the total enrollment in professional-technical courses is concentrated in what is called First Level Technical Training. This training includes some 66 different programs, of which only 14 qualify students for higher training levels within the program. About 75 percent of students are enrolled in courses dealing with electricity and electronics, cosmetology, cooking, woodworking and furniture, mechanics, and clothing (Table 5.9).

Until 1990, the Second Level Professional Training offered supplemental training geared to those who had graduated from the first level or from the CBU.

---

[7] Indeed, it can be shown that UTU students belonged to families with lower incomes than those of secondary education students.

[8] Courses taught off campus by visiting instructors take place in the country's interior, mainly in small towns. These courses have grown significantly, particularly since 1988, when enrollment stood at 1,864 students. By 1991 enrollment had reached 3,973 students. These courses usually deal with non-industrial topics. It is difficult to discern whether they fulfill a training function aimed at labor entry or a social integration function in small communities. For this reason, and because of the small number of students involved, this study does not dwell on these courses.

Table 5.8. Uruguay: Distribution of Enrollment (UTU) in Technical Training by Type of Training, 1987-91
(Percentages)

	1987	1988	1989	1990	1991
Professional training 1st level	42.8	43.4	43.3	39.8	38.1
Professional training 2nd level	20.8	20.8	22.1	1.9	1.8
Technical courses	18.9	19.2	25.1	26.0	27.0
Vocational educ.	—	—	—	25.9	28.2
Others	17.5	16.6	9.6	6.4	4.9
Total	100.0	100.0	100.0	100.0	100.0

Source: Ongoing Survey, Labor University of Uruguay, various issues.

This training accounted for a little more than 20 percent of enrollment in technical education. In 1990, almost all of these courses were replaced with professional courses and their enrollment climbed to 28.2 percent in 1991. Training areas of major importance are marketing and management, which accounted for between 60 percent and 70 percent of enrollment in the past five years (Tables 5.10 and 5.11).

Finally, a series of courses are offered which combine theoretical with technical training and which allow access to university studies. These courses are generally geared to students coming out of the CBU, although it is possible, depending on the completed coursework, to access them from the first level of UTU education. This curriculum includes technical courses whose share of enrollments increased from 19 to 27 percent between 1987 and 1991. The highest enrollments were in the area of business and construction. Enrollment in electricity and electronics courses has been declining, although this area continues to be the most important. These three areas account for 70 percent of enrollments in technical courses (Table 5.12).

In summary, while basic training is general in scope, higher level training is concentrated on management and marketing.

Professional Training Center (COCAP)

COCAP started its courses in 1982. The courses increased in number until 1991 and, starting in 1992, began to decline. Total enrollment during the Center's lifetime amounts to 11,578 students. This training does not compete with that of UTU since it involves short and specialized courses (courses have averaged 49 teaching hours).

COCAP courses are offered on site in Montevideo, in other centers in the

Table 5.9. Uruguay: Distribution of Enrollment in First Level Professional Training by Area of Specialization, 1987-91
(Percentages)

	1987	1988	1989	1990	1991
Clothing	19	21	15	9	13
Electricity and electronics	13	10	12	12	11
Beauty	14	14	18	17	15
Cooking	11	11	13	15	15
Wood and furniture	11	12	13	12	12
Mechanics	9	9	8	15	16
Automotive	7	7	7	—	—
Construction	4	5	3	5	4
Printing	2	1	2	2	2
Agriculture and livestock	2	2	1	1	1
Leather and footwear	1	4	1	2	2
Ceramics and glass	2	4	2	—	—
Maritime	—	—	1	—	—
Crafts	—	—	5	9	9
Others	5	—	—	—	—
Total	100	100	100	100	100

Source: Ongoing Survey, Labor University of Uruguay, various issues.

country's interior, and by visiting teams. Coverage is provided countrywide. The center also provides correspondence courses and a small amount of classroom instruction.

There are two types of courses: those open to all interested people over the age of 18, and those open only to specific workers. The content and implementation of these courses is coordinated with organizations or companies that require specific training. Most of the courses given from 1982 until the present have been on an open enrollment basis and have accounted for 77 percent of the enrollment. Closed courses are organized primarily with public sector organizations.

The training provided is mainly concentrated in the following areas: data processing, areas linked to production (in particular, firefighting, hydraulics, pneumatics, and textiles), home appliance repair, and aspects related to production processes (industrial safety and quality control, in particular) (Table 5.13).

Closed courses organized for private companies were mainly geared to production topics and to the company's areas of specialization. On the other hand, closed courses geared to the public sector focused on data processing and industrial security.

Table 5.10. Uruguay: Distribution of Enrollment in Second Level Professional Training by Area of Specialization, 1987-91

(Percentages)

	1987	1988	1989
Commerce	74	73	65
Advertising	6	6	6
Journalism	6	4	4
Auctioneering	—	—	5
Mechanics	—	—	4
Clothing	—	—	2
Data processing	—	—	2
Automotive	2	2	2
Food preparation	5	6	5
Beauty	1	2	1
Electricity and electronics	4	5	3
Wood and furniture	1	1	—
Others	2	1	1
Total	100	100	100

Source: Ongoing Survey, Labor University of Uruguay, various issues.

Private Training Institutions

In the last decade there has been a trend to create training institutions whose courses, such as those of COCAP, do not supplant those given by established organizations, but rather focus on specialized training. Like COCAP, this system offers open courses of general technical training and a smaller number of courses geared to company needs, mostly specialized training. In 1991, a little more than half of the training institutions had some professional links with companies. Few of the courses provided, however, were financed or sponsored by the companies (18 and 12 percent, respectively). It is interesting to note that 60 percent of the institutions performed intermediation tasks in the labor market.

Uruguay's 80 institutions offered more than 600 courses, some of which were correspondence courses (2 percent of the total). Of these, 75 percent of the institutions granted qualification certificates which required little more than the auditing of courses. The institutions are small. On average each employs 15 individuals, while 68 percent employ fewer than 10, and only five have more than 50 employees.

Almost 90 percent of the courses have a term of one year or less, with the longer courses concentrating in the areas of data processing and management. The latter courses have relatively strict education prerequisites (completed secondary education). The majority, however, are geared for individuals with little formal education.

Table 5.11. Uruguay: Distribution of Enrollment in Professional Education by Area of Specialization, 1987-91
(Percentages)

	1990	1991
Marketing and business	69	62
Communications	12	12
Machine tooling	11	11
Wood and furniture	3	5
Electricity and electronics	2	5
Clothing	1	2
Data processing	1	2
Beauty	1	1
Total	100	100

Source: Ongoing Survey, Labor University of Uruguay, various issues.

Only 18 percent of enrollees are over the age 30, and 29 percent are under 20. More than half of the students have taken data processing courses, mostly involving desktop computers (42 percent of total enrollment). Data processing courses have attracted individuals of all ages, a clear case of a retraining process. Of the courses offered in 1991, 80 percent were first provided in 1985. For the overall course curricula, this percentage is 49 percent. The other two priority training areas, rating much lower in importance, are personal services and management (Table 5.14).

Within the field of personal services, 99 percent of enrollment is in hair-dressing, cosmetology, depilation, etc., while other courses cover services associated with health, dentistry, and nursing. Several of these courses have been created recently but most have been provided since 1980. Also part of the traditional curriculum are courses in management, accounting, and languages. In management, 45 percent of the enrollment is in typing, showing that secretarial skills are very important for women. Male enrollment, on the other hand, is evenly distributed among administration and management, personnel administration, and imports and exports. Another sought-after training area is that of repair services, which focuses on household, visual and audio-visual appliances. These courses have been created recently and their students are mainly men under the age of 30.

Of the courses given in 1991, 95 percent required tuition payments and 28 percent of these involved scholarships. Free courses covered various topics. The average enrollment in these courses varied, with 48 percent of enrollment concentrated in household appliances, audio repair, and video equipment repair courses. Free courses in administration (17 percent of enrollment) also were provided, but practically no computer training.

While free courses allow students from low-income sectors to enroll, they

Table 5.12. Uruguay: Distribution of Enrollment in Technical Courses by Subject, 1987-91

(Percentages)

	1987	1988	1989	1990	1991
Electricity and electronics	34	36	30	31	28
Mechanics	28	20	13	9	9
Automotive	9	9	4	—	—
Farming	7	10	9	9	8
Construction	7	9	19	24	23
Business	—	—	8	13	19
Wood and furniture	7	10	8	6	4
Beauty	2	1	2	2	3
Safety and hygiene	—	—	—	11	—
Construction and naval repair	—	—	3	33	—
Clothing	6	5	4	2	2
Total	100	100	100	100	100

Source: Ongoing Survey, Labor University of Uruguay, various issues.

require certain prior classroom instruction (primary or CBU). Of these students, 60 percent were men, and more than half were under 20 years of age. Less than 10 percent were over the age of 30.

In-House Training

During the past decade, many companies have been compelled to reassign their staff to new tasks. In calculating the tax on company income, this implied a loss of 1.5 times the cost of retraining their workers.

A survey was taken on the training provided and the programs used in the manufacturing industry. Several general evaluations allow an analysis of the new training systems. Of the companies surveyed, 54 percent stated that the training level of their personnel had not improved in the last 10 years, and 62 percent declared that information on training programs had not improved either. However, the percentage of companies that provided some training to their personnel has grown substantially in the 1980s (31 percent prior to 1980 and 56 percent after). Of these companies, 64 percent believed that the know-how acquired resulted in increased productivity.

In analyzing the quality of human resources, 41 percent of the companies identified some type of shortcomings over the last 10 years. These shortcomings pertained to different types of jobs, particularly (a) managers, foremen, and supervisors in the paper, plastics, transport supplies industries, and predominantly, in companies exporting to MERCOSUR; (b) managers and distributors

Table 5.13. Uruguay: Distribution of COCAP Students by Area of Specialization, 1982-92
(Percentages)

Area of specialization	1989	1990	1991	1992	1982-92
Mixed farming	2.4	5.9	5.0	1.9	7.3
Farm machinery	1.2	1.5	0.0	0.0	1.0
Crafts	0.0	0.0	0.0	0.0	0.4
Production supervision	17.3	22.2	5.1	4.4	10.4
Labor supervision	13.3	10.7	16.1	19.3	19.0
Electricity and electronics	4.3	5.2	6.8	7.7	6.3
Mechanics and machinery repair	5.3	7.0	9.1	8.6	7.9
Sanitary and electrical facilities	0.8	0.0	12.5	0.0	2.9
Management	0.0	3.8	3.3	1.7	2.9
Accounting	0.0	2.9	1.4	0.8	1.1
Commerce	1.8	4.2	2.1	5.9	2.6
Hotel management	0.0	1.4	0.6	0.5	0.5
Gastronomy	0.0	0.0	0.0	0.0	0.3
Tourism	0.0	1.3	0.0	0.0	0.3
Repairs	14.1	18.5	12.1	14.3	10.7
Educational services	0.0	0.0	0.0	0.0	2.7
Data processing	39.1	13.7	20.7	34.5	21.3
Others	0.5	1.8	5.3	0.4	2.3
Total	100.0	100.0	100.0	100.0	100.0

Source: Author's calculation based on data from COCAP.

of foodstuffs, chemicals, and transport supplies; and (c) laborers in all fields.

Only 16 percent of the companies (in the tobacco, beverages, textile, chemical, and transport supply industries) declared having introduced changes in their personnel training programs over the last 10 years. On the other hand, as was previously mentioned, 56 percent attempted some training, and a product division of one of the companies claimed to have provided a specialized course. This suggests that, in general, personnel training has not been carried out in a systematic manner. The cause may be due to a lack of a broad managerial perspective on human resources or to the fact that needs were specific and easily identifiable, alleviating the requirement for an overall training program. Table 5.15 details the different programs used, as well as the percentages of companies which availed themselves of the programs.

Companies usually carry out in-house training when they acquire new equipment. However, most companies use outside courses on specialized topics. Such courses have become increasingly attractive during this decade. Demand for courses provided by COCAP seems quite limited and is concentrated in the textile, foods, and transport supply industries. The textile industry, in particular, has made increasing use of the services provided by the institute, while the percent-

Table 5.14. Uruguay: Students Enrolled in Private Institutions by Age and Sex, and by Type of Course, 1991
(Percentages)

	Total	By sex		By age bracket		
		Women	Men	Under 20	20 to 30	Over 30
Farming	1.5	0.8	2.4	3.6	1.0	0.4
Applied arts	0.3	0.4	0.2	0.3	0.4	0.0
Artisanry	0.1	0.1	0.1	0.1	0.0	0.0
Crafts	0.8	1.4	0.2	1.2	0.7	1.0
Production supervision	0.6	0.1	0.7	0.0	0.0	0.3
Labor supervision	1.9	3.1	0.5	2.5	1.3	2.9
Electricity and electronics	1.3	0.0	2.9	2.3	0.9	0.5
Mechanics and mach. repair	2.3	0.0	5.0	4.2	1.1	0.4
Construction	0.2	0.3	0.2	0.1	0.1	0.1
Sanitary and electrical facilities	0.2	0.0	0.5	0.0	0.0	0.0
Management	11.1	12.7	8.9	15.9	7.6	6.4
Accounting	2.1	2.1	1.9	2.4	1.5	1.3
Business	1.9	0.6	2.0	0.0	0.1	0.1
Gastronomy	1.2	1.9	0.3	0.7	0.5	2.2
Tourism	0.2	0.3	0.1	0.2	0.3	0.2
Personal services	11.1	19.5	2.0	12.6	10.2	17.5
Repairs	3.6	0.7	7.1	6.2	3.4	1.5
Educational services	1.1	2.1	0.0	1.2	1.1	1.0
Data processing	53.7	49.5	60.5	40.4	66.3	62.0
Communications	1.4	1.6	1.2	2.2	1.0	0.4
Communications media	1.5	0.9	2.2	1.4	1.5	0.9
Others	1.7	1.9	1.0	2.4	1.1	0.9
Total	100.0	100.0	100.0	100.0	100.0	100.0

Source: Based on the Survey of Private Professional Training Institutions of the National Human Resources Directorate, Ministry of Labor and Social Security.

age of companies in other industry areas interested in COCAP courses has been declining. Also, UTU courses have little attraction for companies, which suggests that demand for technically competent workers is satisfied by the supply which already exists in the market.

An interesting trait to point out is that 15 percent of those surveyed, mostly export firms with more than 100 employees, have sent their workers abroad at some point in time for training. Courses have at times been created at the initiative of the companies themselves by private institutions with which the companies have shown a greater interest in working. Furthermore, 33 percent of the companies have motivated their employees to train through incentives such as pay increases, and 25 percent have used promotion incentives. However, 16 percent did not offer additional benefits to motivate workers since they believed that

Table 5.15. Uruguay: Companies that Used Training Procedures, 1980-90
(Percentages)

Type of course	Percentage of companies
Internal group courses	29.1
Internal individual courses	25.9
UTU	6.9
COCAP	14.2
Outside courses on a specific subject	34.9
Outside courses with a fixed program	19.8
Courses outside the country	15.1
Other courses	10.6

Source: Human Resources Survey.

this training was part of their job. A particular characteristic is that the companies that provided incentives did not perform well in the volume or distribution of their sales.

Personnel training activities have been relatively successful since the percentage of companies that claimed operational shortcomings declined (30 percent) in 1992. These shortcomings were due to low productivity (21 percent), the introduction of new technologies (19 percent), the acquisition of new machinery (14 percent), and inadequate training for recently hired workers (13 percent). It should be noted that the shortcomings were not attributed to education. However, to be successful, training should be geared to individuals who already have a good basic education.

Jobs most at risk are consistently those of unskilled workers for whom companies consider the required courses to be improvements in production, production line processes, supervision, machine operations, and quality control. For technicians and mid-level professionals, shortcomings have been identified in marketing and sales techniques. There continues to be a need, although to a lesser extent, for computer and information processing courses for white-collar workers. This type of skill upgrading seems to have been accomplished successfully.

The cited survey reaffirms the importance assigned to work experience in personnel selection. Experience ranks higher than formal education and specialized training. Formal education seems to be important only in the hiring of professionals and technicians, but even in these cases experience becomes an important factor.

Another important aspect in matching work supply with demand relates to the methods used by companies canvassing for new employees. In this context, distinct procedures have been distinguished which can be classified as objective and subjective. The former includes publishing newspaper ads followed by later screening within the company, and by using the services of personnel placement and selection agencies, the advice of training centers, and company lists. Subjective procedures include hiring friends or relatives and using the recommendations and advice from current staff. This procedure generally does not require a formal analysis of the new employee's background.

Selection by subjective methods is deemed to harm the worker since his personal attributes are not the basis for hiring, leaving those who do not have appropriate contacts at a disadvantage. For its part, the hiring firm, which decides on the number of job candidates, runs the risk of not hiring personnel who possess the required expertise. While subjective methods do not guarantee the best selection, in a restricted environment such as Uruguay's, they can prove to be an effective mechanism for companies; a good recommendation avoids the cost of a search and could secure a good employee.

Based on the data obtained, companies in the manufacturing industry largely use subjective procedures for recruiting their manpower. In the last 10 years, 36 percent of the companies have used these procedures consistently. However, this procedure has also been combined with an intense use of newspaper ads (40 percent of the companies). Objective methods are rarely used. In the last 10 years only 10 percent of companies have consistently used the services of placement agencies and some have made use of company lists, while only 2.6 percent have consulted training centers. The incidence of procedures varies with different industrial sectors. Furthermore, exporting firms, particularly those who sell to MERCOSUR companies, tend to make more consistent use of objective methods than do companies that produce for the domestic market. The importance of objective recruiting methods grows with company size.

Trends in hiring methods do not show significant changes over the last 10 years. Objective personnel recruiting methods have been favored by 5 percent of the companies, while their use has declined in 1.7 percent of companies. However, some industries (machinery and equipment, chemical, textile, food, and footwear) show an increased trend favoring the use of objective methods. Among the different options, a higher percentage of companies availed themselves of placement agencies whose numbers have increased and services diversified, and of the publication of newspaper ads. Consultations with training centers have not increased. However, companies with more than 200 workers are making more use of this option, although in absolute value their number continues to be small.

Strengths and Weaknesses of the Education and Training System

With respect to general education, the state's reaction to evolutionary change consisted of extending compulsory education without significantly altering the curricula. In tertiary education, the merit of private education centers was recognized and greater emphasis was placed on scientific courses as opposed to the humanities. Public sector institutions, however, had difficulty in responding to the new training requirements, not only because of their rigid structure but also because of budget restrictions. These restrictions limited investment in new courses, hiring of qualified teachers, and adoption of new techniques.

In the professional-technical area, UTU faced similar problems, although it introduced two important changes: flexibility to transfer from secondary education to technical training and the ranking of specialization courses. The relative growth in enrollments in administrative training reflects UTU's budgetary constraints, since training in other areas in high demand, such as information science, requires new investments and hiring of teachers. While the diversity in first level courses affords rapid training and labor market entry, the concentration of enrollment in a few courses at the higher levels may be indicative of excessive diversification in the face of budgetary restrictions.

In this context, the reaction of the private sector was positive. Companies took charge of the specific training needs of their employees, although this training was not uniform throughout industrial sectors and exhibited shortcomings. Training did not rely on government assistance; rather, the costs were assumed by the companies. In this regard, the support which the state provided in creating the COCAP, an institution focused on industrial training, is important.

With regard to general technical training, centers were created which provided a range of courses open to students with different prior education requirements. These centers met with widespread acceptance. Featured among the courses offered were information science courses which the UTU curricula lacked. Training was provided which was not job-related. Because most of these courses were on a tuition basis, they excluded low-income groups, as no institutionalized scholarship program was in place. It is interesting to point out that beginning in 1993, a training program created under the jurisdiction of the National Employment Office specifically focused on the unemployed. The program, however, is still ill-defined.

Finally, some shortcomings should be pointed out in the information flows related to personnel selection procedures and in the flows between companies and training centers. (Only the COCAP and several private institutions have attempted to remedy these shortfalls.) These shortcomings will be considered in the following section.

Policy Guidelines

Beginning in the 1970s, a qualitative change occurred in the training requirements of the labor force. The change was the result of the internationalization of certain production criteria and of the trade liberalization process. However, responses which aim to adapt human resources to these new requirements began to be developed only in the 1980s.

The formulation of effective employment policies requires not only an analysis of the characteristics of human resources, but also an assessment of the demand which allows sectoral growth to be quantified in terms of job creation. In this respect, several flexibility indicators presented in this study suggest that wage policies are inadequate in solving imbalances between supply and demand. These imbalances appear to have become more critical in the second half of the past decade. Furthermore, the limitations of a relatively rigid institutional framework are not the main stumbling block for absorbing the target groups into the labor market. This analysis on the topic of labor supply suggests a range of remedial actions which are listed below. These actions directly address identified shortcomings in human resource training (training and experience) and in the link between supply and demand, and aim to alleviate problems of the mentioned target groups.

- To lessen the imbalances identified between the specialized technical training of employees and the requirements of the production sector, a strengthening of fiscal incentive policies seems appropriate. These policies should encourage companies in a sector to coordinate training courses for their workers, so that training can be provided even when it would not be profitable for just one company. In this regard, a precedent exists in the textile industry, where a group of companies formed a specialty training institute.
- Since private training centers operate in several areas, an evaluation of their quality is important. This is helpful in avoiding redundant activities, particularly since retraining courses will be provided by the National Employment Office. This will also guarantee smooth operations for open courses whereby applicants will be able to select these courses on the basis of clear information. Such decisions acquire greater significance in the context of increasingly objective personnel selection procedures by companies.
- The recent creation of the National Employment Office is expected to provide improved information flows, retraining of the unemployed, and the formulation of training programs for all labor. The smooth operation of this institution seems then to be key, since it will be its responsibility to disseminate information and to help in the placement and training of human resources in the reconversion process. For this purpose, it is urgent to identify needs in the different sectors and to interact with the business sector to make efficient use of available resources.
- As UTU is the only public institution providing professional-technical training, its smooth operation is essential. Therefore, it seems important to restructure UTU curricula, focusing on those courses in greater demand.
- In addition to manpower reconversion programs, specific policies should

address the problems of groups that need to reintegrate into the labor market. These policies should include other elements beside training, such as the following considerations:

- Active women make up a highly-educated group which experiences labor segregation and part-time participation in the work force. Short-comings have been noted in the cost and quality of both the public and private preschool and daycare establishment. This suggests the need to extend the coverage of these establishments in order to take better advantage of female manpower, facilitating their full integration into the labor market.
- With regard to young people, the main problem identified is the lack of work experience. Another problem for those who come from lower income households and enter the labor market at an early age is the interruption of their formal education. Moreover, the unskilled experience they acquire does not allow them subsequent access to better paying jobs. One possible solution is to extend the training of target groups (households under the poverty line or those whose basic needs are not met), and to provide social assistance through, for example, a scholarship program. On the other hand, better educated young people who reside longer at home come from higher income families and are highly selective in their job search. For them, lack of experience leads to their underutilization and to long job searches, as well as to discouragement reflected in their high propensity to emigrate. This suggests the formulation of a program providing for paid "stages" (internships) within companies for recent graduates of formal education. It should be pointed out that since 1985, legislation has been proposed (but not enacted) that would facilitate the employment of young people under 30 and a net creation of jobs by exempting firms from social security payroll taxes and from accident insurance premiums.
- Individuals over 50 years of age represent a high percentage of workers who have difficulty in relocating. This problem could be addressed in part by a combination of properly planned initiatives that encourage retirement of older employees and provide adequate company-sponsored training programs.
- Dismissal of government workers raises two issues. On the one hand, their displacement, whether voluntary or through changes in the legislation pertaining to dismissal procedures, would generate strong pressure in the private sector. It is important, therefore, that dismissal processes be carefully carried out. On the other hand, public worker downsizing policies do not seem to take into account the importance of preserving a staff of highly qualified civil servants that can meet the needs of a small country. The indiscriminate drop in real wages and a

careless application of retirement incentives lead to a loss of the state's best human resources. This suggests that the steps currently being taken are a short-term mitigating factor since, at some point, the problem will have to be settled through new negotiation. Thus it is crucial to carry out an evaluation of the needs of the sector and of its current resources, in order to rationalize the downsizing process and avoid the loss of capable employees.

Conclusions

In the last 20 years, Uruguay's economy has undergone various changes in its productive structure, particularly in the industrial sector. Currently, changes are being introduced which are linked to the downsizing of the public sector, economic liberalization and, above all, regional integration. The impact of these changes on the labor market represents one of the country's key research issues.

Furthermore, in the past few decades, there has been a significant increase in the economically active population, particularly due to the incorporation of women and young people into the labor market. These groups have been most severely affected by the current adjustment process. The present unemployment rate for these groups is very high, although their problems in entering the labor market are qualitatively different. Women experience partial incorporation into the labor market and suffer from a relatively high level of segregation. Young people, on the other hand, because they lack experience, face problems in finding their first job.

The analysis of the population's educational level leads to the conclusion that while basic educational background is sufficiently solid to facilitate follow-up training, specialized job training suffers from various shortcomings. Public institutions have responded, though insufficiently, to the new demands, while the private sector has been most dynamic both in creating training centers and in the use of company-run courses. There is, however, little coordination between these efforts.

Furthermore, groups that currently do not face serious unemployment problems could also be affected in the near future. This is particularly true for individuals over the age of 50 who, having a much lower educational level than the average population, would have difficulty in being retrained. The downsizing of government employees will also create additional pressure on the labor market.

The responsibilities entrusted to the National Employment Office are justified by the needs of the private sector. An expeditious assessment of potential changes in production and skill requirements is essential so that remedial actions can be implemented before unemployment climbs further.

In this regard, the promotion of educational training for employed workers seems to be a reasonable course of action. It is also necessary to improve channels of communication between job candidates and companies, and also between companies and training centers.

In summary, future action should consider specific measures for facilitating the entry of young people and women into the labor market, the training of personnel with the least employment potential, the assessment of the sectors affected by labor reconversion and integration, the rationalization of the downsizing of public employees, and the improvement of information channels.

Bibliography

Abuhadba, Mario. 1991. Models of Wage Determination and the Industry Wage Structure in Uruguay. *Análisis Económico* 6.

Administración Nacional de Educación Pública (ANEP), Consejo de Educación Técnico-Profesional. 1992. ¿Quiénes ingresan al ciclo básico único en las escuelas de la Universidad del Trabajo? Montevideo. Mimeo.

Blanchard, O.J., and P. Diamond. 1989. The Beveridge Curve. *Brookings Papers on Economic Activity 1*. The Brookings Institution, Washington, D.C.

Bucheli, Marisa. 1992a. Diferencias sectoriales de salarios en el Uruguay. *SUMA* (no. 12).

_____. 1992b. Los logros educativos y los niveles de ingreso. Document No. 3/92, Department of Economics, School of Social Sciences, Universidad del Republica Oriental de Uruguay, Montevideo.

Cassoni, Adriana. 1993. El proceso de ajuste de salarios. CERES - TINKER, Montevideo. Mimeo.

CEPAL, Oficina de Montevideo. 1992. Enseñanza primaria y ciclo básico de educación media en el Uruguay. Montevideo.

_____. Dirección General de Estadística y Censos 1991. *1a. Encuesta Nacional de la Juventud.* Montevideo.

_____. 1987. Jóvenes desocupados y buscadores de trabajo en Uruguay. Montevideo. Mimeo.

Coe, D.T. 1985. Nominal Wages, the NAIRU and Wage Flexibility. *OECD Economic Studies* (no. 5).

Davrieux, Ariel. 1992. Uruguay: Un desarrollo problemático. Paper presented at the Seminar on Comparative Study of Development Models after 1950 in Small-scale European and Latin American Countries, CEPAL, Montevideo.

Diez de Medina, Rafael. 1992. *La estructura ocupacional y los jóvenes en Uruguay.* Montevideo: CEPAL.

Diez de Medina, Rafael, and M. Rossi. 1991. *La actividad femenina en el mercado laboral de Montevideo*. Montevideo: CEPAL.

Fontana, J. C., N. Niedworok and A. Pellegrino. 1988. *Emigración de uruguayos, colonias en el exterior y perspectivas de retorno*. Montevideo: Ediciones de Banda Oriental.

Klau, F., and A. Mittelstädt. 1986. Labour Market Flexibility. *OECD Economic Studies* (no.6).

Laens, Silvia, *et al.* 1992. *Itinerario de la apertura y condiciones macroeconómicas*. CINVE, Montevideo.

Layard, R., S. Nickell and R. Jackman. 1991. *Unemployment: Macroeconomic Performance and the Labour Market*. Oxford University Press.

Macadar, Luis. 1981. *Uruguay 1974-1980: ¿Un nuevo ensayo de reajuste económico?* CINVE, Montevideo.

Peaguda, Mary, and M. Rossi. 1982. Los diferenciales salariales en la industria manufacturera, estructura y factores explicativos. Instituto de Economía, Facultad de Ciencias Económicas y de Administración, Universidad de la Reública, Montevideo. Mimeo.

Rama, Germán W. 1992. ¿Qué aprenden y quiénes aprenden en las escuelas de Uruguay? Los contextos sociales e institucionales de éxitos y fracasos. CEPAL, Montevideo.

Rama, Germán W., and S. Silveira. 1991. *Políticas de recursos humanos de la industria exportadora de Uruguay. Modernización y desequilibrios*. CEPAL —CINTERFOR/OIT, Montevideo.

Rama, Martin. 1988. ¿Qué es el pleno empleo? Una cuantificación de la desocupación voluntaria, de desequilibrio y de segmentación. *SUMA* (4).

Rodríguez Folle, F. 1986. *Hacia una función de producción para la industria uruguaya*. Working Paper. CERES, Montevideo.

Rossi, Máximo, and R. Tansini. 1992. Ordenamiento y diferenciación salarial en la industria del Uruguay. Un estudio a nivel de plantas industriales. Documento No. 9/92, Department of Economics (F.C.S.).

_____. 1989. *Sesgo tecnológico y demanda factorial en las ramas textil, cuero y química 1976-1986, Uruguay 89.* Montevideo: Instituto de Economía de la Universidad de la República and FESUR.

Tansini, Rubén, and M. Zejan. 1990. Una modelización del sector manufacturero con factores cuasi fijos. *SUMA* (5) 8.

ANNEX

FLEXIBILITY INDICATORS

The analysis of the degree of flexibility of the labor market includes diverse macro and microeconomic elements, as well as factors related to the characteristics and adaptability of the work supply.

The first group of indicators measures the capability of wages to respond to changes—both cyclical and resulting from adverse supply and demand shocks—in the evolution of productivity and relative prices. Figure 5.A.1 shows the relative evolution of productivity and real wages in the manufacturing sector. After 1976, real wages fell more rapidly than average productivity as a result of a deterioration in the terms of trade. Later, the two factors continued along similar paths, until the economic shock of 1983, evidenced by a fairly rapid reaction to the devaluation of the previous year and to the increase in international interest rates. Despite the later recovery, the gap between wages and productivity apparently narrowed, indicating a relatively high degree of flexibility in wage fixing.

Furthermore, the adjustment of nominal wages to inflation is counteracted by the impact exerted on them by the level of unemployment. To the extent that growing labor market pressures induce such an adjustment, this adjustment will evolve within the framework of more flexible wages. The preceding hypothesis will be evaluated using an indicator proposed in Klau and Mittelstädt (1986), which is defined as the ratio of wage elasticity nominal-price for consumers to the wage semi-elasticity nominal unemployment rate, calculated by a wage equation (Table 5.A.1). A large or growing value over time would indicate greater wage response to inflation than to unemployment, that is, lesser flexibility of wage costs. Since this index is not capped, it needs to be compared with the values for other countries. As estimations are not available for Latin America, the figures of developed economies which are published in the cited work will be used.

Values for Uruguay were calculated based on an approximation using a logarithmic-linear equation for the period 1968-91 for Montevideo's private sector, as follows: $tcw = a + a_1u + a_2us + a_3inf + a_4inf_{(-1)} + a5wr_{(-1)}$, where tcw is the nominal salary growth rate; u is the unemployment rate; us is the unemployment rate when labor unions are present; inf is the inflation rate; and wr is the deflated salary for the output deflator.

It can be concluded from the results obtained that the real rigidity indicator of wages is comparatively low for Uruguay even during the period when labor union activity was intense. In the long run, only Japan has a lower indicator, not only as a consequence of the exceptional response of wages to unemployment, but also of the almost instantaneous adjustment to inflation. In Uruguay, both price elasticity and the semi-elastic unemployment rate are relatively high. How-

Figure 5.A.1. Uruguay: Real Wage and Average Productivity of the Manufacturing Sector, 1975-91
(Index 1983=100, normalized)

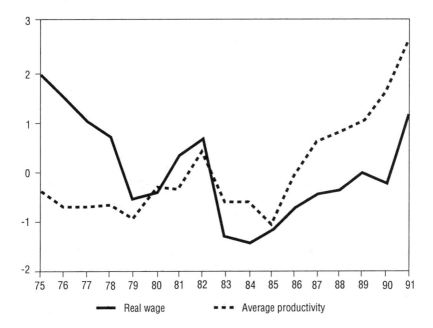

                    ■■■ Real wage   ▪ ▪ ▪ Average productivity

ever, the degree of flexibility introduced by the reappearance of labor unions—which reduced in half the impact of the unemployment rate on the level of nominal salaries—should not be discounted.

Another element which introduces rigidities in the market relates to the level and evolution of non-salary labor costs associated with social security, health insurance, years of service, etc. with respect to total labor costs. To the extent that these represent a fixed cost, even if the rate of growth of nominal salaries were to decline, an increase in contributions would result in an inadequate adjustment of labor costs. However, in Uruguay, this does not seem to be the case: this proportion has declined progressively throughout the past decade, reaching in 1991 almost half of the percentage in 1981.

An additional set of indicators relates to the adaptability of salaries among activity sectors, companies, or trades. If the adjustment processes affect diverse sectors, companies, or workers differently, this should be reflected in a response independent of corresponding labor costs, as evidenced in the analysis on the inter-industrial wage differentials. The studies carried out for Uruguay's industrial sector (Abuhadba, 1991; Bucheli, 1992a; Peaguda and Rossi, 1982; Rossi

Table 5.A.1. Comparison of Indicators of Real Wage Rigidity in Various Countries

Country	Wage-price elasticity	Wage-unemployment semi-elasticity	Real wage stickiness Short-term	Real wage stickiness Long-term
Uruguay	0.66	-1.55[a]	0.43[a]	0.64[a]
		-0.87[b]	0.87[b]	1.31[b]
Japan	0.93	-3.31	0.28	0.28
Canada	0.31	-0.57	0.54	1.67
United States	0.22	-0.33	0.67	3.06
France	0.47	-0.31	1.52	3.03
United Kingdom	0.33	-0.17	1.94	5.82

Sources: Cassoni (1993) and Klau and Mittelstädt (1986).
[a] Refers to period in which unions were inactive.
[b] Refers to periods during which unions operated.

and Tansini, 1992) conclude by confirming the existence of a significant temporary stability related to different kinds of activities in the manufacturing sector.

With one exception, all of the studies, however, deal with relatively short periods of time (maximum 10 years), which may be inadequate for identifying large changes in the wage structure. Therefore, Peaguda and Rossi (1982), who compare the evolution during 40 years, obtain noticeably smaller correlations.

Furthermore and without exception, it is evident from all of the studies that the salary differential spread increased, which implies that salary ranges expanded even when the ordering of the sectors, companies, or worker categories did not change immediately.

It is also important to analyze the behavior of specific groups that have greater labor market entry problems, such as women and young people, since the overall adjustment in wages might not be affecting these groups. In the process, the relative trend in wages for the group, as far as its specific rate of unemployment was concerned, had been surveyed during the 1980s. To approximate the wages, the average income of an individual's main business line in the private sector was used. An average salary ratio was derived between young people under 25 and those over 25 years of age, and another for average income of women and men. Relative unemployment was calculated as the ratio of the unemployment rate for both groups.

For women, a positive relation between relative increases in income and the unemployment rate was observed until 1990 (Figure 5.A.2). In other words, increases in women's salaries with respect to those for men was generally accompanied by an increase in their relative unemployment rate. As for young people (Figure 5.A.3), the result is even clearer. Although their average income deteriorated almost continuously with respect to individuals over the age of 25 until

Figure 5.A.2. Unemployment Rate and Relative Income for Women/Men, 1981-91
(Normalized values)

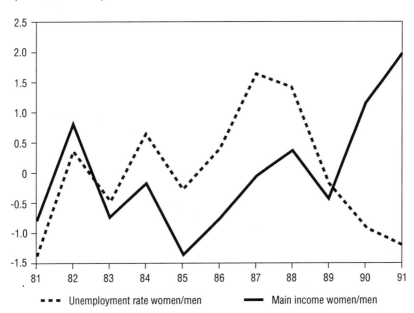

1990, they show an uninterrupted growth in the relative rate of unemployment.

The result of Figure 5.A.2 indicates that some degree of flexibility in female salaries exists, since these respond to specific supply surpluses for the group. As for young people, the results of Figure 5.A.3 seem to invalidate the argument that lower salary levels would diminish their high unemployment level. The unavailability of a large number of observations makes it impossible to carry out a more rigorous analysis for determining the structure of the remaining scatter in the data. However, it is observed that, even if variable within the cycle, the relative incomes of the groups under study have a significant degree of flexibility.

With respect to the adaptability of supply to the demand, it is important to analyze, first, the relative rate of job openings to the unemployment rate. Second, it is interesting to observe the evolution of the structural relationship.

High levels of unemployment, together with a high number of job openings, indicate the lack of labor mobility and therefore market inflexibility. In view of shocks which differentially affect sectors and companies, it is possible that the ratio of available jobs to labor supply could move in opposite directions. This can be estimated using the Beveridge curve. For Montevideo's private sector, the curve indicates that during 1980 and 1981 relatively low unemployment rates and a high number of vacancies were recorded. However, for the period 1983-

Figure 5.A.3. Unemployment Rate and Relative Income for Young Adults/Adults, 1981-91
(Monthly percentages)

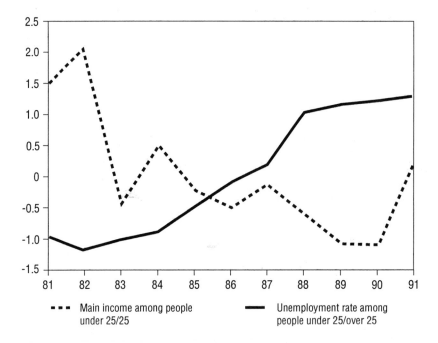

- - - Main income among people
under 25/25

━━━ Unemployment rate among
people under 25/over 25

85, a low vacancy rate and a very high level of unemployment was recorded (Figure 5.A.4). This reflects normal unemployment behavior in a period of disequilibrium, as has been pointed out in other studies (Rama, 1988).

The estimate calculated for the period 1980-90 suggests, however, a tendency in the curve to move outward, which may be due to the persistence of high unemployment rates in the country (Table 5.A.2). In other words, for a constant level of vacancy rate, the unemployment rate is higher. From the table, it would seem that this trend began in 1987.

This result indicates a labor market which becomes more rigid with an increase in sectoral unemployment. The evidence presented so far, however, does not seem to indicate that an inadequate relative salary level is the main cause, nor would correction of the level solve the unemployment problem.

On the one hand, salaries generally adjust themselves relatively quickly to changes in production, with the adjustment being favored by a decline in the relative weight of nonsalaried labor costs. Furthermore, salaries have a significant impact on unemployment despite the fact that the impact declines with labor union activities. On the other hand, there is evidence of a dispersed industrial

Figure 5.A.4. Uruguay: Beveridge Curve, 1980-90
(Rates)

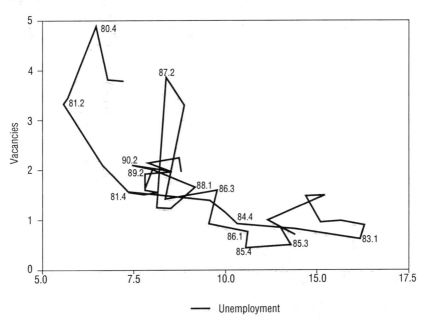

— Unemployment

Table 5.A.2. Uruguay: Results of the Beveridge Curve Estimate, 1980-90

Dependent variable: LU Regressor	Coefficient	Standard error	T-Ratio
C	0.99	0.22	4.56
Q4	-0.08	0.03	-2.20
T	5.93	2.06	2.88
T2	-30.29	9.60	-3.15
TE	41.81	12.98	3.22
LU(-1)	0.50	0.10	4.82
LV	-0.12	0.04	-2.75
Nº obsv.	43		
R²	0.887	S.E. from Regression	0.099
H-Durbin	0.320	Ramsey Test (F(1.35))	0.530
Normality	0.646	Heteroscedasticity (F(1.41))	3.789

where: LU = unemployment rate; LU(-1) = previous period unemployment rate; LV = vacancies rate; C = constant; Q4 = fourth quarter; T = trend (T2 and T3 refer to the square and cube of T, so that the trend is polynomial).

wage structure. Finally, the wages for those economically active groups that en-counter greater problems entering the labor market have evolved with respect to other groups, as a result of their increased contribution to overall unemployment. Thus, it does not seem possible to uphold this wage inflexibility trend.

It should also be pointed out that even in the presence of the above factors, it is possible that the characteristics of labor supply may not be compatible with company requirements, and that the effectiveness of the unemployed in search-ing for jobs may decline. The latter is an alternate explanation for the tendency for workers to move between jobs, which the Beveridge curve shows. This pro-cess is generally associated with extended periods of unemployment and with the consequent loss of human capital. In Uruguay, however, it seems linked to the growing proportion of unemployed young people, a group devoid of appeal because of their lack of work experience. This is a very important factor, as can be seen from several estimates previously carried out (Bucheli, 1992a; Diez de Medina, 1992).

INDEX

Abuhadba, M., 191
Albuquerque, R.C., 34t
ANEP (Administración Nacional de Educación Pública), Uruguay, 172
Apprenticeship programs
Chile, 82, 84, 88
Colombia, 130

Balance of payments
Brazil
during debt crisis, 17-18
deficits related to oil crisis, 14, 17
Uruguay, 148-50
Banco de la República, Colombia, 112
Barandiarán, E., 66
Barros, R.P., 22t
Berry, A., 115
Bivar, W.S., 56t
Bonilla, E., 121
Borba, S., 30
Bosch, M., 87n13
Bucheli, M., 171, 191, 196
Budget deficit
Brazil, 13, 18
Chile, 65, 68
Colombia, 116

Capital flows
Brazil, 17, 19
Colombia, 110, 116
Uruguay, 149-50
Capital markets, Chile, 66, 68-69
Carneiro, D., 16t
Cassoni, Adriana, 192t
CECAP (Center for Training and Production), Uruguay, 168

CEPAL, 171
COCAP (Center for Professional Training), Uruguay, 8, 168, 173-74, 178
Corbo, V., 66
Cortázar, R., 67t
Cottani, J., 67t
Cruzado Plan, Brazil, 20, 24
Currency
Brazil: devaluation and appreciation, 17-18
Colombia: devaluation and revaluation, 113-14, 119
Uruguay: devaluation, 148
See also Exchange rate policy

Debt, external
Brazil
effect of, 18
during oil price shocks (1973-82), 14, 17
Chile, 66-67
Uruguay, 151-52
Decentralization
Chile, 68-69
Colombia, 133
Democratization
Brazil, 14
Uruguay, 152
Diez de Medina, R., 165, 196
DRI (Integrated Rural Development Program), Colombia, 128

Echeverría, C., 81
Economic performance
Brazil, 14, 17-20
Chile, 68, 105t

Colombia
  levels and forecast, 110-14
Uruguay, 148
Economic policy
  Brazil
    structural adjustment (1973-78),
      14, 17
    trade account adjustment, 14
  Colombia (1970-90), 114-17
  Uruguay, 160
  See also Exchange rate policy; Fiscal
    policy; Monetary policy; Stabilization
    program; Structural adjustment; Trade
    policy
Economic shocks
  Brazil, 3, 14, 18
  Chile, 64
  Uruguay, 148-50, 152
  See also Oil price shocks, Brazil
Education, vocational. *See* Training
Educational levels
  effect on employment, 25-27, 39-42,
    46-49
  Brazil
    effect of low, 6
    relation to SENAI training, 39
    relation to unemployment, 25-27
    relation to wage differentials, 28-30
  Chile
    demand during adjustment period, 77,
      79-80
    of structurally-changed labor force,
      77-80
  Colombia, 117-19
    differences, 127
    unemployment by, 117-23
  Uruguay
    differences, 155
    labor force, 155
    of public and private sector
      employees, 167
  See also Human capital; Labor force;
    Labor market; Wages
Education system
  Brazil
    participation, 33, 35-36, 57

quality of, 33, 35-36
    roles of SENAC and SENAI in, 47-48
    structure and spending, 30-34
  Colombia
    career training in formal, 128
    changes, 135
    deficiencies, 127
  Uruguay
    participation, 169-71
    requirements, 167-68
Edwards, A., 66
Edwards, S., 66
Ehrenberg, R., 87n14
Emigration
  Chile, 77
  Uruguay, 152-53, 155, 164
Employment
  Brazil
    distribution in labor categories, 22-23
    informal sector, 49-50
    levels and sectoral distribution
      (1980s), 20-22
    levels of SENAI-trained entrants and
      graduates, 39-41
    sectoral structure (1981-89), 20-22
  Chile
    emergency employment plans, 91-94,
      106t, 107t
    realignment in free-market environ-
      ment, 64
  Colombia
    by education, gender, and age, 117-20,
      122-26
    informal sector, 119
    policy focus on youth and women,
      139-42
    temporary, 118, 121-22
    youth-related programs, 141-42
  Uruguay, 155-60
  See also Unemployment
Employment policy, Uruguay
  formulation, 183-85
  groups targeted by labor policy, 163-67
Employment services
  Chile, 81-82, 91-95, 106t
  Colombia, 134-35, 137-40

Exchange rate policy
    Brazil, 17-18
    Chile, 66, 68
    Colombia, 116
    Uruguay, 148-51
Export promotion
    Brazil, 21
    Colombia, 110
    Uruguay, 148-49

Financial sector
    Chile, 63, 66
    Colombia
        with economic stagnation, 110
        liberalization, 114-15
    Uruguay, 147-49
Fiscal deficit. *See* Budget deficit
Fiscal policy
    Brazil, 18
    Chile, 65
    Uruguay, 152, 161
Flexibility
    Chile
        institutional and legal mechanisms,
            99-100
        social assistance and training, 99
    Uruguay: of economy and wage struc-
        ture, 153-54
Flexibility, labor market
    determinants of labor market, 13, 57,
        65, 69
    with structural adjustment, 2
Fontana, J.C., 153

Galilea, S., 88
Gómez, V.M., 140
Government intervention
    Brazil, 3
    Chile, 64

Hachette, D., 66n2
Harberger, A.C., 66
Horn, R., 129
Human capital
    determinants, 1
    factors influencing development, 6-7

generalized and specialized, 46-47,
    56-57
Chile: depreciation during adjustment,
    77

Illiteracy
    Brazil, 25, 33, 57
    Chile, 93, 106t
    Uruguay, 169
Import substitution
    Brazil, 18,21
    Chile, 64
    Colombia, 110
INACAP (National Institute of Profes-
    sional Training), Chile, 64, 79, 81, 82
Income distribution, Brazil, 24
Indexation, Brazil, 17
Industrial sector
    Brazil
        response to economic shocks, 3
        wages levels in manufacturing, 23-24
    Brazil: institution and on-the-job train-
        ing, 38-43
    Colombia
        career training for, 128-34
        wih economic decline, 110
    Uruguay, 148
Inflation levels
    Brazil, 14, 17-18
    Chile, 65-66, 68
    Colombia, 111
    Uruguay, 151
Informal sector
    Brazil, 7, 23, 49-50, 57
    Colombia, 7, 117, 119, 121, 123, 126
    Uruguay, 156
Inter-American Development Bank, 11
Interest rates, Brazil, 17
Investment, Chile, 63

Jaspersen, F.Z., 2
Jiménez, E., 129

Kalmanovitz, S., 111n4, 112n6
Klau, F., 190, 192t
Kodama, K., 82

Kugler, B., 129

Labor Code, Brazil, 53
Labor force
effects of structural adjustment, 4-5
groups affected by structural adjustment,
4-6, 25-27, 56, 69-79
impact of structural adjustment, 7
Brazil
effect of structural adjustment, 19-20
employment of SENAI-trained graduates, 41-42
participation rates (1980s), 20, 23
training and vocational education,
36-38
Chile
characteristics of employed, 77, 79
composition with structural change,
77-79
retraining of, 64, 96, 108
Colombia
career training programs, 128-34
employment services, 134-35
participation, 117-21
Uruguay: characteristics and participation, 155-60
See also Mobility, labor
Labor Intermediation System, Colombia,
137-38, 141
Labor market
adjustment costs, 46-47
Brazil
distribution by employment type,
22-23
flexibility, 57
influences on behavior, 53-56
regional integration, 49
Chile
change in demand, 64
with international debt crisis, 67-68
participation by age and gender, 72-79
retraining for reentry, 64, 96
Colombia
integration of women, 123
salaried and informal, 117

Uruguay
age distribution, 155-57
current functions, 157-63
economically active population,
158-59
flexibility indicators, 190-96
informal, 156
See also Flexibility, labor market
Labor unions
Brazil, 23
Uruguay, 149, 152, 160
Labor University of Uruguay (UTU),
171-73, 175t, 176t
Langoni, C., 24
Larraín, F., 66
Legislation
Brazil: effect of labor laws, 53-57
Chile
labor law reform, 68
private sector pension funds, 69
Training and Employment Law
(1976), 81
Colombia: labor law reform, 136-37
Uruguay: industrial promotion, 153
Londoño, J.L., 119n7
López, H., 117, 120
Lüders, R., 66n2

Macroeconomic policy, Chile, 65-69, 97
Marques, A.E., 32t
Marshall, J., 67t
Meller, P., 66n3
Mello e Souza, A., 32n4, 33
Ministry of Education, Brazil, 34t
Ministry of Finance, Brazil, 34t
Misas, G., 132
Mittelstädt, A., 190, 192t
Mobility, labor
within a company, 99
determinants of, 68, 98
deterrents to and incentives for, 6-7, 97
with structural adjustment, 2, 13
Monetary policy, Chile, 65

National Employment Office, Uruguay,
148

National Office of Statistics, Colombia, 119

Ocampo, J.A., 117
Oil price shocks, Brazil, 14, 17
OMCs (Municipal Placement Offices), Chile, 95
OPCs (Private Placement Offices), Chile, 95
OTEs (technical implementing agencies), Chile, 82
OTIRs (intermediate technical agencies), Chile, 82, 99-100

Paredes, R., 69n7, 71
Peaguda, M., 191, 192
PEEs (Emergency Employment Plans), Chile, 91-94, 106t
PEM (Minimum Employment Program), Chile, 92
PNR (National Rehabilitation Program), Colombia, 128
POJH (Occupational Program for Heads of Households), Chile, 92
Population growth
  Brazil, 20
  Colombia, 117
  Uruguay, 152
  See also Emigration
PPP (Programs for Public Career Training), Colombia, 130
Private sector
  Chile
    leadership, 63
    private nonprofit training corporations, 82-83
    subsidized training initiatives, 8-9, 64-65, 81-83, 97-98
  Colombia
    assistance of public sector, 143
    employment services, 135
    training programs, 129, 137-38
  Uruguay
    employment and wages in, 155, 157, 160
    training programs of, 8, 147-48

Privatization
  Chile, 64-65
  Colombia, 117
Professional training, Uruguay, 171-82
Psacharopoulos, G., 119n7
Public sector
  Brazil
    educational system, 30-35
    training management by, 7-8
  Chile
    employment decline (1973-77), 66
    with stabilization, 66
  Colombia
    labor force reduction, 117, 119
    training management by, 7-8
    training programs, 129
  Uruguay: employment and wages in, 155-57, 160, 167

Rama, M., 194
Ramírez, M., 117
Ramos,, 22t
Reyes, A., 119
Riveros, L., 66, 71
Rodríguez, P., 121
Rossi, M., 153, 165, 191-92
Rural development. See DRI (Integrated Rural Development Program), Colombia

SALI (Integrated Labor Adaptation Service), Colombia, 138-39
SAL-SP (Labor Adaptation Service for the Public Sector), Colombia, 139-40
Sarmiento, L., 112n5, 113, 117
Savedoff, W.D., 49, 50f
Scholarship program, Chile, 84, 88
Schultz, T.W., 46
Self-employment
  Brazil, 22, 50-52
  Colombia, 123
SENA (National Training Service), Colombia, 8, 126, 128, 129-38, 140-41
SENAC (National Commercial Training Service), Brazil, 43-45, 48
SENAI (National Service of Industrial Training), Brazil

education and training policies, 47-48
education requirements for, 6n5,
    38-43
SENALDE (National Employment Service), Colombia, 134-35, 137
SENCE (National Training and Employment Service), Chile, 81-82, 95
    See also Technical training
SERCOTEC (Technical Cooperation Service), Chile, 79
Services sector
    Brazil, 43-45
    Colombia, 123
Shariff, K., 2n2
Smith, R., 87n14
Social assistance
    Chile, 68-69, 91-94, 98
    coordination with training, 11, 98
Social security system
    Chile, 69
    Colombia, 136
Spending, government
    Brazil
        for education, 31-34
        effect of increased (1985-90), 18
    Chile: for training, 97-98
    Colombia: priorities, 127-28
    Uruguay: for education, 168-69
Stabilization program
    Chile, 65-66
    Uruguay, 149-50, 151, 160
Structural adjustment
    impact of, 7
    Brazil
        process, 14
        regional differences with, 49
    Chile, 65-69
        assistance for unemployed during,
            91-96
        changes influenced by, 97-98
        demographic groups affected by,
            71-72
        human resources with, 69-79
        impact on labor force, 6
        labor force skills mismatch, 64-65,
            70-71

programs to reduce unemployment,
    94-96
Colombia, 3, 109, 116, 142
Uruguay, 147
Subsidies, Chile
    to assist unemployed, 91-94
    to provide training, 81, 83, 87-88, 97-98
    unemployment compensation as, 94-95

Tansini, R., 153, 191-92
Technical training
    Chile, 82, 99-100
    Uruguay, 171-82
Thoumi, F., 115
Trade policy
    Brazil
        with debt crisis and economic shocks,
            17-19
        with democratization (1985-90), 18
    Chile: with structural adjustment, 66-67
    Colombia
        effect of fluctuations, 110-12
        liberalized, 116
    Uruguay: liberalization, 147, 149-50
    See also Exchange rate policy; Export
    promotion; Import substitution
Training programs
    recommendations for, 9-11
    Brazil
        funding for, 38, 42-43
        institutions and on-the-job, 36-38,
            43-45
        public and private vocational, 36-38
    Chile, 79, 81
        investment in SENCE-supervised,
            86-87
        for new skills, 64-65
        role of OTEs, 83-84
        subsidies for company-sponsored, 81,
            83, 85-88, 97-98
        youth training, 11, 84-85, 88, 92t
    Colombia
        career training, 128-29
        career training through SENA,
            129-33, 136-37

funding for SENA programs, 132-33,137
National Training Service (SENA), 126
provided by companies, 140-41
technical, 128-29
Uruguay
change in requirements, 182
company-supported, 177-81
professional-technical, 171
requiring prior education, 168
specialized institutions, 175-77, 179, 181-82
Tuijnman, A.C., 37

Unemployment
Brazil
duration and frequency, 55-56
rates, 20
by region, age, gender, and education, 25-27
Chile
circumstances of high, 63-64, 67-68
social assistance during structural adjustment, 91-96
during structural adjustment, 75-78
with structural adjustment, 70-77
Colombia
by age, gender, and education, 117-25
factors influencing rate of, 122-23
Uruguay
by gender, age, and educational level, 153-55
relation to economic performance, 149-53
See also Employment
Unemployment compensation, Chile, 94-95
Unemployment insurance
Brazil, 53-56
Uruguay, 162-63
United Nations, 35t

Villela, R., 34t
Vocational education. See Training

Wages
Brazil
changing levels, 23-25
differentials and structure, 28-30
formal and informal sector differences, 50-51
regional disparity, 49-50
relation to industrial concentration, 42-43
of SENAI graduates, 41
Chile
by educational level and age, 106t
real, 105t
Colombia: average labor income (1982-92), 120
Uruguay
distribution and levels, 155-57
evolution of real, 153
response to change, 190
Werneck, R., 16t
Women
Brazil: employment rates, 25
Colombia
policy focus on employment for, 139-42
Colombia: work force participation, 121-22
Uruguay
employment policies for, 161-62
labor force participation, 153, 155-57, 165-66
public sector employment, 167
World Bank, 35t, 138-39

Yáñez, J., 71t

Zejan, M., 153
Zerda, A., 88, 112n5, 113, 126, 129, 134